SUPERPLONK

Malcolm Gluck writes the enormously popular Superplonk column in *Weekend Guardian*, a monthly wine column for the Scottish *Sunday Post Magazine*, and is Wine Editor of *Cosmopolitan*. He is also Consultant Wine Editor of *Sainsbury's Magazine* and has written for *She*, *Country Living*, *Independent on Sunday*, and the *Sunday Express*. He is the author (along with Antony Worrall Thompson) of *Supernosh*. His new guide to high street wines, *Gluck's Guide 1995*, is published simultaneously with this new edition of *Superplonk*.

SUPERPLONK

Gluck's Guide to Supermarket Wine

MALCOLM GLUCK

faber and faber
LONDON · BOSTON

First published in 1991
by Faber and Faber Limited
3 Queen Square London WC1N 3AU
Second edition published in 1991
Third edition published in 1992
Fourth edition published in 1993
This new edition first published in 1994

Photoset by Parker Typesetting Service, Leicester
Printed in England by Clays Ltd, St Ives plc

Malcolm Gluck is hereby identified as author of this work in accordance
with Section 77 of the Copyright, Designs and Patents Act 1988

The author and publishers gratefully acknowledge the Estate of
P. G. Wodehouse and Hutchinson Books Ltd for permission to reprint
material (on page 17) from *Meet Mr Mulliner* by P. G. Wodehouse

A CIP record for this book is available from the British Library

ISBN 0-571-17203-2

10 9 8 7 6 5 4 3 2 1

Contents

Introduction

This is the fifth *Superplonk* book I've written and this year it is joined by a sister volume which concerns itself with the high street wine retailers. *This* book concerns itself exclusively with the wine on sale in supermarkets: Asda, Budgen, Co-op, Kwik Save, Littlewoods, Marks & Spencer, Morrisons, Safeway, Sainsbury's, Somerfield, Tesco, Waitrose and, for the first time, the Scottish group William Low.

My two books have in common my love of wine and my determination to unearth the bargain wherever it may be found. Both books also employ my 20-point rating system. From the letters I get, readers find this system invaluable because its basis is value for money. I continue to be the only wine writer who takes the common-sense virtue of value for money into account when rating a wine and the points awarded each wine reflect this.

However, in one crucial respect, all wine, whether it costs £30 a bottle or £3, shares the same glaring weak point, and I would like to take the opportunity afforded by this introduction to expand on this point because it is almost invariably the cause of more defective wines, more disappointing bottles, and more bottles inspiring the purchasers to write to me and complain (in shocked tones wondering how I could have recommended such foul wine in the first place) when what they should have done is to have taken the offending bottle back to the retailer and asked for a replacement or their money back.

This weak point is the one created by that 1¾ inches of tree bark called a cork. Cork is the weakness, cork is the villain, cork is the culprit which gets away with murder. Frequently, it is murder most foul committed before a horde of witnesses. Is it not incredible that so many gifted men and women can make so many wonderful wines for comparatively so little money from so many countries by having so much control over nature and technology, and yet as a result of the faulty method of stoppering their masterpieces a proportion of those wines will be duds? Would a car maker shrug his shoulders and say 'Nothing I can do, squire, it's the nature of the beast' to a customer who complained that the vehicle sometimes refused to go backwards? Would you accept as reasonable the explanation from your newspaper publishers that they're sorry the copy you bought last Wednesday was completely blank but that's the way it is with newsprint and one in every two dozen copies is a dud?

Why do we accept risks with wine that we wouldn't tolerate for one moment with other products and services? The answer is the one which bedevils so much of the business of wine: snobbery, custom, ritual usage and *ignorance*. We drinkers *like* our wines sealed with a cork; screw caps, which serve airlines so well, are shunned (but more about these delightful sealants later) and wine boxes are generally despised. The extracting of the cork has so much ritual about it; so much masculine splendour as we wine wimps screw in that spiral of steel and open up paradise. What a lot of romantic bollocks! We put up with cork, one of the least consistent materials on earth, because we have been seduced into believing that wine wouldn't be wine without it. This is not true, as it happens; winemakers know it and corkmakers know it.

Winemakers are, for the most part, privately concerned about cork; corkmakers simply cannot guarantee a 100 per cent effective product. One reason winemakers don't give great public voice to the shortcomings of cork is that the great majority of wine drinkers simply do not know when most wines are corked anyway and so cork gets away blameless. Even the so-called experts, Master of Wine or whatever, do not necessarily know a corked wine when they come across one because often the defect passed on to the wine by a dodgy cork is assumed to be a characteristic of the wine. Many a wine is condemned as unpleasing when it has, in fact, been slightly soured by its cork. It is only when a wine is truly and incontestably foul that a wine is sent back in a restaurant or taken back to the retailer, and even then we shy British involve ourselves in the embarrassing confrontation this entails only when we have no choice or when our partner on the other side of the table gags in disgust. The whole reason a *sommelier* smells the cork is to detect if there is any taint, yet I have several times refused to accept wines with which wine waiters confessed they could find nothing wrong. This is because cork can be a subtle stealer as well as an almighty bludgeoner of flavour and fruit, and only in light, unwooded, sensitive white wines, rieslings for example or sauvignon blancs or certain sparkling wines, is cork taint detectable by the inexperienced palate when the theft is a subtle one.

In my experience, one in every two dozen wines I try has a defect, sometimes slight, sometimes severe, as a result of a faulty cork, and with Australian wines I would put the figure as high as one in twenty, maybe higher. This average is borne out in tastings I conduct in my own home and in tastings held on retailers' and winery premises. I asked Angela Mount, Somerfield's wine buyer, about cork and she said that in her experience French wines were the worst. 'Of the wines we taste, potentially for listing, certainly the worst offenders are France,' she told me. 'I get the highest incidence of corked wines from French wines, followed by

Portugal. Compared to France, the incidence of corked wines from the new world including Australia is low.'

Even when she buys wines out of her own money, the professional can get caught out. 'I bought half a case of Raimat Tempranillo as a customer from one of our own stores because I wanted some good Spanish wine at home,' she told me with a wry smile. 'Every bottle was corked. So with my buyer's hat on I started checking things out and Raimat admitted that they had some problems. They said it was the barrels. I said it was the corks. We delisted the wine on that basis.'

Last year, the Aussies sold us close on 60 million bottles of wine, so if my average is in any way reliable, and I fully accept that my experience may not be a statistically meaningful one in this context, then 3 million of those bottles were not giving their purchasers the pleasure their makers intended. With barrel-fermented or aged red wines the defects are more easily hidden, and no one except the winemaker him or herself, knowing every nuance of the aroma and the flavour structure of the wine he or she has made, can confirm cork taint when it is extremely slight.

Peter Bright, a winemaker based in Portugal, but who is making wine all over the world, told me: 'Australia is very sensitive to the cork problem because Australia has got very high internal standards.' Yet even winemakers can get it wrong. Steve Daniel, an Oddbins wine buyer and one of the fastest corked-bottle spotters around, told me that he once had to submit a wine to laboratory testing to prove it was corked because its maker refused to accept anything was wrong with the wine. The lab confirmed cork taint.

The history of wine is full of instances where Mankind accepts a defective product as the norm: from the oxidized liquid, almost acetic acid itself, handed out as the wine ration to Roman troops (hence the story of the vinegar offered to Christ on the cross), to the wickedly crude wines drunk in the eighteenth and nineteenth centuries which had to be fortified with brandy to become palatable. Wine drinkers have often had their palates accustomed to characteristics which were in truth defects, or considered defects by others, and today many a French champagne expert considers the aged champagne favoured by many Brits as a barbaric aberration, and that the character admired by these drinkers is nothing less than faultiness. The wines of Montilla are oxidized to suit the local palate and Madeira is deliberated baked; both wines undergo tortures which in other wines would produce unacceptable products. I am also personally of the opinion that many a corked bottle of port is cheerfully consumed, even by the knowledgeable, but the corkiness has been so subtle, masked as it is by a fortified red wine of considerable age, that only its maker would, or should, immediately spot it. It is interesting to note in this regard that several leading port shippers, Cockburns in particular, have felt sufficiently concerned about corks to introduce bottles, from the 1991 vintage on, with less variation than before in diameter along the whole length of the neck, and are using a shorter but fractionally wider cork. This will form a tighter seal and prevent what Cockburns call 'canals' forming in the cork which cause seepage. This is good news. (Especially with regard to Cockburns. The 1991 vintage is one of the most brilliant I have tasted – rating 16 points – and by 2006 and beyond, when it would start to reach maturity, I would expect to see this wine nudging 20. But not, of course, if seepage took place.)

Corked wine is a disgrace. How does it happen? How can it be detected? What could be done to prevent it?

We have the word cork in our language courtesy of the Latin *Quercus suber*. The first word means oak, the second cork, but in our role as the greatest linguistic thief on earth it is the first bit we have harvested, trimmed and polished to incorporate into our tongue in much the same way as the cork oak itself is relieved of its bark, which is then hewn into small roundels to become wine stoppers. The beauty of cork is its extraordinary lightness and elasticity; within five minutes of a faultless cork being squeezed into the open neck of a wine bottle it has expanded sufficiently to form an airtight seal and will last under the right conditions for thirty years or more. This elasticity is a feature of all corks made from a single piece of bark, as well as being present, to a lesser degree, in the 'composite' corks made from several pieces of bark, glued together, which are used for many wines nowadays. No other material in nature works in quite the same way, and no other bark.

Quercus suber grows mainly in Portugal, but there are also plantings in Spain, Algeria and Sardinia. (Portugal, in fact, grows 53 per cent of the world's cork but is actually responsible for 75 per cent of total world production of the finished cork product.) The cork tree grows nowhere else. Unlike other species of oak, or any other trees for that matter, the bark of *Quercus suber* is uniquely capable of being stripped off without hurting the tree itself. Trees are exogens, which means their trunk growth takes place outside, and this occurs annually via a glutinous substance called cambium which lies beneath the bark which is part of the tree itself. However, between this cambium and the bark there is sap, so if you strip the bark you damage the tree. *Quercus suber*'s quirk is that the sap, the lifeblood, is *under* the cambium, not above, so the outer layers of the bark are not part of the tree but form only a protective skin which may be harvested every decade or so without harm to the tree. These harvests take place in summer, the cambium quickly reasserts itself, and the layer of trunk which carries the sap is not harmed and the bark regrows. To look at the end results of a cork harvest is to be witness to the least exciting harvest time you can imagine; great knobbled and gnarled convex strips lie about the ground looking like the shed, fungoid-grey skins of gigantic and very mouldy ancient alligators who led distinctly miserable lives. Unlike other bark, cork is not brittle but soft and yielding and this is because its structure is composed of aerated cells. In the average cork there are more than a million of these cells, which is why a cork is so light: half its bulk is air. Bark from different trees is not all the same quality, it needs meticulous seasoning over several months and, in some cases, as long as one year, and is prey to fungus. Yet this bark becomes transformed to become a significant part of one of mankind's most profound pleasures and, in some cases, greatest treasures.

There are several problems with corks. The cheaper composite corks, constructed from glued-together chunks, can leak the glue which holds them together and so contaminate the wine. This leakage is a rarer phenomenon nowadays than once it was because manufacturing methods have improved. Composites used to be manufactured like one long sausage, extruded through a machine. Now individual moulds are used which result in the use of less glue, and the cork is compressed at high temperature to theoretically get rid of any cork smell. The use of conglomerate corks is almost invariably restricted to fast-moving supermarket and high street wines which are not cellared and are therefore in contact with cork for a comparatively short time.

However, taint still occurs too regularly with composites for comfort. These corks can also cause problems by their refusal to budge from their necks without resorting to arm-wrestling techniques. This is, of course, because they are less elastic than whole corks and liable to become unyielding lumps.

A small percentage in every batch of all corks will also have interior faults undetectable either by machine or by the human eye, and these faults will develop over time and permit air to get to the wine. This fault is readily detected when the wine is poured because the fruit has oxidized; it is tart, it is sharp and unappealing and, whether white or red, the wine is distinctly 'not right'. With older, oak-aged, distinguished red wines the power and concentration of the fruit is not so much rendered undrinkable by a faulty cork as simply dulled and lacking in the brilliance which should be there by right. The wine waiter and the restaurant manager, who was urgently called over to arbitrate when I refused to accept a Château Margaux 1947 at an official dinner at the Café Royal, both hopped about in fury at my rejection of a wine which was perfectly drinkable but evidently not the wine it should have been. The cork looked in excellent health for one at the end of its life; but had a microscope been taken to it I am quite sure it would have revealed an infinitesimally small defect which, over thirty years, permitted the robbery to take place at an arthritically slow rate. This wine confirmed Peter Bright's opinion that 'You've got the small percentage of your wines that are corked, but you've got this other percentage with cork influence so subtle that the wine just doesn't taste that good. It's "had the nose lopped off it", as we say. The problem is trichlorophenyls and the threshold is about five parts per trillion. These are very powerful aromatic substances and they block the olfactory nerve – they come up and they put a blanket on it. It's not a case of them smelling bad. It's like smelling an empty glass. It's not so much an active smell itself, it's smell blockage.'

The biggest problem which can be caused by a cork is a result of the process which enables wine stoppers to be manufactured from it in the first place. After the oak bark has been removed from the tree it is cleaned with chlorine bleach, but if the cork is not totally free of moisture, as can happen, then the cork is contaminated within and a chemical called 2-4-6 trichloranisole (TCA) develops to a greater or lesser degree. When this undetectably sick cork comes into contact with a bottle of wine it passes on its taint. It can smell of mushrooms, dusty books, or that horrid musty smell which comes from the opened drawer of a long-neglected desk. The degree of taint need only be incredibly small, a few nanograms per litre (10 g g/L), for it to be picked up by smell or taste.

The Common Market, concerned about the cork industry, has set up working groups in various member countries to both properly identify all the compounds which may cause cork taint, and also to look in depth at cork forestation and manufacture. The ultimate objective is to eliminate the taint and with it the estimated 2 per cent annual EU product wastage due to corkage (which works out at about £438 million a year). However, if the bureaucratic juggernaut behind this initiative lumbers as ponderously as it has done with other matters then drinkers have a long time to wait before a 100 per cent pure natural cork is produced.

My advice to anyone who opens a bottle of wine and finds the contents wildly unpalatable or fitting any of the subtler descriptions above is to go back to the supermarket or wine shop and get a replacement or your money back. If the cork smells musty or unpleasant then without doubt the cork has either robbed the wine of its fruit or passed on an over-smell of its own. It seems to me that a wine which has been lying on its side, kissing cork for four or five years, has had as much of itself in contact with that cork as it had in contact with wood, during its time in the barrel. Winemakers make a lot of fuss about their barrels and the wonderful influence of wood. Isn't it time they kicked up a ruckus about cork – the thing which can be equally as influential as wood, but only for the worse?

Twelve years ago in Australia the wine producer McWilliams discovered that a couple of hundred thousand bottles of one of its wines had been spoilt by duff corks and received several million dollars in compensation. Every wine producer has a bad cork story. They just don't care too much to tell them – because the ending is always a funny wine. When I was in Alsace in early spring I asked Jean Hugel, whose family company has been making some of the world's greatest late harvest wines for over 300 years, about cork and he was guarded, although he did say they had once, back in the late fifties, gone through a 100,000 batch of which 10 per cent were faulty. Asked whether he would dump cork if somebody came up with a better way of sealing wine, he said this:

'The cork, the noise, it adds poetry. You could seal very well without cork, with a screw cap. For wines, simple wines which are drunk fast, I wouldn't see any difference to putting a screw cap on. But for the moment, especially for ageing the great wines, we don't see another system of closing the bottle.'

On the other hand, Peter Bright reckons screw caps would keep wine fresh and uncontaminated for as long as needed. 'But it needs guts on a producer's part to dump the cork. I remember years ago when Pewsey Vale riesling in Australia came with a screw cap and every single bottle had to be withdrawn. The consumer hated the idea.'

As it happens, a British company, MCG Closures Limited, which makes the screw caps of the sort you see on spirit bottles, held a comparative wine-tasting for wine writers and people in the trade in March this year. This company had arranged for certain bottles of wine to be both bottled in the normal way by a driven cork and also in the way MCG would like to see all wine stoppered – with a screw cap. Eight wines were on display for the assembled experts to taste: 3 French, 2

Australian, 1 Canadian, 1 English, and 1 South African. The result was that no one present could truly and knowledgeably tell much difference between a bottle sealed with a cork and a bottle sealed with a screw cap, and those of us who thought we could spot the difference did so on the basis that the screw-capped wine was the fresher of the two. I guessed wrong 50 per cent of the time and so did everyone else more or less. The wines were of the '92 and '93 vintage. If the tasting proved anything it was that a screw cap is as good as any cork yet runs no risk of contamination, and it ought to result in cheaper wines. Corks can cost anything from £60 a thousand to £120 a thousand (around 12p each), but in some wines the corks can cost as much as 15p each. The screw cap, if it was widely adopted, would reduce these costs considerably.

Is the screw cap, then, the next revolution on the wine horizon? Tesco is talking to the Germans about replacing the corks on certain of its biggest selling lines with screw caps. Safeway also say they 'need to look closely at screw caps'. Waitrose is rumoured to be considering introducing a couple of bottles with screw caps. Other retailers are also looking at doing the same thing. What holds most of them back is their nervousness about customers' reactions and the possible criticism of wine commentators. As far as I'm concerned they have nothing to worry about. I only wish that the revolution would spread to a wider range of wines – especially wines of a greater perceived quality and value than fast-moving Germans. When I have asked winemakers if they thought their wines would keep just as well with a screw cap as with a cork, not one of them has said no.

I find corkscrews a nuisance and the ritual of cork removal irritating, and I would love to store all my wine standing up where I can read the labels (with a screw cap there's no need to lay the bottles down because there is no cork to keep moist).

However, will consumers put retailers under enough pressure
to get rid of cork? Will they complain enough on grounds of
lost quality? Certainly the closure manufacturers, if the polite
and gentle souls at MCG are anything to go by, will put little
pressure on wine producers on grounds of cost. I tried my
utmost at the MCG tasting to get the company to reveal how
much cheaper it must be to seal with a screw cap, but all they
would tell me was that a screw cap wouldn't be any more
expensive than a composite cork.

However, perhaps what MCG knows in its heart is that
screw caps will never replace corks in wines. The rituals of
storing wine lying down and removing the cork with a corkscrew are too sacred to be disturbed. What then can we
replace cork with? Cork, of course. Synthetic cork. A brilliant
substance which copies cork's virtues with none of its vices.

And this substance, I can reveal, exists. It is a cork, 38mm
long, made from lightweight, food-approved vinyl acetate
polymer, a form of plastic. It is made under a patented process
by the Novembal company, less than 50 kilometres from
Mâcon, and it imitates the colour of cork precisely, accepts a
corkscrew in the same way, and can be removed without
straining. It won't attract weevils (like natural cork), or go
mouldy under the capsule, and it'll never deposit cork dust in
your wine. It also creates a 100 per cent airtight seal. It can be
used in any bottle of wine, from the cheapest *vin ordinaire* to
the most expensive *vin de garde* (which might expect to be
cellared for decades). It is a beautiful product. It totally solves
the problem of corked wine because it is *a truly 100 per cent
neutral stopper*. The only small drawback is that once it is
removed from the neck of a bottle it cannot be put back with
ease. Plastic lacks the superb degree of springiness of natural
cork.

But it will never be the thief that natural cork is. It will never steal a wine's fruit or foul up a wine so completely it is undrinkable. It will never occasion a single reader writing to me wondering if I have lost my olfactory marbles.

Why is this cork not inside every single bottle of wine on sale? Ask Marks & Spencer. It is this remarkable establishment which knows as much about the plastic cork as anyone in this country; for the store has, discreetly, been using the Novembal product in certain of its cheaper German wines for five years, and on its French Country red and white wines for a somewhat shorter period. The store plans to extend its use to as many as three dozen wines.

Jane Kay, Marks & Sparks resident oenologist and wine boffin, told me this: 'I was horrified by the state of the cork industry in Portugal when I visited it. Part of the problem stems from the fact that over 50 per cent of corks come from 300/400 different companies, some employing half-a-dozen to ten people. It's a backward industry, some of it part-time. There is, as a result, not enough control between cork producer and cork buyer. It's only recently that the producers would even admit there was a problem in the first place.'

For Janet Lee of Tesco the problem starts with the stripping of trees at too young an age. 'Eight-and-a-half years instead of ten,' she says. But does this mean the store will abandon cork and go over to plastic? Only on a small experimental basis as yet. At Safeway there is much the same air of caution. Wine chief Liz Robertson is not over-enamoured with fake cork, though the store's own-label *vin blanc* and *vin rouge* both sport plastic. But 'We're not terribly thrilled about plastic corks, no,' she told me and went on to explain that she found plastic corks 'stuttered' as they left the bottle. Over long contact with alcohol perhaps? I think what Mrs Robertson means is that the plastic cork doesn't emerge from the bottle neck quite as smoothly as the natural product. She thinks screw caps are a better solution to the problem of duff corks and she also believes that the combination of the American determination to solve the problem, along with the EC study group, will lead to improvements in cork harvesting and production. 'There's no way we at Safeway will be sitting still on this matter,' she went on to say. 'Something needs to be done. There has to be change here. What we've all realized in the wine trade is that the problem isn't going to go away. It needs concerted action. Bringing all the cork producers together would help. Things will improve. But in the short term we're looking at the screw-cap route as a possible solution.'

Over at the Co-op there was a degree of surprise when I telephoned Paul Bastard, wine buyer, and asked him his feelings about the plastic cork I had just removed, with no audible stutter, from his store's bottle of Touraine Sauvignon Blanc. 'I didn't know we had one,' he said, taken aback. 'We've been wanting to do something about cork, and we've been looking at screw caps, but we're a bit timorous about taking the step. But a plastic cork? I'll investigate and phone you back.' When he did phone back it was to tell me he was pleased to be part of the revolution. Personally, I am delighted to be able to promise every single purchaser of the Co-op's Domaine du Clos du Bourg Sauvignon de Touraine 1992 a terrific wine for £3.35 with never a corked bottle.

Asda is very keen on plastic. It estimates that annual product wastage due to cork taint is as high as 5 per cent. This represents, in the store's own words, a substantial loss in customer satisfaction and profit. As a result, Asda has been using the plastic cork for some time. In this period only two customers have 'commented' on the use of plastic, and no corkage has ever been reported. Nick Dymoke Marr, one half of Asda's wine-buying team, told me that the store had started using them about a year ago on some red and white Côtes de Roussillon and Corbières. 'The only real complaint we've had in one year was a customer who said she found it difficult to put the cork back in the bottle once if had been taken out,' he told me. 'Our technical guys are currently in the process of briefing our Italian suppliers, our German suppliers, and our other French generic suppliers and asking them to investigate corks further. We're looking at rolling it out over the next eighteen months or so.'

Why abandon the conventional cork?

'Because we get a lot of cork problems. Particularly on wines that are quite neutral like Frascati. If it's something that's fairly heavy going like Bulgarian cabernet, most people probably wouldn't notice. They wouldn't see the fault in it that we saw. But with something like Frascati, where customers are coming in week after week buying the same bottle of wine, if it doesn't taste like it ought to then customers are very perceptive. The people we buy our Frascati from are going to start using plastic corks.'

What was the German reaction to plastic? Weren't they keen on the new technology involved?

'The Germans,' said Mr Dymoke Marr, 'have got slight problems. They heat the necks of the bottles as they go along the line, to keep a good seal for the cork, and the plastic melts as it goes into the top of the bottle. We're going to try and find a way of getting around that. But it's certainly something that's an on-going project and we feel important to the business.'

Is it cheaper to seal a wine bottle with a plastic cork? Apparently not. But money isn't a consideration as far as Asda are concerned if it eliminates customers' dissatisfaction.

'Plastic is marginally more expensive – a fraction of a penny. And if you're talking about bottling tens of thousands of cases of wine that's a significant on-cost. But anything we can do to move away from faulty wine has got to be worthwhile.'

Amen to that. I find it revealing that no customer has ever complained about the cork on the grounds that it didn't seem like the real thing. No one, it seems, thought the difference worth remarking and I believe that no one would unless he was looking out for it. The plastic cork has the lightness and the feel of cork and it's embossed in the same way. I guess the only frustrated customers were those who tried to hammer the cork back in the bottle, but maybe most drinkers, quite sensibly, would settle for sealing any bottle intended for reuse with one of the rubber seals you can buy for pennies and which will become the norm when plastic corks are adopted worldwide.

And I do not doubt for one nano-second that this will come to pass. M & S, Asda and all the other supermarkets and wine retailers who are looking at the plastic cork are on the threshold of the biggest revolution in wine production methods since the modern style glass wine bottle was made possible by the blast furnaces of the inventive Sir Kenelm Digby in Gloucestershire, in the 1630s.

When this happens we will all get to drink wines free of any cork faults. More people will get to enjoy the wines they buy as their makers intended them to be enjoyed. And I will never receive another letter asking why a certain wine I have recommended smells like the interior of a laundry basket.

So, if the wine doesn't taste right, take it back. All the supermarkets in this book are staffed by agreeable human beings who will honour your rights under the Return of Goods Act and either give you your money back or replace the wine. If this happened with every bottle of corked wine sold then retailers would have no choice but to put pressure on their suppliers to mend their ways *and change to plastic corks*.

The cork is dying! Long live the cork!

How this guide works

Each supermarket in this guide is separately listed in alphabetical order. Each has its own introduction, with the wines logically arranged by country of origin, red and white (including rosés). Each wine's name is as printed on its label.

Each wine is rated on points out of 20. In practice, wines scoring less than 10 points are not included although sometimes, because a particular bottle has really got my goat and scored so miserably I feel readers might be amused by its inclusion, I stick in a low pointer. Over the past five years, you may be interested to know, this miserable vinous underclass has assaulted my palate in steadily decreasing numbers. Indeed, the rise in the quality of wines overall is reflected in this year's rating figures; higher ratings appear more frequently and in a few cases I have even been forced to tack on a further half-point, such has been the increase in complexity without an appreciable hike in prices.

An excellent supermarket wine can be so characterized because of its price, not only because it is rewarding to drink. I have made it unmistakably clear in my introduction to this book how much value for money is taken on board when I rate a wine. I expect expensive wines to be good but I do not always expect good wines to be expensive. Thus, a brilliant £10 bottle may not offer better value than a £3 wine because, although the pricier wine is more impressive, it is not, in my eyes, anywhere near three times as impressive.

The full scoring system, from my initial tasting and scoring point of view, works as follows:

20 Is outstanding and faultless in all departments: smell, taste and finish in the throat. Worth the price, even if you have to take out a second mortgage.

19 A superb wine. Almost perfect.

18 An excellent wine of clear complexity but lacking the sublime finesse for the top, yet fabulously good value.

17 An exciting, well-made wine at an affordable price.

16 Very good wine indeed. Good enough for *any* dinner party. Not expensive.

15 For the money, a great mouthful with real style.

14 The top end of everyday drinking wine. Well-made and to be seriously recommended at the price.

13 Good wine, not badly made. Not great, but very drinkable.

12 Everyday drinking wine at a sensible price.

11 Drinkable, but not a wine to dwell on.

10 Average wine (at a low price), yet still a passable mouthful. Also, wines which are expensive and, though drinkable, do not justify their high price.

9 Cheap plonk. Acceptable for parties in dustbin-sized dispensers.

8 Rough stuff. Feeble value.

7 Good for pickling onions.

6 Hardly drinkable except by desperate thirsts on an icy night by a raging bonfire.

5   Wine with all its defects and mass-manufacturing methods showing.

4   Not good at any price.

3   A palate polluter and barely drinkable.

2   Rat poison. Not to be recommended to anyone, even winos.

1   Beyond the pale. Awful. Even Lucretia Borgia wouldn't serve it.

For easy reference a condensed version of these ratings is to be found on the very last page of the book.

Prices

I cannot guarantee the price of any wine in this guide for all the usual trite reasons: inflation, economic conditions overseas, the narrow margins on some supermarket wines making it difficult to maintain consistent prices for very long and, of course, the existence of those freebooters at the Exchequer who are liable to up taxes which the supermarkets cannot help but pass on to the consumer. To get around this problem a price banding code is assigned to each wine:

A Under £2.50   B £2.50–£3.50   C £3.50–£5
D £5–£7   E £7–£10   F £10–£13
G £13–£20   H Over £20

Acknowledgements

I wrote in the acknowledgements to this book last year that I
worked alone, but this is, blessedly, no longer strictly true. I
taste alone and I *write* alone but I am grateful for the growth
of extra limbs and another brain for this year's book in the
shape of Linda Peskin, who organizes tastings for me and
helps me stay afloat amongst the ceaseless tide of my corres-
pondence, scribbled tasting notes, and train, tube, bus and
airline tickets. It is also a relief to find myself supported by
the sage advice of Sarah Lutyens and Felicity Rubinstein.
To be encouraged by Sarah Gleadell and Belinda Matthews
and energized by Angela Smith is also a delight, and I recognize I also owe a debt to many other people at Faber and
Faber who regard this lilliputian tome as some sort of mission. I must thank here, for grasping several nettles so resol-
utely, Tim Davies and Jonathan Tilston. I must also thank
Matthew Evans for so instructively pouring a bottle of red
wine over my only pair of white linen trousers. I would also
like to say a big thank you to all those supermarket wine
buyers who make my life easier when I do not always find it
easy to return the compliment. I would particularly like to
single out Janet Lee of Tesco, Liz Robertson of Safeway,
Mike Connolly of Sainsbury, Angela Mount of Somerfield
and Stuart Purdie of Morrisons. I would also like to thank
Jane Kay of Marks & Spencer, and Nick Dymoke Marr and
Robin Cooke of Asda. I am in debt to *Weekend Guardian* as
ever and to all those of its readers who write to me and keep
me on my toes, never letting me forget that my first duty is to
them as it is equally to the purchasers of this book. In many
ways I lead the life of Riley, whoever he was and however he

earned his immortality, and I regard this life to be licensed by my devotion, only occasionally wavering during periods of heavy research, to my readers' interests.

Asda

The Morecambe & Wise of British supermarket wine buying are still at it and in superb form. Asda made several cuts last year, including flogging off its superbly equipped laboratory, but Philip Clive and Nick Dymoke Marr have continued to be amongst the most entertaining wine buyers around. It would, of course, be commercial suicide for Asda to give two such tireless souls the heave-ho, for it is extremely doubtful if any other two wine buyers could do their job when the competition employs three and four times that number of buyers. These two guys are not only doing a grand job buying wine, they're also doing an innovative job of presenting it.

For Asda, where wine is concerned, is now showing the most radically different face to the world of any supermarket. Mr Dymoke Marr, who exhibits enthusiasm, floridity and expansiveness of personality (along with the beginnings of a pair of Edwardian sideburns), explained it to me in these words.

'We're putting together a package of initiatives,' he started formally (as though he couldn't quite believe himself what he was about to tell me), 'which we think are going to have a dramatic effect on our wine sales. The key to it is the complete moving away from country of origin on our shelves. We will merchandise white wines by how dry or how sweet they are and red wines by how light or how full. Four stores began the experiment, for up to six months, the longest of which was Edinburgh. All the tests that we've done on it in terms of sales, profit, and what our customers think of it are totally positive. We now intend to go national. There are now fifteen pilot stores around the country, which happened around 25 July this year, and following the success of these, every store will be organized this way over 1995.'

I expressed a measure of scepticism. I was really wondering how a reader might find a wine I had recommended if it couldn't be found under country of origin.

'Consumer research tells us that people come into the store and they either say "I'm going to buy a bottle of Frascati because that's what I always buy" or they say "I like a dry wine and I want to spend about £3". The two primary thoughts in their mind which steer them to either buying or not are what is it going to cost me and what does it taste like. The fact that it comes from France, Italy or Spain . . .'

But what if a customer wanted to buy a wine that somebody had recommended? A bead of sweat had broken out on my brow. Was this the end of the supermarket wine writer as we know him?

'I spent a day out at our Burnley store the other week and there wasn't one person who found it confusing,' he said, throwing me a lifeline. 'I was really surprised. I thought there would be at least a handful who said it was a real nightmare. So I think as an on-going thing this is going to be reasonably revolutionary, because nobody else has done it in this country.'

I left the subject alone. I'm not entirely convinced moving away from country of origin is a good idea. But I'm prepared to be persuaded and I'm looking forward to my postbag. I brought up the fact that he had mentioned a package of initiatives. Could he reveal further goodies contained in this?

'One of the other things we tested last year,' Nick expanded, 'was a training course which was sponsored by Stowells of Chelsea. Fifteen regional courses which every wine department supervisor attended. They were three-day courses ending with the Wine and Spirit Education Trust certificate exam. 214 people sat the exam and only twelve people failed. We got seventy 'A' grades as well. Totally stunning results and very encouraging because the way I view Asda is that we've got fifty brilliant stores that are really doing the right thing and selling a lot of wine, we've got fifty stores where we're not very far from getting to that level, we've got fifty stores where we've got a lot of work to do and we've got fifty stores where we're struggling badly. So training for us is really key. Philip and I can put the most brilliant range of wines on the shelf but at the end of the day somebody has to sell it to the customer and we can't just leave it up to people to come in and stick it in their basket.'

I got that queasy feeling again. The feeling when it suddenly dawns on you that maybe you don't have a future in your chosen line of work. I asked Nick if all these initiatives didn't change somewhat the basic nature of the supermarket.

'Yeah, it does. Because the supermarket industry is going to have to watch really closely what people like Oddbins, Threshers, Victoria Wine are doing in the high street. Threshers particularly and up in the north Cellar 5 as well. That's our heartland, we've got a hell of a lot of stores up there, and our customers – like Morrisons and Kwik Save – patronize these high street retailers. You know what's interesting about this? We get less of our customers through our wine department than our competitors. That gives us more potential than our competitors. If we can get 5 per cent more of our shoppers per week to walk through our wine department that's an amazing result for our business.'

Strength returned. I was still in business. Maybe enough wine drinkers would continue to read my book to keep the roof over my head and the goldfish in breadcrumbs. But would these drinkers be Asda customers? What was there to tell Asda's customers, potential as well as actual, about the actual wines in the store?

'We've been through a range-reduction exercise over the last twelve months. But we've not made our range any less interesting than it was. In some ways it's actually more interesting because of wines like Moroccan red, which we're actually selling a lot of. Now that to me is a real success. It proves we don't need a colossal range like Tesco's. They've got something like 600 different wines. We've got 300 and there's still room for manoeuvre. Like bag-in box, for instance. We turned a slide into a growth in spite of reducing the range from twenty-seven to eighteen. We kept the boxes like the Cape red and the Cape white which we're flogging for nine-and-a-half quid, which is brilliant value for money, and we're in the process of putting together some things like Spanish bag-in-box and Hungarian chardonnay. All under £10. From a 7 per cent year on year decline in box sales, the most recent figures show a growth of about 15 per cent.'

You see how easy it is to like these Asda blokes? They're frank with you. I like their openness and their genuine desire to chance their arms. Like that Moroccan red. Or, more exotically considering the price, Barolo. By one of those coincidences which makes life such a rich, Koestlerian tapestry I found myself taking an Asda Barolo to watch Arsenal play Turin on the box. Barolo of course is Turin's house wine. The match was a meagre, plodding affair, barely fit to set beside a wine so generous and individual; it finished with more aplomb than any forward on the pitch, offered more variety, and it paraded richer, more silky skills. The wine has a liquorice undertone which is subtle and understated at first and then it wallops you with a soupy fruit which is softly dazzling without being brash. It has a lovely refined balance to it. Mind you, the wine ought to be good. It costs £8.49 a bottle, but then since it has been bought by Asda to replace, in Mr Dymoke Marr's words, 'some more expensive rather naff

burgundies and Bordeaux', it should be judged in this context
– and judge it in this context I have and I'm happy, therefore,
to rate it highly. I know of no burgundy or Bordeaux under
eight and a half quid I could more pleasurably drink. It takes
an hour before it comes on strong but then so did Arsenal.
The wine is made by Fratelli Cavalotto, a name well regarded
by Barolo aficionados, and it comes from a single vineyard,
Bricco Boschis. It's called Cavalotto Barolo 1988. Another
handsome Italian red from Asda, part of the same naff Frog
replacement package as the Barolo, is Rosso delle Minere
Montescudaio 1990 at £6.99. This wine is from the little
appreciated area of Montescudaio, the other side of Chianti,
towards Livorno on the coast, and uses a proportion of the
same grape variety as Chianti, the sangiovese, along with
trebbiano and malvasia. It has black cherry and blackcurrant
fruit in an overall earthy style and has a delicious dry and
bitter, almost almondy, finish. It's a lovely wine.

Now the revealing thing about these bottles is in Mr
Dymoke Marr telling me that they were bought to replace
more fashionable wines which weren't so hot. This tells us
that we have here a wine buyer who is using his taste, judge-
ment, and knowledge of his customers not only to pander to
their well-established prejudices but to lead them down paths
less familiar yet ones less expensive to tread and richer in
experience. Asda, more so than its major competitors, enjoys
these well-judged rushes of blood to the head. Look how
they've re-arranged their wine shelves. This is the strength of
a two-man wine department: no committees.

This is not to suggest that the store ignores the more
familiar paths. Indeed, Asda may have a mere three quarters
of a case of red bordeaux on its list, for example, but the
bottles are carefully chosen. In Château de Paranchère,
Mayne de Grissac, and in particular Haut-Saric, the store is

offering some of the best value under-a-fiver clarets of anyone – clarets with true richness and complexity. We will pass over the red and white burgundies, pause briefly at the Beaujolais (the Morgon and B-Villages aren't bad), appreciate the red Rhônes, examine with little interest the white Loires, and plunder with enthusiasm the French regional reds. Germany is represented, battling hard to keep its quality bottles (of which there is a half-dozen) in front of an indifferent consumer's nose, Italy is a favourite hunting ground of our two buyers (see above) and so is Spain. Portugal has only Dão and Bairrada of any real interest to offer, the USA is very weakly represented (no loss here, though, for the bargain hunter), but Australia has eighteen representatives including palate-arousing western Australian wines. Chile is good, South Africa is also sound but could improve hugely, Bulgaria is heavily in there, and so is Hungary. There is an excellent choice of sparkling wines.

I think I've managed to find the pick of this list amongst the wines which follow and I must say I've enjoyed the trip. For a wine buying department you could pack into a telephone box and leave room for a third and urgent caller, Messrs Clive and Dymoke Marr are performing a minor miracle. But, lads, can't you get stuck into Portugal a bit more? And you might poke about New Zealand with more profit, too. Tremendous bargains in these places. And what about Hawaii and Zimbabwe? What could better support the theory that arranging wines by country of origin is out of date than a Hawaiian sparkling wine and a Zimbabwean rosé?

I look forward to seeing these wines on Asda's shelves. They were meant for one another.

ARGENTINIAN WINE – *red*

**Argentinian Trapiche Cabernet Sauvignon
1990** 13 £B

AUSTRALIAN WINE – *red*

Berri Estates Cabernet Sauvignon/Shiraz 1990 14 £C

Berri Estates Cabernet Sauvignon/Shiraz 1992 15 £C
Sweet finish to the dry fruit. Balanced, full (yet not over-blown), perfect style of fruit for all manner of grilled meats.

Fairview Estate Shiraz 1992 14 £C
Soft seductive fruit with a touch of spice (cinnamon toast? Surely not).

**Goundrey Windy Hill Cabernet Sauvignon
1988** 15 £D
Tangy and rich. Strong, purposeful wine with fruit and acid well balanced, stylish. Savoury polish to the fruit. Will suit strong food.

**Goundrey Windy Hill Cabernet Sauvignon
1989** 13 £E
Interesting aroma and mature fruit.

Hardy's Nottage Hill Cabernet Sauvignon 1992 14 £C

Oxford Landing Cabernet/Shiraz 1992 12 £C

Penfolds Bin 35 Shiraz Cabernet 1991 15 £C
Terrific. Savoury, bold, convincing, stylish.

Rowanbrook Cabernet Sauvignon Reserve 1991 15 £C
A lot of pleasure here, for the fruit has a sweet blackcurrant finish to the dryness of the style which is quite delicious.

South Australia Shiraz 1992   12 £C

South Australian Cabernet Sauvignon 1989   15 £C

South Eastern Australia Shiraz Cabernet 1992   16 £B
Vivid structure. It hits the palate like softly machined leather. Lots of fruitiness to engage all the taste buds. Has an elegant strawberry finish.

South Eastern Australian Shiraz/Cabernet
1990   14 £B

AUSTRALIAN WINE – *white*

Goundrey Estate Langton Chardonnay 1993   15 £C

Goundrey Langton Semillon/Sauvignon Blanc
Mount Barber   13 £C

Hardy's R.R. 1994   10 £C

Hill Smith Old Triangle Riesling 1993   12 £C

Mitchelton Marsanne 1993   12 £C

Mitchelton Un-Oaked Marsanne 1992   14 £C
Agreeably unflamboyant.

Mitchelton Un-Oaked Marsanne 1993   14 £C
Rich and fruitily riveting. Lovely grilled chicken wine.

Orlando St Hilary Chardonnay 1993   15 £D
A very classy product: woody (without a forestry commission
licence), fruity (in the old-fashioned French style), balanced.

Oxford Landing Chardonnay 1993   12 £C

Oxford Landing Sauvignon Blanc 1993   14 £C
Excellent performance in a fringe theatre mould but at close
to West End prices. Still, there's no doubting the fruit, its
balanced effect on the palate and the overall style.

South Australian Chardonnay 1993   13 £C

South Eastern Australia Semillon Chardonnay
1993   15 £B
Always an impressive blend from Asda this wine, and the '93
is no exception: rich, full yet fresh, lingering finish, this is
superbly stylish for the money.

BULGARIAN WINE – *red*

Burgas Country Red Cabernet/Merlot   14 £A
Solid plonk.

Merlot 1990   11 £B

Oriachovitza Cabernet Sauvignon Reserve
1989   12 £B
Eucalyptus and dilute blackcurrant.

Oriachovitza Cabernet Sauvignon Reserve
1990   16 £B
Wonderful minty, ripe blackcurrant and plum fruit, dry yet
finishing sweetly and naturally. True class for a silly price.

BULGARIAN WINE – *white*

Preslav Chardonnay Sauvignon Vintage Blend   14   £B
Rich, almost full-blooded fruit but held back by its east
European manners. Great food wine.

Preslav Vintage Blend Chardonnay/Sauvignon
1992   11   £B

CHILEAN WINE – *red*

Cabernet/Merlot (Asda)   14   £B
Rich beefy blend. A veritable stew of a wine; a curiously ripe
yet dry combination of characterful fruitiness. Very good food
wine. Will ride roasts especially well.

Caliterra Cabernet Sauvignon 1991   14   £B
Very good value.

Rowanbrook Cabernet/Malbec 1992   14   £B

Rowanbrook Cabernet Sauvignon, Mataquito Valley
1990   15   £C
Appealing sweet blackcurrant finish to soft, fruity wine which
is of appeal to grilled and roast meat dishes.

Rowanbrook Cabernet/Malbec 1993   15.5   £B
Elegant, complex, deep; most attractively textured and fruited.

CHILEAN WINE – *white and rosé*

Caliterra Chardonnay 1992   14 £C
Lovely melon/lemon style. Again, not huge. A touch expensive but it has got style.

Caliterra Chardonnay Cunco 1993   15 £C
Delicious, slightly woody fruit which is very controlled and fine.

Chilean Sauvignon Blanc 1993 (Asda)   14 £B

Rowanbrook Chardonnay Reserve 1992   16.5 £C
Wonderful melon/lemon fruit with pineapple acidity. Terrific buttery quality to the texture and the wood integration is nigh perfection. A very good wine indeed for the money to shame many a white burgundy maker.

Santa Helena Chilean Rosé 1992   15 £B

Santa Helena Rosé 1994   15 £B
One of the fleshiest rosés around for the money. Lovely fruit.

Sauvignon Blanc 1992 (Asda)   15 £B
Ooh! What delicious fruit here – like squashy melon and bananas – but undercut and freshened by good vibrant acidity. Great structure.

ENGLISH WINE – *white*

Denbies English White Wine 1992   15 £B
Possibly the finest wine made in Surrey.

FRENCH WINE – *red*

Beaujolais (Asda) 12 £B
Cheap and cheerful.

Beaujolais-Villages Domaine des Ronze 1993 12 £C

Cabernet Sauvignon Vin de Pays d'Oc 14 £B
Typical baked clay dryness of the grape but not the austerity
which this sometimes implies. Lovely soft fruit with buried
flavours. Great with roast meat. Under three quid, this is
some bottle: rich and captivatingly blackcurrant, and pos-
sessed of considerable style.

Cahors (Asda) 13 £B
This isn't a Cahors! It's been prettified with merlot so it's soft
and cuddly instead of bristling with fierce 100% auxerrois
fruit. Shame!

Château Balac Cru Bourgeois AC Haut-Medoc
1990 13 £D

Château de Cabriac Corbières 1991 14 £B
Drinking brilliantly now, this vintage, having been softened
and opened up.

Château de Parenchère AC Bordeaux Supérieur
1990 14 £D
Good style. But put it down for a couple of years and see how
much better it gets.

Château du Bois de la Garde, Côtes du Rhône
1989 13 £C

Château Haut-Saric, Bordeaux 1990 14 £B

Château Haut-Saric, Bordeaux 1992   15   £B
Drinking softly and sweetly.

Château La Ramière, Côtes du Rhône 1992   13   £C
Very tasty. Good earthy fruit.

**Château Mayne de Grissac, Côtes de Bourg
1990**   13   £C
Rather a spiky little wine which needs to soften considerably
to be comfortable on the tongue. Lay down for next year?

Château Plaisance AC Côtes de Bourg 1990   13   £C

Château Val-Joanis Côtes du Luberon 1990   15   £C
Under four quid but punching in the six-quid-middle-weight
Côtes-du-Rhône league.

Château Vieux Georget 1990   11   £C

**Châteauneuf-du-Pape, Château Fines Roches
1988**   13   £D

Claret, Asda   14   £B
If you want soft, ripe, approachable claret at a rock-bottom
price, this is your bottle.

Domaine de Barjac, Vin de Pays du Gard 1990   12   £B

Domaine de Barjac Vin de Pays du Gard 1992   13   £B
Blackcurrant jam without sugar.

**Domaine de Grangeneuve, Coteaux du
Tricastin**   13   £C

Fitou (Asda)   13   £B
Dry, earthy, pleasant fruit: excellent value bottle.

Fleurie Domaine Verpoix 1993   11   £D
Some attractive fruit here. The price lets it down.

Fleurie Prince de Bruillez 1993	12	£D

French Vin de Pays Rouge Carafe	10	£B

**Mas Segala Côtes du Roussillon Villages
1993**　　　　　　　　　　　　　　16.5　£C
Superb logan-, black- and raspberry-flavoured wine of real
character and forceful style whilst offering soft texture of
considerable class. Very impressive for the money. Has a
violet-scented touch to it quite individual and exotic like a
quirky C-du-P. Has developing tannins which mean this wine
will age well for 2/3 years and more.

Merlot, Vin de Pays d'Oc (Asda)	13	£B

Morgon, Michel Jambon 1991	12	£D

Pinot Noir Bourgogne 1992 (Asda)	12	£C

Pinot Noir Vin de Pays 1992　　　　　　13　£C
This is a sporting try but the grape is not the most suited to
the area. It's a bit like seeing a sprinter hurdling: starts well
but stumbles at the finish.

**Pinot Noir Vin de Pays Producteurs de Limoux
1992**　　　　　　　　　　　　　　　　10　£C

Red Burgundy 1992 (Asda)	10	£C

Saint-Laurent Vin Pays de l'Hérault 1993　　15　£B
Lovely chewy tannins, coal-edged and rich. Great wine to
keep for a year or two or to drink now with spicy sausages.

Santenay, Foulot, Château Perruchot 1993	11	£E

St-Chinian (Asda)　　　　　　　　　　13　£B
Also available in a 1.5 litre bottle for £5.49. A dry, full-bodied

red. This wine will benefit from laying down for another 6
months to a year (in the big bottle).

St-Emilion (Asda)	13	£C

Stylish, dry, good weight of fruit.

St-Laurent, Vin de Pays d'Hérault 1991	13	£B

Syrah, Vin de Pays des Collines Rhondaniens (Asda)	13	£C

Vin de Pays Cabernet Sauvignon (Asda)	13	£B

Vin de Pays des Bouches du Rhône (Asda)	12	£B

Vin de Pays des Côtes de Gascogne	12	£C

Vin de Pays Merlot (Asda)	14	£B

A lot of rich fruit for the money, dry and full of flavour.

FRENCH WINE – *white*

Blanc de Blancs (Asda)	11	£A

Bourgogne Pinot Noir 1992 (Asda)	12	£C

Burgundy 1993 (Asda)	10	£C

Chablis 1992 (Asda)	14	£D

Very good stuff, very good, but why can't it be cheaper? It's
steely and lean and very authentic but the price is out of step
with the rest of the act, which is very modern.

Chablis Premier Cru 'Les Fourchaumes' 1992	15	£E

Delicious, expensive, will develop well over the next 4/5
years. Hugely drinkable now for rich layabouts.

Chardonnay Bourgogne 1992 (Asda)   12   £C

Chardonnay, Vin de Pays d'Oc (Asda)   12   £C

Château Fondarzac Entre deux Mers 1993   14   £C
Oysters and this? Laurel and Hardy.

**Chenin, Vin de Pays de la Haute Vallée de l'Aude
1990**   14   £B
An excellently balanced wine of some character. Great value.
Very modern in style, clean and fresh. Don't go near muscadet when you can pick up quality like this at so much less.

Corbières Blanc 1993 (Asda)   13   £B

Côtes de Duras Sauvignon Blanc (Asda)   12   £B
Of some use when shellfish are around.

Domaine des Deux Roches St-Veran 1993   13   £D
Some style and burgundian class.

Domaine St François Sauvignon Blanc 1993   14   £B
Gooseberry deliciousness. Aromatic and delightfully thirst-
quenching.

Fortant Sauvignon Blanc Vin de Pays d'Oc 1993 14 £C
Only falls a bit short on the finish, otherwise it's a very good,
good-value, sauvignon blanc.

French Vin de Pays Blanc Carafe   10   £B
Flash packet, feeble booze.

Le Pigoulet Vin de Pays du Gers 1993   15   £B
Perfect little glug: modest, fruity (with lurking pear-drop
aromas and flavours), fresh and hugely appealing.

Montagny Domaine de Montorge 1992   12   £D

Montagny Premier Cru 'Les Coères'
Domaine de Montorge 1989   11   £D

Muscadet, Domaine Gautron 1992   11   £C

Muscadet Sur Lie Domaine Guy Bossard 1993   13   £C

Muscat Cuvée Henry Peyrottes   15   £B
*The effect is instant and gratifying. As I drained my first glass, it
seemed to me that a torchlight procession, of whose existence I had
hitherto not been aware, had begun to march down my throat and
explore the recesses of my stomach. The second glass, though slightly
too heavily charged with molten lava, was extremely palatable. It
helped the torchlight procession along by adding to it a brass band of
singular sweetness of tone. And with the third somebody began to
touch off fireworks in my head.* Thank you, Sir Pelham Grenville
Wodehouse.

Pouilly-Fumé, Domaine Patrick Coulbois 1992   11   £E

Puligny-Montrachet Domaine Carillon 1988   10   £F

Sancerre La Porte du Caillou H. Bourgeois
1992   12   £E

Vin de Pays Chardonnay (Asda)   11   £C

Vin de Pays des Côtes de Gascogne (Asda)   15   £B
Pineapples and peaches crisply conceived. Excellent quaffer.

Vin de Pays des Côtes de Gascogne, Cap de Bosc
1991   14   £B
A superbly fruity and generous wine. Lush style. Very
attractive.

Vouvray, Domaine de l'Epinay N.V.   11   £D

GERMAN WINE – *white*

Bereich Bernkastel (Asda)	11	£B

**Bretzenheimer Vogelsang Riesling Spätlese
Schloss**   12   £D

Deidesheimer Hofstuck Kabinett 1993   10   £B

Flonheimer Adelberg 1993   14   £B

**Graacher Himmelreich Riesling Kabinett,
Reichsgraf Von Kesselstatt**   14   £D
Superb, clean, flinty, lemon-rich wine. Brilliant value aperitif.
As invigorating to the taste buds as a fresh spring day to the
soul. Put down for 3/5 years.

**Herxheimer Himmelreich Huxelrebe Beerenauslese
1988 (half)**   14   £E

**Hochheimer Holle Riesling Kabinett Geheimrat
Aschrott 1992**   13   £C
Good but developing. Pity to drink it until 1998.

Mainzer Domherr Spätlese 1993 (Asda)   12   £B

**Niersteiner Petenthal Riesling Auslese Graf
Wolff Metternich**   12   £D
Sweet and simpering. Will pick up some character by 1999.

**Niersteiner Rosenberg Riesling Kabinett,
Metternich 1991**   13   £C

Niersteiner Spiegelberg Kabinett 1993 (Asda)   14   £B
I'd happily accept this as an aperitif any day.

**Wiltinger Braunfels Riesling Kabinett, Von
Volxem 1992**   12   £C

Wiltinger Scharzberg 1992   10   £B

HUNGARIAN WINE – *red*

Hungarian Cabernet Sauvignon 1993 (Asda)   14   £B
Has some real flavour and style.

Hungarian Merlot/Kekfrancos, Dunavar (3 litre) 8   £E
Connoisseur collection! One smell of it and I fled.

Hungarian Merlot 1993 (Asda)   14   £B
Nice smokey fruit. Very agreeable glug.

Kekfrancos 1993 (Asda)   14   £B
Lots of soft ripe fruit which, though dourly introduced, aromatically responds once the fruit is on the tongue.

Villany Hills Cabernet Sauvignon 1992   15   £B
Touch of leather on the bouquet, rich fruit, dry and brambley
to the tongue, with good balancing acidity and a firm finish.
Excellent value for money. Has soft but noticeable tannins
which impart a pleasant grip to the wine, and I dare say the
wine would age well for a couple of years. Excellent roast and
grilled food wine.

Villany Hills Merlot 1992   12   £B
Some spiciness about the fruit.

HUNGARIAN WINE – *white*

Chardonnay Mescsekaljou 1992   13   £B
Decent firmness of fruit which is a touch sweet to finish.

Hungarian Chardonnay 1993 (Asda)   15   £B
Dry touches to a recognizably chardonnay melony fruitiness
make this a bargain for the money and an admirable partner for
light pastas.

**Hungarian Chardonnay Reserve Mecsekaljou
1993**   14   £B
Why Private Reserve on the label? I am suspicious of these
pretensions – especially when the words are little better than
lies (the wine is not private and it is not reserved). That said, it is
brimful of ripe pear/melon fruit.

Muscat 1993 (Asda)   13   £B
Brilliant aperitif.

Pinot Blanc 1993 (Asda)   13   £B
This is very far from unpleasant but it has a woodiness lurking
in the fruit and insufficient acidic balance to provide a counter-
weight.

Sauvignon Blanc Iveltelini, Dunavar (3 litre)   12   £E

ITALIAN WINE – *red*

Barbera d'Asti Cantine Gemma 1990   15   £C
Baked apple and curranty undertones to the ripe fruit which
offers violets, plums and an overall splendid sense of balance.

Bardolino (Asda)   12   £B

Barolo Bricco Boschis Cavalotto 1988   16   £E
For a detailed description of this wine, see pp.4–5.

Barolo Cavalotto Giuseppe   13   £E
A very soft-shouldered Barolo, most accommodating to the
tender-palated – unlike many Barolos which are heavy mon-
sters reeking of liquorice.

Carbone, Aglianico del Vulture 1988   15   £C

Chianti 1993 (Asda)   12   £B

Chianti Classico 1990 (Asda)   13   £C

Chianti 'Colli Senesi' 1992   15   £B
Delicious stealthy fruit (creeps up on you softly).

Ciro Rosso Classico 1992   12   £C

Montepulciano d'Abruzzo, Cantine Tollo 1993   14   £A
Lovely squashy fruit. Spread it on bread.

Quercia Al Poggio Chianti Classico 1990   16   £C
A superb Chianti Classico by any standards, with typical
terracotta (baked earth) fruit, yet in this example the fruit is so
soft it makes the tongue weep for more.

Rosso delle Minere Montescudaio 1990   15   £D
This wine is from the little-appreciated area of Montescudaio
the other side of Chianti, towards Livorno on the coast, and
uses a proportion of the same grape variety as Chianti, the
sangiovese, along with trebbiano and malvasia. It has black
cherry and blackcurrant fruit in an overall earthy style and has a
delicious dry and bitter, almost almondy, finish. It's a lovely wine.

Sangiovese delle Marche   13 £B

Sangiovese di Romagna 'Riva' 1993   15 £A
Best bottle of plonk I've tasted in a while. It'll sit very nicely on
the dining table beside a plateful of spaghetti. Soft, gluggable
to the point of indecency, this is a modern curiosity (made by a
Chilean based wine maker).

Sicilian Rosso (Asda)   13 £B
Nice, sweet, bruised fruit touch to the wine.

ITALIAN WINE – *white*

Frascati (Asda)   11 £B

Frascati Superiore (Asda)   13 £B
Some rich fruit here, curiously.

Orvieto Classico Cardeto 1992   14 £B
As good as they get for Orvieto: balanced, clean, fresh.

Pinot Grigio 'Ca'Pradai' Bidoli 1993   15 £B
Ye Gods! Fruit in a pinot grigio! (A delicious touch of apricot
no less.) This phenomenal happenchance is as unusual as
finding a hen with teeth.

Sicilian Bianco (Asda)   15 £B
Nutty and crisp – like a Stephen Fry one-liner. Also superb
value.

Soave Classico 'Corte Olive' Lenotti 1993   14 £B
Think all Soave is junk? Taste this. It has style, fruit, balance
and finish.

Verdicchio delle Marche (Asda)   13 £B

Vino da Tavola Bianco (Asda)   14 £B
White table wine certainly sounds a more romantic proposition in the Italian language and this example can sit on
swankier tables than most. Has melons and lemons chiming
together most harmoniously.

MOROCCAN WINE – *red*

Moroccan Red Wine, Domaine Mellil   16 £B
Touch of mint to this virile beauty. A lovely, ripe, full bottle of
dry yet vivaciously fruity wine.

PORTUGUESE WINE – *red*

Barraida 1990 (Asda)   13 £B
Curious appley touch to the fruit.

Dão 1992 (Asda)   15 £B

Douro 1991 (Asda)   13 £B
Rather overripe and sweetly raisiny.

PORTUGUESE WINE – *white*

Douro 1990/91 (Asda)   13 £B
Excellent value under £3.

Vinho Verde   13 £B

ROMANIAN WINE – *red*

Romanian Cellars Pinot Noir/Merlot 1990 16 £B
Brilliant combo with deep chocolatey fruit undercut by a
blackcurrant figginess which finishes with a soft, rich, velvet
texture. Good with spicy sausages and mash.

Romanian Pinot Noir 1986 13 £B
Won't somebody take pity on this one? It's been hanging
around Asda's shelves for the devil of a long time.

SOUTH AFRICAN WINE – *red*

Clearsprings Cape Red 13 £B
Soft plum with hints of raspberry. But it is dry, though
beautifully rounded on the finish. Also available in 3 litres.

Fairview Estate Shiraz 1992 12 £C

Kanonkop Bouwland Red 1992 15 £C
A big, rich, rounded, berried wine with an underlying ripeness
of tone which curiously never invades the dryness of the wine
or dilutes its power.

Landskroom Estate Pinotage 1993 15 £C
Soft, with a lush sweet touch to the subtly smokey fruit.
Delicious wine to pour down a thirsty throat.

SOUTH AFRICAN WINE – *white and rosé*

Asda Cape White   13   £B
Modern fruit-drop fruit.

Astonvale Robertson Chardonnay 1993   14   £C
Modern style of fruitiness which mingles soft and hard fruit
aromas and flavours to telling effect.

Astonvale Robertson Valley Chardonnay 1992   13   £C
Not wholly convincing as other Robertson chardonnays (not
much delicious citrus quality).

Fairview Estate Dry Rosé 1994   12   £B
Inoffensive.

Fairview Estate Dry Rosé, Paarl 1993   10   £B

Fairview Estate Gewürztraminer 1994   13   £C
Delicious and very effective aperitif.

**Spes Bona Chardonnay, Van Louveren,
Robertson 1993**   14   £C
Delicious, stylish, fruity and well-crafted. Good fruit, not
over-rich or gawky. Nice balance. Touch of mint perhaps, but
this passes for elegance.

Van Louveren Sauvignon Blanc 1994   14   £B
Subtly nutty undertones to steely fruit. Great fish wine. Needs
more time in bottle? Possibly.

SPANISH WINE – *red*

Bodegas Campillo, Rioja Crianza 1988 16 £C
Without a hint of the cramped, woody undertones of the usual
beast, this example is dry, the fruit gushing with flavour. A
wine of considerable strength of character and style.

Don Darias 14 £B
Exuberantly flows the Don.

Late-Bottled Vintage Port (Asda) 13 £D
Try it with blue cheese, for it has a touch of sweetness to
tackle the most astringent Stilton.

León 1986 (Asda) 16 £B
Suede fruit! Drinking brilliantly, soft yet dry.

Navarra (Asda) 13 £B

Ribera del Duero Señorio de Nava 1987 14 £D
Maturely reposing, the fruit is assertive without being gawky
or loose-limbed. A very together wine. Excellent with cheese
and biscuits.

Rioja 1990 (Asda) 15 £B
Vanilla and mint, softly compressed. Delicious if you like
those flavours.

Torres Coronas 1990 12 £C

Valencia Red (Asda) 13 £A
Soft and fruity. Well, sort of . . .

Viña Albali, Valdepeñas 1990 13 £B

SPANISH WINE – *white*

Fino Sherry Quinta Osborne y Cía   15   £D
Bone-dry perfection. Salty, clean and superb.

La Mancha (Asda)   12   £A

Moscatel de Valencia   15   £B
One of the best-value pud plonks on the planet.

Rioja Campillo 1988   15   £C
Superb the way the fruit dallies with dryness then pulls back
without upsetting the balance.

Valencia Dry (Asda)   14   £A
Nutty and fruity (though not massively so). Makes an excellent
first course wine – salads, soups, etc.

USA WINE – *red*

Sebastiani Merlot   13   £C
Delicious, soft fruit.

USA WINE – *white*

Dunnewood North Coast Chardonnay 1991   14   £C
Rich forward fruit, attractive lemon finish. Delicious.

Dunnewood North Coast Chardonnay 1992   13   £C
Might have a touch too much unintegrated wood for some people.

Sebastiani Chardonnay 13 £C
Heavy, oily, woody quality of considerable appeal to chicken and fish stew eaters.

SPARKLING WINE/CHAMPAGNE

Asti Spumante (Asda) 10 £C
Peachy and sweet.

Blanquette Methode Ancestrale 13 £C
Granny will love this.

Cava (Asda) 14 £C
Soft, earthy, delicious. Very stylish.

Champagne Brut (Asda) 13 £F
Lovely lemony aperitif.

Champagne Rosé Brut (Asda) 14 £F

Scharffenberger Brut California 13 £E

Varichon et Clerc Sparkling Chardonnay 14 £C
Soft and peachy, this makes an excellent aperitif. But champagne it ain't.

Budgen

There isn't a lot to say about Budgen. Budgen doesn't say a lot about itself. However, I can tell northern readers that Budgen is not a collective noun for cage birds but a group of southern, town-based supermarkets of modest size and aspiration. The objective here, apart from maximizing profit (though this took a dent this year which couldn't have been welcome news to the store's new German partner), is to fill that niche left somewhat empty when the big boys decided to concentrate on vast out of town superstores with astrodome-sized car parks. However, since Tesco has successfully attacked this sector of the market with its metro store concept and Sainsbury is beginning to stir itself, Budgen faces terrifying competitors of inordinate ambition. Do the wine shelves offer a real alternative to the Tesco shopper? Or does Budgen merely fill the easiest vacuum – the vacuum of convenience and accessibility to those without transport?

Indeed, is there anything of real interest to the wine drinker happening at Budgen? When I spoke to wine buyer Tony Finnerty he assured me there was. 'New World wines have worked tremendously well for us over the last twelve months. I'm also looking for more eastern European wines as well which are becoming a lot more interesting now.'

Okay, but aren't your customers still stuck in lambrusco and liebfraumilch?

'Price is still the biggest problem. So for most people lambrusco, liebfraumilch and vin de table still work well. Saying that, we are creating a lot more sales now via our cut price special exercise. Every two weeks we create a theme around a specific country like America, or alternatively we

gear it towards a food. If we're promoting steak, for instance, I
will recommend a red wine. What I'm trying to do is get away
from the £1.99 wines.'

And are customers responding to this? They're prepared to
spend more on higher priced wines?

'The first one we had a success with was a Minervois which
normally retails about £3.99. I brought it down to £2.99 – a
big cut but the point was we were still selling wine above the
£1.99 barrier. People came and picked it up. And when the
Minervois returned to its normal retail price sales stayed high.
We've done it with two or three similar wines.'

Isn't it all about confidence?

'Yes. People are experimenting a lot more with wines they
wouldn't have touched before. We're giving them more infor-
mation about the wine and also recommendations where possible of what to eat with it. We're trying to do a lot more food
and wine orientation together because my philosophy is that
we have a whole store full of food and wine so let's get them
together and sell them together as a package. We are getting
some good responses. We're getting a lot of feedback from
customers – positive letters as opposed to negative which is
quite encouraging. We seem to be getting the message across
that Budgen has good prices and ranges as well. It's taking
time because I basically do everything, as you know! But we're
getting there.'

Mr Finnerty, who talks with the earthy enthusiasm of a 1st
division football manager anxious to see his team in the
Premier division but recognizing he's short of a few key
players, is certainly getting there. He's not frightened of
introducing his customers to unusual wines. The dry white
Tokaji, for example, isn't overwhelmingly my cup of cocoa
exactly, but it was refreshing to see it on the shelves. I can
think of many a Premier division supermarket wine buyer who

would shy away from even considering such a wine. The store needs non-run-of-the-mill wines like this (though with better value and more exciting fruit) in order to help make Budgen a first choice for customers, not an alternative only to be considered when you can't be fagged to go to the superstore. Convenience is a great attraction, but if it's the only reason for customers to buy then in the long run you'll never be able to expand your profits fast enough to fund innovation and keep competitive.

Wine is a trigger department. It can be *the* trigger department. A terrific wine at a terrific price can be the sole reason for customers to patronize a store, and if they stay to do the weekly shop then the beginnings of a relationship can be forged. I would guess that both Morrisons and Somerfield have found regular new customers by coming up with bargain bottles and Mr Finnerty needs to do the same.

The store also needs to *tell* people what's going on. That means keeping not only professional boozers like me regularly informed about new wines and new developments, but also the customers. The customer constantly needs to face new offers, attractive deals, interesting food partners for the wines. The wine shelves are among the most exciting, many times *the* most exciting, which customers encounter. That's why the wine is always left to last. Many a shopper who meticulously makes a list of things she needs will deliberately leave wine off. She wants to be surprised when she gets to the shelves. She wants to enjoy experimenting, to see what's on offer rather than buying the same old bottle she bought last week. In this sort of mood, two or three bottles may go into the trolley and one of them may be a complete shot in the dark.

And I say she rather than he because I don't think men shop for wine in quite the same way. Men enjoy browsing, it is true, but more often than not they've got a specific wine in mind, or a wine they've heard about from friends, or a wine they've discovered reading the wine pages of a newspaper. Are we men bigger stick-in-the-muds than women? Do we need more reassurance before we buy? It's possible.

Budgen needs to capitalize on the small but vital sense of adventure inherent in shopping. And Mr Finnerty is ideally placed to provide it. More wines like the whizz-bangingly fruity £2.39 Bordeaux Blanc please sir!

AUSTRALIAN WINE – *red*

Brown Brothers Tarrango 1993	15	£C

All singing, all dancing fruit. A sort of joyous Aussie Beaujolais.

Jacob's Creek Dry Red	13	£C

AUSTRALIAN WINE – *white*

Hardy's R.R. Medium White 1993	10	£C
Riverina/Budgen SE Australian Semillon	12	£B

AUSTRIAN WINE – *white*

Winzerhaus Grüner Veltliner 1991	14	£C

Winzerhaus Grüner Veltliner 1993   14 £C
With its engaging rich edge to the ripe fruit, this is a well-
balanced and well-made wine.

CHILEAN WINE – *red*

Underraga Pinot Noir 1990   14 £C
This is a much better vintage than the previous year: deeper,
richer, more stylish.

FRENCH WINE – *red*

Abbaye St-Hilaire, Coteaux Varois 1992   14 £C
Deliciously dry and plummy with gentle savoury undertones.
Excellent with grilled meat and vegetables.

Budgens Claret, Dulong   13 £B
Good style wine.

Château Bassanel, Minervois 1992   14 £C
Good fruit pickings here, and some weight and seriousness –
although this is essentially a simple, quaffing wine. Dry.

Château Caudeval, Fronton 1992   12 £C

Château de Malijay, Côtes du Rhône 1992   13 £C
Soft and highly drinkable.

Chinon, Les Bernières 1993   13 £C
Pleasant.

Costières de Nîmes　　　　13　£C
Attractive. Earthy.

Côtes du Rhône Villages　　　　13　£C

Delas Crozes-Hermitage　　　　10　£C

Faugères, Jean Jean　　　　13　£C
Very meaty. Great pasta wine.

Geminian Cabernet Sauvignon, Vin de Pays d'Oc　　　　12　£C

Geminian Merlot, Vin de Pays d'Oc 1993　　　　12　£C
Apples and plums. Very dry.

Le Haut Colombier, Vin de Pays de la Drôme 1992　　　　13　£B
Touch of sweet fruit to it. It's a really Rhône style structure and feel.

Madiran, Domaine de Fitère　　　　12　£C
Good cheap claret type.

Tuilerie du Bosc, Côtes de St-Mont, 1992　　　　13　£C
Seriously fruited stuff.

Vin de Pays des Coteaux de l'Ardèche, 1991　　　　12　£B
Nice dry cherry fruit.

FRENCH WINE – *white and rosé*

Blanc de Blancs Cuvée Speciale　　　　10　£B

Bordeaux Blanc 1992   15   £B
A solid, fruity, well-made bargain. Lots of melony fruit and
freshness. Remarkable price for the level of fruit on offer.

Château le Gardera, Bordeaux Blanc 1992   13   £D

Corbières Blanc de Blancs 1990   13   £B
Outright bargain. Not as determinedly keen-eyed as it might
be but attractively fruity all the same in a quiet way.

Côtes de Provence Rosé   10   £C

**Domaine de Villeroy-Castellas Sauvignon
Blanc**   11   £C

**Domaine l'Argentier Terret, CdP Côtes de
Thau**   14   £C
Ripe, rounded fruit, well polished and deep. Very forceful
style of wine.

Geminian Sauvignon Blanc, Vin de Pays d'Oc   13   £C
Keen and fresh. Good shellfish wine.

Gewürztraminer Gisselbrecht 1989   14   £C
Expensive but lovely. Spicy lychee fruit plus clean acidity.

**Le Bonnefois, Vin de Pays des Côtes de
Gascogne**   13   £B
Delicious fruit. Very good value.

Les Chasseignes, Sancerre 1993   11   £D

Listel, Domaine de Bosquet-Canet   11   £C

Muscadet Sur Lie, Domaine du Bois Breton
1992   9   £C

Muscat, Vin de Pays Catalan   10   £C

Pinot Blanc Gisselbrecht	12	£C
Tuilerie du Bosc, Côtes de St-Mont 1992	12	£C

GERMAN WINE – *white*

Baden Gewürztraminer Reserve, Badischer 12 £C
Some spicy fruit here.

Bereich Bernkastel 1993 11 £B

Flonheimer Adelberg Auslese 14 £C
Delicious aperitif; lemony undertones, touched with honey.
Fantastic value.

Klusserather St Michael Kabinett 1992 12 £B
Some attractive touches here make this a good aperitif.

Longuicher Probstberg Kabinett 11 £C

Schmitt vom Schmitt Niersteiner Spätlese
1992 11 £C

Schmitt vom Schmitt Pinot Blanc 1992 14 £C
Forget the fact that it's German. Think of it as Swiss or
Alsatian. A delicious, dry wine of sound class and weighted
fruit.

HUNGARIAN WINE – *red*

Cabernet Sauvignon 13 £B

Merlot	12	£B
Nagyrede Rouge 1993	10	£A

HUNGARIAN WINE – *white*

Chardonnay	10	£B

Château Megyer Tokaji Furmint 1993   10   £C
This is potentially very interesting – a dry wine with Tokaji on
the label – but it is a mite dull and not great value.

Nagyrede Selection Blanc 1993 (half)	11	£A
Sauvignon Blanc	10	£A

ITALIAN WINE – *red*

Merlot del Veneto, Vino da Tavola Gambellara   14   £B
Soft, cherry fruit of great appeal.

ITALIAN WINE – *white*

Lugana Villa Flora 1993	14	£C

Tocai del Veneto, Vino da Tavola Gambellara   13   £B
Brilliant value. Has a curiously cosmetic quality (undertone)
to the fruit.

NEW ZEALAND – *red*

Montana Cabernet Sauvignon 12 £C

PORTUGUESE WINE – *red*

Dão Dom Ferraz 13 £B
Great fast food wine. But then Mr Ferraz is an incredibly fast driver.

Dom Ferraz Reserva, Dão 1989 14 £B

Tinto de Anfora 1988 14 £D
One of the classiest and most satisfying wines of Portugal, and in a great vintage not available everywhere (it has been replaced by the '89). Made from satin and figs by an Australian.

PORTUGUESE WINE – *white*

Lezíria Medium Dry White, Almeirim 14 £B

SOUTH AFRICAN WINE – *red*

Table Mountain 1992 13 £B

SPANISH WINE – *red*

Don Carvi Navarra   12 £C

Gran Condal Rioja, Gran Reserva 1981   15 £C
So rich and soupy you could pour it over grouse. Has late
middle-aged fruit with vanilla hints undercutting the
dryness.

Marqués de Caro Reserva 1988   11 £B

Raimat Tempranillo   14 £D
Utterly ravishing wine of deep richness and suave fruit.

Viña Albali 1983   13 £C

USA WINE – *red*

Sutter Home Merlot 1992   13 £C
Good with rich food.

USA WINE – *white and rosé*

Glen Ellen Proprietor's Reserve Chardonnay   15 £C
Gorgeous style – buttery chardonnay (in the Aussie mould)
with a touch of New Zealand citricity. Delightful Californian
sum of the parts.

Inglenook Charbono   14 £C
Madeira coloured, dry as charcoal, some dried curranty fruit.

Interesting specimen of a rare breed. Probably good with spicy sausages as burnt as it is.

Sutter Home White Zinfandel Rosé 1992   12   £C
Chilled, very chilled, with oysters and lemon. Might work.

SPARKLING WINE/CHAMPAGNE

Flinders Creek Brut, Australia   12   £C
Good fruit, good price, good structure . . . until the finish. It doesn't have one. Pity.

Flinders Creek Brut Rosé, Australia   14   £C
Bargain rosé with a fresh finish of cherry and strawberry. Dry.

Lindauer, New Zealand   13   £D
Good fizzer.

Seaview Brut   15   £D
Where available for under £5, one of the best sparklers on the market: stylish, refined, and quite delicious.

Co-op

The Co-op is the largest undertaker in Britain yet it has been burying the wrong people for years. It should have buried Tesco and Sainsbury. Six years ago it was neck and neck with those two giants, but now both these two are streets ahead in terms of annual sales and are burying the Co-op. The organization has also come under increasingly severe competition from Morrisons, Safeway, Asda and Kwik Save, each of which has achieved growth since 1988, while the Co-op has failed to match this dynamism.

I wish things were otherwise with the dear old Co-op. I admire the ethical financial principles underlying the Co-op's approach to business, and with 4,650 shops, run by over forty individual Co-ops, all part of the same movement in sentiment if not in management (therein lying its problems caused by an enfeebling inability to marshal all its strength under one directorial board and so compete with its single-minded giant competition head to head), it is broad enough to compete with anyone. But breadth is not enough. Depth is the other crucial attribute. And this is what the organization lacks. Instead of being forty-odd individual Co-ops there should be just one. Instead of the two giant umbrella bodies – the Co-operative Wholesale Society and the Co-operative Retail Society – it would make competitive sense to have just one.

Does this affect the way the wine buying department performs? Of course. The wine department of any truly competitive supermarket chain is a trigger department. It is constantly fighting its corner with the occasional £1.99 cut-throat bargain, an irregular stream of £2.49 cheapies, and a constant supply of £2.99 to £3.49 New World wines of good fruit with distinctive flavours. That is the reality which brings customers in, keeps them coming, keeps them buying not just the wine, but all the other things they need to run their households. It is the ability to manage this supply of wine to hundreds of stores which, via promotions and publicity, thousands of customers have been persuaded to visit that lies at the heart of retail management skills, but the Co-op cannot act in so tightly focused a manner because different Co-ops make different decisions. If they were all brought under one wine buying and directing team then the big boys would have a real fight on their hands. You have to look after the customers, in every little detail, and this is where the Co-op's depth does not match its breadth.

Earlier this year, I received a letter from a *Guardian* reader complaining that certain Co-op wines I had recommended were unknown to the branches he visited. He also wrote to the Co-op asking for an explanation. A week short of two months later he received a reply: 'Apologies for the late reply to your letter,' the first paragraph said, 'it has gone round the houses before it landed on my desk.' Gone round the houses? You mean the first person to receive it didn't think that serious customer disappointment was important enough to concern her (or him) and just passed the letter on? This is what I mean by lack of depth.

The Co-op undoubtedly possess, however, healthy wine buying skills. It is the only retailer whose wines are bought by a doctor, though what manner of doctorate Arabella Woodrow possesses I have never thought to ask, but I can tell you she has her finger firmly on the £2.99-and-below pulse.

Example: she went shopping in Italy earlier this year. On a very tight budget. She returned with a terrific red by the name of Principato, a blend of schiara, lambrusco and merlot (see page 51). Principato costs £2.65. It's a great bargain and well worth its rating.

After a trip to Spain, the good doctor returned with two further highly drinkable wines: Valle de Monterray, a deliciously fruity, well-balanced white with a touch of melon (excellent fish 'n chip wine) which costs £2.49, and Tempranillo Oak-Aged which has a gentle smoky quality shrouding a creamy structure of fruit, and this is another bargain at £2.79.

These wines are good enough, and well priced enough, to stand on any major retailer's shelves. The Co-op needs more of them. It needs to promote them. It needs to make it difficult for people to visit the competition without getting the feeling that they are wasting their money.

As far as I'm concerned I can't wait for the marriage of the two big Co-op groups. I'll even throw confetti and buy the happy couple a wedding present.

AUSTRALIAN WINE – *red*

Australian Red (Co-op)   13   £B
From the Co-op comes a pair of young hopefuls grown in the Murrumbidgee irrigation area of New South Wales. Australian Red has a cherry side to its fruit, making it suitable for light chilling and drinking with salads.

Cabernet Sauvignon   13   £C
Great with a richly stuffed roast fowl.

Château Reynella Cabernet/Merlot 1991   14   £D
Wonderful! A real wine at last!

| Jacaranda Hill Shiraz/Cabernet 1992 | 12 | £B |

| Shiraz | 14 | £C |
Famous bruising Aussie style.

AUSTRALIAN WINE – *white*

| Australian White (Co-op) | 14 | £B |
Has some bite and freshness, suggesting semillon in its make-up perhaps, and is a simple fish wine. At heart, a simple quaffing wine.

| Jacaranda Hill Semillon/Chardonnay 1992 | 14 | £B |
Excellent fruit style and feel.

| McWilliams Bin 101 Semillon 1984 | 11 | £C |
Too old and tired.

| Moondah Brook Chenin Blanc 1992 | 15 | £C |
Utterly captivating wine. Fabulous steel-jacketed melon fruit.

BULGARIAN WINE – *red*

| Cabernet Sauvignon | 11 | £B |

| Suhindol Merlot/Gamza | 12 | £B |

BULGARIAN WINE – *white*

Preslav Chardonnay	11	£B
Welchriesling and Misket	12	£B

CHILEAN WINE – *red*

Cabernet Sauvignon   15   £B
Coffee and chocolate fruit.

CHILEAN WINE – *white*

Peteroa Sauvignon Blanc 1993   14   £B
Excellent balanced fruit and acid. Terrific shellfish wine.

Sauvignon Blanc   13   £B
Good value for a simple fruity wine. Somewhat quiet to finish
but a very likeable style.

ENGLISH WINE – *white*

English Table Wine   14   £C
Excellent as before – but pricey. Still worthy of support.

FRENCH WINE – *red*

Anjou Rouge	12	£C

Bergerac Rouge	13	£B

Cahors	14	£C

Made by the highly regarded Rigal brothers who are negociants as well as making their own wine at Château St-Didier in Parnac. This wine is blackcurrant and coal tar and is well dry yet has soft fruit – indeed the smiling softness of the fruit is curiously counterpointed by a typical scowl of Cahors dryness, and the whole adds up to a pleasantly balanced personality.

Château Cissac 1983	11	£E

Château Cissac 1987	10	£E

Château Laurençon, Bordeaux Supérieur 1992	13	£C

Château Pierrousselle, Bordeaux 1993	14	£C

An agreeable cabernet sauvignon and merlot mix which is dry, gently blackcurranty, young yet never green or gawky, smooth, and very well priced.

Châteauneuf-du-Pape, Cellier des Princes **1991**	10	£E

Claret	12	£B

Corbières	11	£B

Costières de Nîmes	13	£B

Earthy, soft, dry, edgily nutty with blackcurrant and plum fruit. Good value.

Côtes de Provence Rouge	11	£C

Côtes du Luberon   13   £B
Attractive, gentle charcoal/rubber bouquet, plus a good dollop of cheering fruit. Good value.

Côtes du Rhône   11   £B

Côtes du Roussillon   11   £B

Côtes du Ventoux   11   £B

Domaine de Hautrive, Côtes du Rhône Villages 12   £C

Domaine St-Julien, Merlot, VdP d'Oc 1992   14   £B
Deep, rich and bitter, with tannic fruit-berry flavour. A brilliant and interesting food wine.

Fitou   12   £B

Jules Vignon, Côtes du Beaune Villages   11   £D

Médoc   12   £C

**Montbazillac Domaine de Haut-Rauly 1990,
(half)**   13   £C
A good and very useful half bottle.

Morgon, Les Charmes 1992   11   £D

Vacqueyras, Cuvée du Marquis de Fonseguille   14   £D
Soft, approachable, utterly plum-in-the-mouth well-spoken
for a downtrodden Rhône bumpkin. Most attractive dry
finish.

Vin de Pays de Cassan   14   £B
Cheap, fruity, supple, soft. Wonderfully drinkable. Stylis-
tically, Chianti meets Côtes-du-Rhône.

Vin de Pays de l'Aude   11   £B

Vin de Pays de l'Hérault Rouge	12	£B
Vin de Table Red (1 litre)	11	£B

FRENCH WINE – *white and rosé*

Alsace Gewürztraminer   14   £C
Lychee and grapefruit to the nose, mulled fruit, richly edged
for the mouth, spicy tickle in the throat. An interesting aperitif, or to drink solo with a book, or for mild Chinese food.

Alsace Pinot Blanc	13	£C
Anjou Blanc	13	£B
Bergerac Blanc	11	£B
Blanc de Blancs	11	£B
Bordeaux Blanc Medium Dry	12	£B
Chardonnay Fleur du Moulin, VdP d'Oc 1993	12	£C

Château Pierrousselle Entre-Deux-Mers 1993   15   £C
Distinguished feel to the wine. Yet the modern ripe fruit has a
fresh edge and a gentle nuttiness. Excellent fish wine.

Côtes du Roussillon Blanc	10	£B

Côtes du Roussillon (Vignerons Catalans)   13   £B
No great depth or sophistication but utterly guzzleable.
Attractive melon fruit (totally predictably) but with a good
balancing acidity (not so predictably).

Domaine du Clos du Bourg, Touraine
Sauvignon   15   £B
Delicious nutty fish wine yet with enough depth of dry, leafy
fruit to be enjoyed on its own. Has the brilliant new plastic
cork (see introduction).

Lurton Cabernet Sauvignon Blanc de Noirs
1992   10   £C

Muscadet Sur Lie, Domaine de la Haute   12   £B

Premières Côtes de Bordeaux   11   £B

Rosé d'Anjou   12   £B
A pleasant little rosé.

Vin de Pays des Côtes de Gascogne   12   £B

Vin de Pays des Côtes des Pyrénées Orientales 13 £B

Vouvray, Domaine Les Perruches 1992   11   £D

GERMAN WINE – *red*

Nussdorfer Bischofskreuz Rotwein, Pfalz   15   £B
Soft as peach fuzz, with dry plummy fruit with a kind of cassis
edge. So surprised to find itself a red wine grown in German
soil that it forgot to develop tannin.

GERMAN WINE – *white*

Baden Dry 14 £B
One of the most agreeable of this increasingly agreeable wine:
soft, fruity, yet fresh. Good value.

Bernkasteler Kurfustlay 12 £B

Hock Deutscher Tafelwein 11 £A

Liebfraumilch 10 £A

Morio-Muskat Rheinhessen 12 £B
Pleasing minor aperitif for little outlay.

Mosel Deutscher Tafelwein 11 £B

Niersteiner Gutes Domtal (1.5 litres) 13 £C

Oppenheimer Krotenbrunnen 11 £B

Piesporter Michelsberg 12 £B

Rudesheimer Rosengarten 12 £B

St Ursula Galerie Pinot Blanc Trocken 11 £C

St Ursula Galerie Riesling, Pfalz 1993 13 £C
Good fish wine.

Trocken Rheinpfalz 14 £B
A bargain at just over £3. Attractive fragrance of green grass
and lemon. Good weight of fruit, balanced, fresh to finish.

**Westhofener Bergkloster Auslese, St Ursula
1992** 14 £C
Rich, gently honeyed. Try it as a complex alternative to
liebfraumilch with a bunch of grapes and cheese.

HUNGARIAN WINE – *red*

| Co-op Hungarian Red Country Wine, Balaton | 12 | £B |

| Hungarian Merlot 1992 | 14 | £B |

An extremely quaffable merlot of soft, yet tannic, savoury
fruit. Most agreeable.

HUNGARIAN WINE – *white*

Hungarian White Country Wine, Nagyrede
(Co-op)   14   £B
Delicious fruit for the money. Gooseberry/melon/musky
peach. Good with food or solo.

ITALIAN WINE – *red*

| Barbera del Piemonte | 11 | £B |

| Chianti | 10 | £B |

| Merlot del Veneto | 13 | £B |

Cherries! Who'll buy my sweet cherries?

| Montepulciano d'Abruzzo 1992 | 11 | £B |

| Principato (Co-op) | 14 | £B |

A blend of schiara, lambrusco and merlot. Dry yet ripe, with a
light cherry fruitiness which is never frivolous but rather
serious in the length and richness of the finish, this is not only

a marvellous pasta, pizza, and risotto wine but something which could stand up to much posher fare (though that said, I must say I regard risotto as one of the poshest treats imaginable, and a first class example made with mushrooms with a bottle of Principato would make me a happy man any day of the week).

San Roseda Valpolicella Classico 1991	11	£C
Sicilian Red	13	£B

Excellent rubbery fruit with a candied cherry finish. Soft, fruity, subtle vivacity. Delicious with rabbit stew.

Valpolicella	12	£A
Vino da Tavola Barbera del Piemonte	12	£B
Vino da Tavola Trebbiano (Co-op)	8	£B

ITALIAN WINE – *white*

Bianco di Custoza	12	£C

Nice-ish weight of fruit, fair-ish balance, fresh-ish finish. If like your wine with lots of ish, this ish for you.

Chardonnay Atesino	11	£B
Frascati Superiore	11	£B
Lazio Country White	11	£B
Orvieto Secco	12	£C
Sicilian White	11	£B

Rather fruitless.

Soave	10	£B

Trebbiano dell'Emilia	13	£B

Excellent value for a calm, unfussy wine useful as an aperitif
or with mild fish dishes.

MOLDOVAN WINE – *red*

Taraclia de Moldova Cabernet Sauvignon 1990	14	£B

NEW ZEALAND WINE – *white*

Forest Flower Fruity Wine 1993	13	£C

PORTUGUESE WINE – *red*

Bairrada Tinto 1990	14	£B

Excellent. Dry, punchy fruit.

Douro	15	£B

Another wonderful slurp from the land of happy smiling
peasant wines (pricewise) which have rich aristocratic natures
(tastewise). Lovely blackberry fruit here.

Douro Tinto 1990	15	£B

Even better than before.

Quinta da Alorna Tinto	12	£A

Smith Woodhouse 10-year-old Tawny Port   15   £E
Tawny in name but not in nature; vigorous, lean, beautifully
blushing, unbloody and unbowed by its time in cask which
failed to darken it cheeks or diminish its fruity, nutty, curranty
character which will partner cheese brilliantly. Worth the
money to experience one glass.

Vinho de Mesa Santos   15   £B
Typical baked figs and earth aromatically which completely
belie the creamy fruit flavour. Delicious. Astoundingly good
value.

PORTUGUESE WINE – *white and rosé*

Bairrada Branco 1991   13   £B
Good soft fruit and style. Some energy here.

Portuguese Rosé   10   £B

Vinho Verde   11   £B

ROMANIAN WINE – *red*

**Dealul Mare Cabernet Sauvignon Special
Reserve**   15   £B
Rich, delicious, bright-berried softness. Great fruit and great
price.

SOUTH AFRICAN WINE – *red*

Cape Red   14   £B
'Ripened under burning African skies.' What rubbish! Sweet
finishing, dry fruit. Excellent value.

SOUTH AFRICAN WINE – *white*

Cape White   13   £B
Some floral fruit here.

SPANISH WINE – *red*

Pozuelo Crianza 1990   14   £C
Dry and vaguely rich, like a middle-aged playboy whose age is
impossible to guess.

Rioja Crianza   12   £C

Tempranillo Oak-Aged (Co-op)   15   £B
Brilliant value fruit, tinged with vanilla, bright, dry, savoury.

Valdepeñas   11   £B

Valencia Red   12   £A

SPANISH WINE – *white*

Moscatel de Valencia   16   £B
Marmalade and toffee caramel – rich and exciting. Fabulous
value for the Christmas pud.

Valencia White   14   £A
Good level of fruit – balanced.

Valle de Monterrey, Vino de la Tierra (Co-op)   14   £A
A deliciously fruity, well balanced white with a touch of melon
(excellent fish 'n' chip wine).

USA WINE – *red*

California Ruby Cabernet (Co-op)   14.5   £B
Bargain dry fruit – curiously plummy and cherryish, but
attractive. Brilliant pasta wine.

USA WINE – *white*

California Colombard   11   £B

SPARKLING WINE/CHAMPAGNE

Cava   15   £C
Excellent style – not a whiff of the vegetal aroma and fruit.
Just fruit, acid (very refreshing) and bubbles.

Daniel le Brun NV, New Zealand   14   £E
Excellent chardonnay style

De Clairveaux Champagne Brut NV   12   £F

Liebfraumilch   10   £C

Sparkling Chardonnay, Italian   11   £C

Sparkling Saumur   13   £D

Veuve Honorian Champagne Brut NV   12   £E

Kwik Save

I wandered into a brothel on the way to the annual Kwik Save wine tasting. It was almost the highlight of my afternoon. The bordello's street number was clearly the one on the Kwik Save invitation, but when I ventured inside and up the stairs and asked a young woman, busy making a bed, where the tasting was she laughed and said where would I like it to be? I rapidly sussed the error of my admission and fled.

I found the right address five minutes later and among the sixty-one wines I tasted I found a case, a round dozen of them, worthy of 14 points and more.

Without doubt Kwik Save has made strides. In hiring wine consultant Angela Muir it made its first step in the right direction, and this has paid off over the past two years. It now has 790-odd licensed stores, and the proportion of its business attributable to wine is increasing monthly. It claims wine sales overall have almost doubled since Ms Muir took up her consultancy.

I must confess to finding the idea of Angela Muir and Kwik Save a partnership of seemingly opposing styles which would make an appealing scenario for a TV play by Mike Leigh. Her ladyship is middle class, refined, charming, and reminds me of the bustling headmistress of my primary school. She has the precise, modulated, Master of Wine tones of someone purchasing rare vintages for the Fortnum & Mason wine list. Kwik Save are a bunch of down-to-earth no-nonsense toughs, and I dare say the office cleaner hoovering up after a board meeting finds several blasphemies and a pile of dropped aitches among the cigar butts.

Kwik Save customers are nervous about wine, finding

£2.99 a border beyond which madness lies, and Ms Muir has set about demolishing this barrier, whilst trying to find decent wines under it, as enthusiastically as any committed primary school headmistress would set about correcting her pupils' manners.

She has enjoyed only a relative measure of success. Two Australians proved popular and both cost over £3, yet similar priced New Zealanders were 'left to die quietly on the shelves' in her own phrase. On this basis, therefore, Kwik Save ought to be one of my havens, for £2.99 as a price point has my full approval. But the range is still struggling to find coherence and overall quality. There are some outstanding wines, but not enough. I found one 16-pointer and five 15-pointers, but there should be a dozen more at least.

The problem, of course, is finding the wines. If you are Sainsbury, or Safeway, or Tesco, you can cut your suppliers to match the under £2.99 cloth. You are, as a supermarket giant, first in the queue for winemakers' attentions. You can buy huge quantities of bargain wine which suddenly become available, you can initiate ideas with flying winemakers to make under £3 wines all over the world, you can rely on a prime network of publicity chaps to set about making a fuss when the wines hit the shelves, and you have the support of several colleagues all doing the same thing. Not at Kwik Save. Kwik Save will never invest in these things because these things cost money and that money would inevitably find its way on to the price tickets. Kwik Save is about saving money, or more properly, spending less than you would elsewhere, and Ms Muir is facing this fact and buying accordingly, and it is tough work.

So, no 1993 Beaujolais or Rhône wines. 'Bad value,' says Angela. Instead she turned to vin de pays and South Africa. Eastern Europe was another natural place to look, taking

advantage of flying winemakers Kim Milne and Nick Butler in
Hungary. Australia figures greatly, and increasingly South
Africa, but not yet Chile to any great degree.

In one respect, I find Kwik Save customers infuriatingly
unadventurous and not as cost conscious as they might
imagine. It is apparently a fact that they buy quantities of
champagne, and the store has the ubiquitous Moët & Chandon on sale at £16.99 which even Tesco price at £18.55.
There is also a Kwik Save champagne called Louis Raymond
on sale at £7.89. Yet both these wines are poor value when
compared with several supermarket own-label Cavas and
sparkling Aussies at £4.99.

I will regard it as a breakthrough, not when Kwik Save
customers break the £3 barrier, but when they give up buying
champagne altogether. It is only stale custom and perceived
status which keeps champagne flowing at Kwik Save, for
champagne is not a value for money commodity.

When Kwik Save's customers recognize this and turn to
bargain bubblies then Ms Muir will have a real success on her
hands.

AUSTRALIAN WINE – *red*

Angove's Butterfly Ridge Cabernet   13   £B

AUSTRALIAN WINE – *white*

Angove's Chardonnay 1992   13   £C

Angove's Chardonnay 1993, S Australia   15   £C
Lush wood and ripe fruit well married.

BULGARIAN WINE – *red*

Cabernet Sauvignon 1990, Burgas   15   £B
Juicy fruit but has a serious side. Great roast food wine for lots
of guests.

Iambol Merlot/Pamid 1992   13   £A

Lovico Suhindol Cabernet Sauvignon/Merlot   12   £A

Oriachovitza Cabernet Sauvignon Reserve   16   £B
Wonderful minty, ripe blackcurrant and plum fruit, dry yet
finishing sweetly and naturally. True class for a silly price.

BULGARIAN WINE – *white*

Bear Ridge 1993   13   £A

CHILEAN WINE – *red*

San Pedro Chilean Red   10   £B

FRENCH WINE – *red*

Cabernet Sauvignon, Vin de Pays d'Oc 1993	10	£B
Château Fontcaude, St-Chinian 1993 Lush, soft fruit. Delicious style.	15	£B
Claret	12	£B
Côtes du Ventoux 1993	11	£B
Merlot, Domaine Resclause, Vin de Pays d'Oc 1993 Excellent value, very soft ripe fruit.	14	£B
Minervois 1993 Good party glug.	13	£B
Rouge de France	12	£A
Rouge de France, Selection Cuvée	10	£A
Steep Ridge, Vin de Pays d'Oc Grenache/Shiraz 1993	13	£A
Vin de Pays de l'Hérault	12	£B

FRENCH WINE – *white and rosé*

Blanc de France Lots of melony fruit well put together.	14	£A
Bordeaux Blanc Cuvée VE 1992 Competently made, some good fruit and style. Good price.	13	£B

| Bordeaux Sauvignon 1993 | 10 | £B |

| Comtesse de Lorancy | 15 | £A |
Lots of rich, fairly riveting fruit.

| Côtes du Ventoux 1993 | 10 | £B |

| Côtes du Ventoux Rosé 1993 | 12 | £B |

| Domaine de la Gravenne, Vin de Pays d'Oc Sur Lie, 1993 | 13 | £B |
Melon, sour, full, curious.

| Muscadet 1993 | 10 | £B |

| Rosé de France, Selection Cuvée | 9 | £A |

| Steep Ridge Chardonnay/Sauvignon, Vin de Pays 1993 | 12 | £B |

| VdP des Côtes de Gascogne, Cuvée 1993 | 14 | £A |
Good glugging stuff.

| Vin de Pays de l'Hérault | 13 | £B |

GERMAN WINE – *white*

| Hock 1993, Deutscher Tafelwein, Rhein, K. | 8 | £A |

| Morio Muskat, Pfalz 1993 | 14 | £A |
I would never refuse a well-chilled glass of this floral wine as an aperitif.

HUNGARIAN WINE – *red*

Hungarian Merlot 1993   12   £A

HUNGARIAN WINE – *white*

Hungarian Chardonnay, Balaton Boglar 1993   11   £B

Hungarian Country Wine, Balaton Boglar 1993   12   £A

ITALIAN WINE – *red*

Arietta, Montepulciano d'Abruzzo 1993   13   £A
Some attractive sweet fruit.

Il Paesano, Merlot del Veneto   13   £B
Light and juicy. Fun.

Valpolicella, Cantina Sociale di Soave 1993   10   £B

ITALIAN WINE – *white*

Frascati Superiore, Villa Pani 1993   12   £B

Gabbia d'Oro   10   £A

Soave, Cantine Sociale di Soave, 1993   10   £B

PORTUGUESE WINE – *red*

Lezíria Red 10 £A
Not tasting so hot, this sample.

PORTUGUESE WINE – *white*

Lezíria White 14 £A
Still a great bargain for the fruit and structure on offer.

SOUTH AFRICAN WINE – *red*

Clearsprings Cape Red, Simonsvlei 13 £B
Good clean, well-polished fruit.

Silver Hills, South African Red 1991 13 £B
Some curiously attractive fruit.

SOUTH AFRICAN WINE – *white*

Clearsprings Cape 11 £B

Silver Hills, Stellenbosch 1993 13 £B

SPANISH WINE – *red*

Flamenco	12	£A
Promesa Tinto	8	£A

SPANISH WINE – *white*

Castillo de Liria Moscatel, Valencia   15   £B
Have it with hard cheese and hard fruit or even strawberries
and cream.

USA WINE – *red*

Maxfield Vineyards Cabernet Sauvignon   14   £B
Like the Premium Red, but a lot chewier and richer-edged.
Both are bimbo reds.

Maxfield Vineyards Premium Red   14   £B
Delicious full cherry/overripe blackberry fruit, soft and very
lush. Excellent value. A delicious quaff.

USA WINE – *white*

**Maxfield Vineyards Californian Premium
White**   11   £B

SPARKLING WINE/CHAMPAGNE

Champagne Brut, Louis Raymond 13 £E
Lemony, light style.

Littlewoods

Braving the ugliest, noisiest, nastiest street in the United Kingdom (unless you care to relieve yourself of the brutality at street level and look upwards and catch some of the superb Victorian and Edwardian buildings still remaining uncorrupted) the intrepid superplonker wends his way along London's Oxford Street to the Littlewoods store by the Circus station. This is no place for a wine writer, but then this begs the question – is Littlewoods the place for wine? The short, but enigmatic, answer is – it depends. There is no reason in the world for anyone to buy a bottle of wine at Littlewoods unless she is actually in the store buying something else, and whilst this something used to be anything from luggage to lingerie, the store has also now extended its repertoire to include on its premises the Iceland food-chain. The reason, then, to buy wine at Littlewoods is if you're looking for a bottle to accompany the food you've bought from Iceland. I asked Littlewoods' wine buyer Ian Duffy about this.

'Yes, the people we're mainly selling the wines to are the people who come in for food,' he revealed. 'We have a fairly even split between those stores that have food and those stores that don't, and we do see a difference in the sort of customers we get in each. In the new food halls with Iceland we see a much younger, much more adventurous customer.'

And they're interested in newer wines? Not the old favourites like, yawn yawn, liebfraumilch and lambrusco?

'Yes. The people coming into the market experiment more. So the German and lambrusco business is not as buoyant as it was, but it's still a massive market. There are a lot of people, younger people, who want to find something that's got a lot of

69

fruit, but drier. They're prepared to experiment. Their average age is probably 30–40 rather than 50–60 as used to be, and it is predominantly female.'

Nothing new here? Only if you compare Mr Duffy's words with the same sort of thing being said by lots of professional wine buyers as they grapple with the new world of wine now flowing over the British palate. But I think there is a quiet revolution behind his words. Wine is being consciously linked with food by more Britons than ever before. This is a very continental attitude. Our wine-producing partners in the Common Market all see wine as an adjunct to food. It is only in Britain that we entertain the idea of serious drinking without at least an accompanying tidbit at our elbows. Or rather used to. With wine displacing beer for the first time as the nation's favourite tipple, here is concrete confirmation that the linking of wine with food is catching on with everyone. The sort of wine you need to go with food is not liebfraumilch or lambrusco which merely go with a sweet tooth. It is the new world of robust fruity wine. Littlewoods can now spread its wine net further, and Mr Duffy, who carries a lean and hungry, almost quixotic expression, matching his bustling arrangement of limbs, is cheerfully wielding this net to good effect.

'We see the opportunities in our business being generally new world, specifically Australia, with eastern Europe for value for money, and for the same reason Spain, and to a lesser degree Italy. The losers in the business at the moment tend to be Germany to some degree, and to a larger degree France.'

I remarked that I'd been impressed with some of the New World wines he'd shown me and that I'd given more of his wines high marks than ever before.

'If you look at what we've shown you today, there are two

things which I hope would be evident to you. There are a lot more new wines than you've been used to seeing us launch and the bulk of those new wines are from the New World. We've responded to the change in our customer profile by trebling our range of New World wine. We're actually going to display New World in a section by itself to highlight what we've got. There will be a wider range in New World, especially Australia, than we've got elsewhere.' Ian Duffy sounds more positive than at any time in the past three years. He likes his new big net.

'Twenty years ago when people first experienced red wine it was likely to be claret. Claret is very distinctive in its style. Customers got used to it. But the new people coming into today's market haven't got that preconceived idea and aren't being brought along in the same way. When you taste certain inexpensive Australian wines and you compare them with some clarets, you know as well as I do which you'd buy from a personal point of view. And that's going to be the view of 90 per cent of my customers.'

Is Littlewoods going to try to compete with the major supermarkets with New World wines?

'We try to compete at supermarket prices, but in the high street. Our locational competition is the traditional off-licence. But our range and pricing is different. In a lot of city centres our competitors are Co-ops and Somerfields.'

It's good to know Littlewoods is changing. Everything does. I look out from the third floor and see the delicious scalloped windows of the pre-First World War building, originally a department store, across the street and wonder if those windows, like white lidless eyes, ever gaze down at the horrors beneath and wonder 'who would have thought it would have ever come to this?' But come to this it has and so 224 years after James Cook, son of a farmhand, discovered the delights of Australia, Littlewoods has done so as well.

AUSTRALIAN WINE – *red*

A. Garrett Black Shiraz 1992   14   £D
Spiciness and fruit. Good food wine.

Hardy's Coonawarra Cabernet Sauvignon   16   £D
Opulent, ripe fruit with figs, liquorice and chocolate, and a
very distant echo of mint.

Hardy's Shiraz/Cabernet Sauvignon 1993   14   £B
Lots of fruit for the money.

Jacob's Creek Dry Red   13   £C
Full-bodied, but not too overdeveloped – complementary to
carnivores' favourites like steak and onions.

Misty Morning Australian Red   13   £B
Soft, very soft.

Orlando RF Cabernet Sauvignon 1991   14   £C
Dry, rather serious.

Windsor Ridge Cabernet Sauvignon   11   £C

Windsor Ridge Shiraz   9   £B
Worst shiraz I've ever tasted.

AUSTRALIAN WINE – *white*

A. Garrett Fumé Blanc 1993   15   £D
Lime and pineapple with a heavier fruit of some exotic but
unknown breed in the centre. Delicious.

Hardy's Padthaway Chardonnay 1993   13   £D
Rich fruit which is so smooth, almost oily, it rolls down the throat like melted butter.

Hardy's R.R. Medium White 1993   12   £B

Hardy's Semillon/Chardonnay   13   £B

Jacob's Creek Medium Dry White   11   £C

Misty Morning Australian White   13.5 £B
Well-fruited, well-priced.

Orlando RF Chardonnay 1992   15   £C
Superb balance of melony fruit, lightly smoky, and citric acidity. Lovely wine.

Windsor Ridge Chardonnay   13   £C
Some good fruit here. Rather woody (balsa, not oak).

Windsor Ridge Sauvignon Blanc   14   £C
Perfect little sauvignon blanc for the money: fresh, fruity, and eminently respectable.

Windsor Ridge Semillon   13   £B
How long can this pleasant number stay the bargain it is for under £3?

BULGARIAN WINE – *red*

Bulgarian Cabernet Sauvignon   12   £B

Cabernet Sauvignon 1989   12   £B
Some pulpy blackcurrant fruit.

CHILEAN WINE – *white*

Andes Peaks Sauvignon Blanc 1993   14.5   £B
Soft yet fresh: elegant. Very good value.

FRENCH WINE – *red*

Beaujolais (Littlewoods)   8   £B

Château d'Aigueville Rouge 1991   13   £B
A cheap, very approachable Côtes du Rhône of likeable fruitiness and flavour.

Claret Bordeaux Rouge   9   £B

Claret (Littlewoods)   14   £B
Soft with only a hint of tannin.

Corbières 1991   10   £B

Corbières (Littlewoods)   13   £B
Light, inexpensive, very sound. Good with pasta.

Côtes du Rhône   10   £B

Côtes du Roussillon Villages 1991   10   £A

Fitou   13   £C
Attractive, soft, plummy fruit with an earthy edge.

Minervois 1990   10   £B

Vin de Pays de l'Aude Red   10   £B

Vin de Pays Pyrénées Orientales Red   13   £B

Vin de Table de l'Aude Red	12	£B

Very friendly introduction to dry red wine.

Vin de Table Red (Littlewoods)	12	£B

FRENCH WINE – *white and rosé*

Bordeaux Blanc (Littlewoods)	11	£B

Château d'Aigueville Blanc	12	£C

Rather flatter than at Sainsbury? Not as fruity or as balanced.

Domaine de Lalanne – Côtes de Gascogne	13	£B

Very attractive fruit. Melon drops.

Le Moulin, Vin de Pays Pyrénées Orientales	10	£B

Muscadet Sèvre-et-Maine 1992	11	£B

Cheapest muscadet on the market? Not a lot more one can say.

Premier Côtes de Bordeaux	10	£C

Rosé d'Anjou 1991	9	£B

Not special.

Rosé d'Anjou (Littlewoods)	13	£B

Vin de Pays de l'Aude (Littlewoods)	11	£B

Vin de Pays de Vaucluse	9	£B

Vin de Table Dry White (Littlewoods)	10	£B

Dry, struggling to be fruity.

Vin de Table Medium (Littlewoods)	10	£B

GERMAN WINE – *white*

Bereich Niersteiner 1990 13 £B
An easy-going aperitif.

Hock 11 £A

Liebfraumilch 1992 13 £B
Very attractive example of the breed with an undercurrent of
acidity preventing the sweetness from dominating.

Morio Muskat 13 £A
A simple aperitif of remarkable acidic/fruit balance. Outstanding value for money.

Mosel Kabinett 1991 10 £B

Piesporter Michelsberg 1992 11 £B

Rheinpfalz Morio Muscat 1990 12 £B

St Johanner Abtei Auslese, Rudolf Müller 1989 14 £C
Honey and bitter almonds, almost marzipan, make this an
appealing companion for an apple or a chunk of cheese.

HUNGARIAN WINE – *red*

Cabernet Sauvignon 13 £B

Hungarian Merlot 1990 9 £A

HUNGARIAN WINE – *white*

Chardonnay	10	£B
Gewürztraminer	10	£B

This was the wine Attila, sweeping across Hungary's Great Plain, inflicted as the supreme punishment upon those of his warriors who had displeased him. It has improved some since the infamous Hun's time, but only relatively.

Olasz Riesling	12	£B
Sauvignon Blanc	12	£B

ITALIAN WINE – *red*

Chianti Il Borgo	10	£B
Valpolicella Il Borgo	11	£B

ITALIAN WINE – *white*

Frascati Il Borgo	8	£C
Lambrusco White	8	£B
Soave Il Borgo	11	£B

PORTUGUESE WINE – *red*

Bairrada 13 £B
Decently fruity drinking to go with rich poultry dishes.

Bairrada Red 1987 12 £C
Over the hill. Tasted better.

ROMANIAN WINE – *red*

Pinot Noir 1987 14 £B
Brilliant bargain fruit, soft, vegetal and instantly appealing.

Romanian Cabernet Sauvignon 1985 15 £B
Gamey and rich with dried strawberry fruit. Delicious.

Romanian Pinot Noir 1988 14 £B
Light cherry and strawberry fruit.

ROMANIAN WINE – *white*

Transylvania Pinot Gris 1992 14 £B
Lovely, bright and breezy aperitif.

SPANISH WINE – *red*

Carreras Cabernet Sauvignon 10 £B

Marqués de Cáceres Rioja 1989   14.5   £C
Full of flavour without blowsiness.

Rioja Romancero Red 1987   12   £C
Vanilla aroma, quite flaky, but the fruit is not blowsy or big but
rather demure. Odd beast, really.

SPANISH WINE – *white*

Carreras Chardonnay   10   £B

Carreras Sauvignon Blanc   9   £B

USA WINE – *red*

Altamira Cabernet Sauvignon 1991   12   £B
Rich-edged soft fruit. Good with food.

Silver Peak California Red   13   £B
Bright cherry fruit with a touch of apple.

USA WINE – *white*

Altamira Sauvignon Blanc 1992   10   £B
Slightly stewed beany flavour creeping up into the fruit – not
noticeable with food.

Silver Peak Californian White   13   £B
Good flavour here.

SPARKLING WINE/CHAMPAGNE

Asti Spumanti, Martini   10   £D
Terribly sweet young thing.

Cavalino Sparkling Moscato, Italy   6   £A
5% alcohol and quite horrible. Probably best poured over ice-cream.

Flutelle Vin Mousseux   13   £C
Not as lush or wittily lemonic as it has been. And still very close to a fiver.

Mosigny Champagne (Littlewoods)   11   £F
Solid, rather than exciting.

William Low

R.I.P. 1868–1994

Bill Low. Great name for a supermarket! It has a deliciously inexpensive, down-to-earth ring to it, and now it is no more. With several score branches spread over Scotland and the north (the most southerly being Loughborough), the temptation for Tesco to buy the company was too great, and although Sainsbury did their professional best to make the purchase as expensive as possible William Low is on the way out – after 126 years.

In due course it seems highly likely that all Low stores will become Tesco's, but as far as I am concerned I shall treat Low's wines as a separate entry. Tesco's purchase of Low is good news for wine drinkers although whether all of the more flamboyant wine purchases on the Low shelves will have a long-term future remains to be seen. For there is, it must be said, nothing low about the wines or low about the reach of the store's extremely able wine buyer, Kevin Wilson. Mr Wilson is a high aiming hero in fact and in the eyes of some of his suppliers he is a superhero. Looking at some of the wines he has chosen it's easy to see why.

He is the only supermarket buyer brave enough to have chanced his arm on Priorato, the world's most off-puttingly fruity wine sporting the world's most off-puttingly fruity label. Yet there the bottle is, on Low's shelves for £4.99, staring bloodily out at the customers like revolutionary graffiti written in gore, and woe betide any gentle palate which ventures inside. Priorato I rate highly, with food it's terrific, but it is patently so rich, raisiny and subtly yet lip-curlingly oxidized that the taste of this northern Spanish curiosity, a truly local wine with a distinctly regional and bristling impenetrable accent, is off-putting. But not to Mr Wilson or, I dare say, the more daredevil of his customers.

And what of Scotland's one white wine? It is called Domaine du Pigeonnier, a dry Bergerac Blanc, and the fair hands of Jon and Liz Alexander, tracing their Scots lineage back to the 1400s, are responsible for its manufacture from semillon and sauvignon grapes grown in their own vineyard, and a very pleasant drink it is too. It has an attractive modern aroma, suggesting maximum extraction of perfume (and colour) by allowing the grape skins to spend time in contact with the juice, piles on a good weight of subtle melon fruit and offers a good finish. Not a typical Bergerac. It has more bonny fruit and less bony dryness of the type – but this is all to the good. An excellent glugging aperitif and a suitable contender for Robert Burns's 'Go fetch to me a pint o' wine, An' fill it in a silver tassie.' William Low is the only place in the British Isles you can find this wine.

Really interesting wines dot the Low list like cherries in a rich cake. Some of these cherries are unripe, like Cathy Corison's Napa Valley Cabernet Sauvignon, some are waiting to ripen, as with Rainer Lingenfelder's Riesling, and some are gloriously perfect picking, like Hedges Cellars Cabernet/ Merlot from Washington State. Even Mr Wilson's poorly rated wines are interesting.

But some are highly rated bargains, like the £3.29 Sangiovese di Toscana Rocca delle Macie 1993. This wine, blended by Angie Muir who also helps out at Kwik Save, is a corker of a wine for the money. And I agree with Mr Wilson when he says that it 'offers the consumer a truer reflection of the sangiovese variety than the overcropped wines you tend to find from Emilia Romagna'.

The store also looks after its customers in other ways. I believe it was the first supermarket to introduce a 10 per cent discount for customers buying twelve bottles or more. This discount applies to mixed cases as well as to wines on promotion. As a matter of interest, this scheme would reduce the price of that Sangiovese di Toscana to £2.96 a bottle.

If that isn't a thundering great bargain then nothing is.

AUSTRALIAN WINE – *red*

Château Reynella Cabernet Merlot 1992   17   £D
A dazzlingly misleading wine. It aromatically sets you up for tar and violets, soothes the tongue with satiny, cassis-like fruit, then wallop ... the long arching upper-cut of rich fruitiness pierces the throat with such exquisite force it leaves a lingering wound.

Hardy's Stamp Series Shiraz/Cabernet
Sauvignon 1991   13   £B

Penfolds Bin 2 Shiraz/Mataro 1991 (half)   14   £A
Meaty, strong, soft, dry – a useful half bottle.

Penfolds Bin 35 Shiraz/Cabernet 1992   15   £C
Ripe, soft fruit with some development ahead of it. Attractive berry flavours, well structured and balanced. Very drinkable now but a 17/18-pointer in 3/4 years.

AUSTRALIAN WINE – *white*

Chardonnay, Meadowbank Vineyard Tasmania
1992   11   £E
Scores 11 at the moment because the wood is somewhat raw.

David Wynn SE Australia Dry White 1992   14.5   £C
Gentle stickiness on the fruit, like a muted toffee-apple.
Delightful to sip unaccompanied.

Normans South Australia Chenin Blanc 1992   14   £C
Interesting and tasty.

Penfolds Bin 21 Semillon/Chardonnay 1993   15   £C
Fresh and lively yet a dollop of pineappley melon keeps
intruding. Delicious refreshing wine.

Penfolds Bin 202 South Australian Riesling
1993   14   £C
Superb, rich aperitif. Delicious.

Penfolds Koonunga Hill Chardonnay 1992   14   £C
Full lush fruit plus a ticklish dollop of lemon zest. Delicious,
but getting pricey near a fiver.

AUSTRIAN WINE – *white*

Lenz Moser Pinot Blanc 1991   15   £C
Delicious dry, fruity wine, with a graceful introduction via a
toasty aroma through to a clean finish. A balanced, elegantly
structured wine at a bargain price.

BULGARIAN WINE – *red*

Sliven Country Red Wine, Merlot/Pinot Noir   14.5   £B
Very bright and breezy. Soft fruit, smashingly allied to apple-
skin fresh acidity. Superb value for light dishes (cold meats) or
drinking any time.

CHILEAN WINE – *white*

Caliterra Chardonnay 1992   14   £C
Lovely melon/lemon style. Again, not huge. A touch expensive but it has got style.

Caliterra Chardonnay Cunco 1993   15   £C
Delicious, slightly woody fruit which is very controlled and
fine.

FRENCH WINE – *red*

Château de Rabouchet, Bordeaux 1991   14.5   £C
Solid, gently hairy fruit, with a suggestion of spice and savour-
iness to it. Balanced, well made. Will improve for a few years
yet.

Château Laroze 1989, Grand Cru St-Emilion   11   £F

Château Peyrou, Côtes de Castillon 1989   15.5   £D
The first vintage of a graduate oenologist, Catherine Papon,
this is a perfectly mature chocolate claret with the Castillon

brusqueness to the tannins, but they are delicious, rich tannins helping the fruit to a satisfying drinkability and dryness.

**Cuvée de la Commanderie du Bontemps, Médoc
1986** 12 £C

Figaro, Vin de Pays de l'Hérault 1993 14 £B
Good rich fruit, deliciously dry and earthy.

Gamay, Cuvée Palombet 1992 8 £B

**Merlot, Vin de Pays des Coteaux de l'Ardèche
1992** 12 £B

Palombet Cepage Gamay 1992 8 £B
Barely drinkable bilge-water.

Sirius Red 10 £D
Some weight of fruit but rather disappointing structure. Some aroma, too, but ill-defined. A formula wine made to a recipe, like tinned food.

FRENCH WINE – *white and rosé*

Anjou Blanc, Château de Passavant 1992 14 £C
An interesting Frog with princely ambitions. An attractive, dry wine with the quaint softness yet freshness of chenin blanc grapes, it hints at a sweetness it doesn't possess. A delightful wine for light Oriental fish dishes and European leaf salads.

Bergerac Blanc, Domaine du Pigeonnier 1992 14 £C
Attractive modern aroma suggesting maximum extraction of perfume via good skin contact. Good weight of subtle melon

fruit and a good finish. Not a typical Bergerac, has more fruit
and is less bone dry. My first Scottish wine!!

Château du Trignon, Côtes du Rhône Blanc
1992   13 £C
Wonderful with trout! But the fruit could be more vivacious.

Château Thieuley, Bordeaux 1993   15 £C
Delicious fruit with gentle leafy and grassy character glinting
through. Superb shellfish wine.

Château Thieuley, Bordeaux Clairet Rosé 1993 12 £C

Côtes de Duras, Domaine la Roche 1992   13 £C
Lots of fruit, expensive. Not so vividly balanced as these wines
usually are.

Granite Ridge Sauvignon Chardonnay, Vin de
Pays du Comte Tolosan   12 £C
An okay wine of some merit which an Australian nom-
enclature does little to heighten.

Mouton Cadet 1991   10 £C
Hold your breath and listen: 'Beautiful straw colour with gold
highlights. The generous nose is forward and full, with notes
of grilled almonds. On the palate the wine is round and well
evolved, combining body and fruit. Well structured, with great
aromatic complexity. Very good length, offering richness,
finesse and balance.' So say the Rothschilds about this, their
wine. All I can say is they should have added a rider about this
drinkable but crazily overpriced wine going extremely well
with fish, particularly codswallop.

Sirius White   9 £D
Serious woody nose. Sticky fruit with acid all out of kilter.
Weedy finish. Expensive crap.

**Syrah Rosé Domaine de Laporte, Vin de Pays
Catalan 1992**   11   £B

**Viognier, Vin de Pays des Coteaux de l'Ardèche
1992**   13   £C
Delicious but rather muted.

GERMAN WINE – *white*

Riesling Kabinett, Lingenfelder 1992   13   £C
Open for at least half a day to thicken; but this really should
not be drunk for at least five years.

**Wiltinger Klosterburg Riesling Kabinett, Van
Volxem 1989**   13   £C
A distinguished aperitif for riesling lovers.

HUNGARIAN WINE – *red*

Bull's Blood   13   £C

Cabernet Sauvignon   13   £B

Merlot   14   £B
The Villany region's merlot seems to be one of best bargains
of any wine list on which it appears. A great soft-hearted pasta
wine.

HUNGARIAN WINE – *white*

Chardonnay 1992   15   £B
Elegantly subtle touches of butter with an almond finish.
Old-fashioned in style and structure (including the price), and
heartening to drink without food or to accompany salads, fish,
chicken, and vegetable dishes. Marta Domokos of the Kiskoros winery, whose wine this is, may not fly like some
winemakers in Hungary, but she surely soars.

Pinot Blanc, Nagyrede 1992   12   £B
Tries hard, but its softly, softly approach to the acidity does
not balance out the fruit, so while it is a cheap, drinkable wine
it has no hugely attractive features.

ITALIAN WINE – *red*

Chianti 1992   13   £B
Well-made fruit in good order.

Chianti Classico, Rocca delle Macie 1990   13   £C

Rosso Piceno, Umani Ronchi   13   £B

Sangiovese di Toscana, Rocca delle Macia 1993   15   £B
Only the Italians can produce fruit which is all soft and
yielding but then suddenly unleashes, as it's about to disappear down the throat, quiet yet determined tannins which
won't let go of the teeth.

ITALIAN WINE – *white*

Gavi, Michele Chiarlo 1992 10 £D

Teresa Rizzi Chardonnay, Vino da Tavola delle Tre Venezie 12 £B

Terre di Ginestra 1991 13 £C
Cataratto is the grape variety which makes this wine and there is nothing catty or ratty about it.

Villa Fontana, Fontana Candida 1992 13 £C
Good example of Frascati. One of the better ones.

NEW ZEALAND WINE – *red*

Timara Cabernet Sauvignon/Merlot 1990 12 £C

NEW ZEALAND WINE – *white*

Montana Sauvignon Blanc 1992 14 £C
Marvellous new-mown grass aromas plus a lemon zestiness. It feels like spring!

Sauvignon Blanc, Rothesay Vineyard, Collards 1993 16 £D
Curiously but undeniably delish. Wonderful grassy scents, with a rich waxy/honey centre which is always dry. It finishes with sour asparagus. Odd? Yep. But worth cultivating.

Timara Chardonnay/Semillon 1992 13 £C

SPANISH WINE – *red*

Castillo de Liria Valencia   14   £B
An excellent mix of soft fruits at a bargain price.

Don Darias   14   £B
You know how sometimes you meet an upfront fruity person
whose ribald sense of humour almost makes you blush but
you can't help yourself falling completely under his or her
spell? So it is with this wine.

Priorato Vini Negri, Scala Dei 1988   15   £C
Rich, raisiny, subtly oxidised, this is a true peasants' brew of
such toughness (tannins) that it can be opened 12 hours
beforehand. Will be a delight with spicy, highly flavoured food
like pepper stew with chorizo. An uncommon wine from the
wild regions of Catalonia, this is a brave try for Wm Low.

Torres Coronas 1989   13   £C

Viña Albali, Reserva, Valdepeñas 1987   15   £C
Creamy, touch of vanilla. Delicious.

SPANISH WINE – *white*

Castillo de Liria Moscatel, Valencia   15   £B
Have it with hard cheese and hard fruit or even strawberries
and cream.

Don Darias   14   £B
With a spicy fish stew or curry, this is the wine.

Torres Viña Sol 1992   12   £C

USA WINE – *red*

**Cabernet Merlot, Hedges Cellars, Washington
State 1993**   18   £D
A truly luxurious wine without ostentation. It has perfect
fruit/acid balance, soft yet assertive tannins and a velvety
cassis fruit.

**Cabernet Sauvignon, Corison, Napa Valley
1990**   10   £G
There are £3 Portuguese reds with more complexity.

Glen Ellen Merlot 1990   16   £C
The universe's most perfect roast chicken wine in a bottle
labelled like a cross between golden shag pipe tobacco and
malt whisky. But this at least has the virtue of keeping sales
down and thus the price. Comes from an ambitious vineyard
in California and its arresting cedary aroma leads to a soft, dry
fruit with a dark cherry-liqueur edge to its general earthiness
and it goes with a plain roast chicken (a flavoursome beast,
mind, not one that's been barred from sowing a few wild oats)
like Torville with Dean.

USA WINE – *white*

**Fumé Chardonnay, Hedges Cellars, Washington
State 1992**   15   £D
Tasty, soft, impressive.

SPARKLING WINE/CHAMPAGNE

Angas Brut Rosé, Australia   15   £D

Anna de Cordoniu Chardonnay, Spain 1989   16   £E
Stunning sparkler of great character: complete, full, elegant,
classy.

Asti Martini   10   £D
Terribly sweet young thing.

Cava Cristal Brut Castellblanch, Spain   12   £D

Chardonnay Santi Vino Spumante Brut, Italy   13   £C
Dry, nutty. Some attractive fruit here for the money.

Cordoniu Napa   15   £E
An impressive sparkling wine made in California by a Cava
producer from Penedes in northern Spain. It is delightfully
classy bubbly, gently citric, with a soft coating of fruit and it
stands comparison with the usual examplars, yet costs £8.99
or thereabouts.

Cuvée Napa, Mumm California   13   £E
Quiet, not explosive, and rather like a reasonably made
champagne.

Green Point Vineyards Brut, Australia 1989   13   £E
Delicious, and exactly like a decent champagne but not a great
one.

Mercier Champagne   11   £G

Seaview Brut 15 £D

Where available for under £5, one of the best sparklers on the market: stylish, refined, and quite delicious.

Seppelts 1er Cuvée Brut 15 £D

Lovely fizz, light and handsome.

Marks & Spencer

This store is so adored by its customers that I am quite sure it could charge admission. 20 pence would be sufficient and it would raise £150 million a year by so doing, and it could either devote these proceeds to charity or use them to run a lottery. 'Added value' is M & S's *cri de coeur* and its customers hand over the dosh by the bucket load to buy this idea.

Until this year, I have never been 100 per cent convinced that this so-called added value had any connection with the wine side whatsoever. The food side has no equal with its added-value seductions. We all know how deliciously time- and trouble-saving it is to have that M & S prepared *moules marinières* waiting for us in the fridge when we totter home after a day's slog, but the M & S Chablis we might open to go with it, at £6.99, seems a bit steep. What is required is a £1.99 bottle emanating from a French winery which trucked up the grapes from La Mancha in Spain. M & S, however, will have nothing to do with such wines at such prices. They cannot make an acceptable profit margin on them and therefore the cheapest 75cl, full-strength bottle of wine in the store is £2.99. Indeed, there are eighteen such bottles quivering on this edge of £3, and so the nervous soul who finds solace at the likes of Kwik Save will find no embarrassment at putting his hand in his pocket and finding enough loose change for an M & S wine, costing little more than a packet of fags.

Indeed, the M & S duo of wine buyer Chris Murphy and technical expert Jane Kay (the only oenologist employed by any retail group) has created some real sparks of their own in 1994. This is undoubtedly due to the new-found out-of-recession confidence of M & S customers who are leading the way in being prepared to pay not only a fiver and above for wines from countries they have visited, but also around a fiver for wines from countries they only see portrayed in TV series. Though that said, I doubt anyone in the cast of *Neighbours* will ever get to taste a more complex, more deliciously minty Coonawarra Cabernet Sauvignon 1989 than the special blend at M & S, not to mention a snazzier 1992 McLaren Vale Shiraz, or a more blackcurrany 1992 south-eastern Australian Cabernet Sauvignon (Langhorne Creek 1992). Each is something of a bargain at £4.99, demonstrating that value for money is not purely a function of price but a more complex equation involving greater pleasure for less outlay.

And in applying this equation, Chris & Jane (and where have we heard these names before, where successful partnerships are concerned?) have struck gold not only in the New World, but also in the old. Hugh Ryman has turned in a nice little Spanish white for them (also available at Majestic Wine Warehouses) called Concha de Barbera, a superb Moscatel de Valencia which is a Beaumes-de-Venise taste-alike for half the price, a mind-bogglingly tasty red from Raimat in Spain using merlot in the blend (and a wine which is one of the highest scoring in this book), several useful red Bordeaux and an absolutely brilliant red Rhône (Domaine André Mejan '90).

The only pity is that the last wine is only available mail order, but then Monsieur Mejan's vineyard is barely ten acres, so it's hardly surprising it couldn't make enough to satisfy the store's shelves. M & S has some attractive wines on its mail-order list (and these are indicated in the listing which follows).

It also has some interesting wines in the new wine shop concept that the company is fast establishing in certain branches. Over fifty stores now have a wine shop on the premises with people on hand to offer advice who can also arrange tastings. These wine shops will offer the range of wines on sale everywhere, but certain wines, more expensive and more upmarket, will only be available at these new shops. Did I say 'interesting'? I mean Noel Coward's way of saying 'interesting'.

Many of the wines to be found only in M & S wine shops are boring, considering the expense involved. Most are Old Worlders of course and, frankly, many are a step backwards. Who needs a fairly interesting Meursault at £14.99 when the store has a palate-grippingly brilliant Rothbury Estate Chardonnay/Semillon for £4.99? Who in their right mind spends £12.99 on an iffy Volnay when (s)he can get away with a positively wonderful Dão Garrafeira for £3.99? Only the '91 Ducru-Beaucaillou at £18 is a truly lovely wine and at that price it ought to be.

The answer to the question 'who needs?' is two-fold: first, there are certain porridge-brained twerps who just have to spend a lot of money on a label rather than a wine and, second, it's a nice earner for the store. I suppose if it keeps Chris & Jane happy I shouldn't grumble.

They are, after all, doing us proud around £5 and under. And I for one am extremely pleased they're putting most of the best efforts into this area, even though the £1.99 bottle is beyond them.

What is not beyond them is the desire to have every aspect of quality control under their aegis. 'We cannot bear to sell things which may not be perfect because an aspect of manufacture has been beyond our control,' Mr Murphy told me heroically. Thus, no store is more exercised about cork, for the store recognizes that the method of sealing wine with the bark of a tree is a flawed process, and one of Jane Kay's specific assignments has been to develop the use of the plastic cork with suppliers. The introduction to this book goes into greater detail about the whole history of cork and M & S's involvement in its (I hope) demise.

If the store does receive wide acceptance of the plastic cork, and persuades more winemakers to use it, then M & S will see this century out as the pioneers of the most revolutionary step wine has taken since the introduction of the glass bottle some centuries ago. M & S has a history of wine innovation. Arguably it was the first retailer to use a flying winemaker – though he employed a motor car – when Jacques Lurton was hired to freelance the making of a Bordeaux Blanc de Blancs in 1988.

But replacing natural cork with a better plastic substitute is not just innovation. It is revolution. And it is a revolution long overdue. Natural cork contaminates an appreciable percentage of wine and spoils drinkers' enjoyment. The plastic cork will end the occurrence of the corked bottle forever and the receipt by me of letters from disgruntled readers inquiring why I have recommended a wine which tasted either foul upon opening or failed to develop any appreciable fruit.

It tasted foul, I reply, because it was faulty. It was faulty because the cork contaminated it. It failed to develop any fruit because the cork had stolen it. I will die a happy man if my one small contribution to civilized living has been to encourage more people to complain about corked wines, thus putting pressure on wine retailers to push their suppliers into doing something about the problem.

The something which needs to be done – must be done – is the full introduction of plastic corks. M & S has successfully led many revolutions in food and wine retailing and I see no reason why they can't be totally successful at the head of this one.

AUSTRALIAN WINE – *red*

Bin 37, Orlando 1990   15   £C
A whopping great, tarry, soft, berried beast of style and vim.

Cabernet Sauvignon Bin 37 Orlando 1990   14   £C

Coldstream Hills Cabernet Sauvignon 1990   11   £E

Coonawarra Cabernet Sauvignon 1989   15   £C
Cough linctus aroma with a dusty drawer undertone. Ripe
tarry fruit, big and rich. Great stuff. Has an ineffable and
irreverent quality of devil-may-care fruitiness.

Cotton Ridge   13   £B
A wholly successful alliance of grenache, shiraz and malbec
grape varieties.

Glenbawn Estate Shiraz/Cabernet 1992   15   £C
This rich pudding of a wine, with a real fruit centre, has a
sweet finish to its slightly smoky plum and blackberry flavours
and it's a truly seductive potion.

Langhorn Creek Cabernet Sauvignon 1992   14.5   £C
Very approachable blackcurranty fruit with a faint hint of a
green pea.

Len Evans Cabernet Sauvignon 1990   14   £D
Big and soft and immensely approachable. Stylish and finely
tuned, it offers lots of rich fruit.

**Lindemans Bin 37 Australian Cabernet
Sauvignon 1991**   16   £C
Has a fruity, digestive-biscuit heart to the lush, soft fruit.
Lovely. Has touches of leather and yet manages to achieve
massive drinkability.

McLaren Vale Shiraz 1992　　　　　　　15.5　£C
Bright, up-front fruit, coconutty and woody. Lovely fresh
balancing acidity. Lush and soft style, though, not pert. An
attractive glug all by itself. Faint spicy overtones. Has barks
and berries in amorous confusion.

McWilliams Australian Shiraz/Cabernet　　12　£C
Not as impressive as once it was.

**McWilliams Coonawarra Cabernet Sauvignon
1989**　　　　　　　　　　　　　　　15　£C
Hints of mint to the fruit, which is soft and very yielding.
Delicious.

Pheasant Gully Shiraz　　　　　　　　12　£C

AUSTRALIAN WINE – *white and rosé*

Australian Chardonnay Blanc de Blancs 1990　12　£E

Australian Medium Dry 1992　　　　　　11　£C
This is an own-label version of yet another Aussie assault on
an established U.K. wine market niche – in this case
Liebfraumilch. The grape here is Rhine riesling, as it is
so-called down under, and it makes a pleasant, easy quaffing
off-dry tipple for tenderfoots yet to graduate to drier wines. I
am all in favour of this progression to more complex wine as
the drinker's palate matures, but I think that the price of
edging up towards £4 is high. This wine should be 80 pence
cheaper to really scupper the German sweetheart.

Cotton Ridge Dry White   12   £B
A quiet Australian! Nothing wrong with that, but it does make
this an unusual Oz white with its demure fruit. Not as ring-a-
ding with fruit as we've come to expect from this neck of the
planet.

Hunter Valley Chardonnay/Semillon 1992   15   £C
Rich fruit to start, then muted melon, then gentle citric
flavours. Delicious.

Len Evans Chardonnay 1992   16   £D
Woody and rich, upfront and tasty. Very good with rich
seafood dishes.

**Lindemans Australian Medium Dry, SE
Australia**   15   £C
Aromatic, forceful, never sweet, this is a deliciously fruity
wine.

Lindemans Bin 65 Australian Chardonnay 1993 16   £C
Balanced, elegant, full of fruit, which impinges on the taste
buds like crystallized melon and lemon.

McWilliams Australian Rosé   13   £C
Pleasant, uncomplicated.

**McWilliams Australian Semillon/Chardonnay,
SE Australia**   15   £C
Brilliant depth of flavour and crisp, tangy acids: melony,
lemon, fresh. Lovely stuff.

Pheasant Gully Colombard   11   £C

Pheasant Gully Colombard, McWilliams   13   £C

Riverina Chardonnay 1992   12   £C

Rothbury Estate Chardonnay/Semillon 1992   15   £C
Masses of good aromatic rich fruit plus a nice bite to the
balancing acidity. A delicious drop of character-building
drinking – a thoughtful wine to enjoy by itself.

Rothbury Estate Chardonnay/Semillon 1993   17   £C
Magnificent glug of wooded fruit combined with classy acids
to provide a remarkable under-a-fiver experience. Ripe and
rippling with flavour.

Semillon/Chardonnay   12   £C

BULGARIAN WINE – *red*

**Bulgarian Cabernet Sauvignon, Svichtov Region
1990**   15   £B
Excellent fruit; balanced, dry, full and rather elegant.

FRENCH WINE – *red*

Beaujolais 1992   11   £C

Beaujolais AC, Cellier des Samsons 1992   12   £C

Beaujolais-Villages AC, G. Duboeuf 1992   12   £C
Quite pleasant, I suppose.

Beaune Premier Cru Clos de la Feguine 1991   14   £G
A rich, burnt toffee-fruited wine of impressive weight of fruit.

Bordeaux Matured in Oak, AC Bordeaux 1990   14   £C
Again, as with so many M&S clarets, this is deliciously soft, approachable stuff.

Cabernet Sauvignon, Chais Beaucairois   11   £B

Cabernet Sauvignon, Vin de Pays d'Oc   14   £B
Savoury dry fruit, rounded to finish. Superb roast food wine.

Château Cos d'Estourel, St-Estèphe 1987   13   £G
Not a bad stab at making an Aussie-style Shiraz. Touch overpriced, though, at £19.99.

Château Ducru Beaucaillou 1991   16   £G
Violet-fruited touches. Lots of tannin. Great shape. Will be magnificent in 12–15 years.

Château Gazin, Pomerol 1987   13   £G

Château Grand Mayne, St-Emilion 1985   16   £G
Old style, classic, dry, very fine stuff. Tastes like a crusader has been pickled in it. Delicious.

Château l'Hospitalet, Pomerol 1988   14   £F
Like a Fronsac. Can't say better than that.

Château Lacousse, Classic Claret, AC Bordeaux 1993   14   £C
Lovely soft wine. None of the usual austere tannins.

Château Lynch Bages, Pauillac 1987   13   £G

Château Pichon-Longueville-Baron, Pauillac 1987   15   £G
Brilliant in 10 years.

Châteauneuf-du-Pape AC, Les Couversets 1991   15   £E
A lovely herby example.

Classic Claret, Château Lacousse 1991   14   £C

A glugging claret, skilfully blended from merlot and cabernet sauvignon, with a delightful dry, tannic edge which is never harsh and always chewy and flavoursome. This is exactly the sort of wine a leading retail buyer, who wishes to remain anonymous, was referring to when he said, 'It's all about getting the blinkered Bordeaux to make softer wines. They make such hard inaccessible stuff. Give me fruit!' This wine gives to to him, without sacrificing any of the typicity which makes claret claret.

Côtes de St-Mont 1989   13   £B

Côtes du Rhône (1 litre)   13   £C

Domaine La Côte aux Loups, Bourgogne Passetoutgrains   14   £C

How wonderful to see this wine on sale in a UK supermarket (ooops . . . sorry Lord Marks, I mean *store*)! How refreshing to find a drinkable burgundy under four quid! It's a light, fruity burgundy to be sure but then it's a blend of gamay (the beaujolais grape) and pinot noir (the burgundy grape) and this famous blend, usually though not always roughly 70 per cent gamay and 30 per cent pinot, has the official title Passetoutgrains, and it has been a stock restaurant wine in the region for decades. This is an excellent example at a fair price (though £3 would be better) for it is no bossy-boots burgundy with fat price tags and no guts, but a decent, gently earthy burgundy of spirit and style. I should add that the usual proportions of the blend have not been observed in this example, for it is a mere 10 per cent gamay and 90 per cent pinot noir. I was surprised at these proportions when I discovered it because it was not apparent to me upon tasting.

**Domaine Mont Rose Cabernet Syrah , Vin de
Pays d'Oc 1993**   16   £C
Has touches of earthiness (old world) with ripe forward fruit
(new world). It really works. Superb little wine.

Domaine Roche Blanche 1993   14   £C
This is a hugely attractive, fruity wine of softness and flavour
which only fails to score 2 points more because its finish is a
touch weak.

**Domaine St Pierre, Vin de Pays de l'Hérault
1993**   12   £B
You either like bubble gum or you hate it. I feel moderately
encouraged by this example.

Fitou 1991   14   £C
Real fruity earth. Great rustic glug. Great spicy food wine.

Fleurie AC, Cellier des Samsons 1993   13   £D
Not bad.

French Country   13   £B

**French Full Red, Côtes du Roussillon Villages
(1 litre)**   12   £C

**Gamay, Vin de Pays des Coteaux de l'Ardèche
1993**   12   £C
Good beginner's wine: no tannin, no acid, just gluggable fruit
by the dessertspoonful.

Gevrey Chambertin, J. M. Boillot 1989   12   £G

House red, Vin de Table, Tresch   12   £B
Sweet as a fruit-drop and almost as endearing.

La Petite Propriété, Vin de Pays de l'Aude 1992 12   £B

Lirac, Domaine André Mejan 1990 18 £D
The ultimate in sweet fruit earthiness and flavour. Lovely rich
wine with the unique Rhône characteristics of soft berries and
brisk, terse, rustic tannins. Superb. Available by mail order
only.

Margaux 1989 15 £D
This is good value for Margaux lovers for it is a deliciously
serious claret, with its credentials all in order, yet is also soft
and drinkable, tasty and bright. No ragged edges, no dis-
agreeably hard tannins, this is undoubtedly the fruits of
M & S wine buyer Chris Murphy's determination to get
immediately drinkable wines from his Bordeaux suppliers.

Margaux AC, Roger Joanne 1991 15 £D
Hugely elegant and rich.

Merlot, Christian Moueix 1989 14 £D

Moueix Merlot, AC Bordeaux 1990 16 £D
Aromatic, tarry, dry, blackberry and fig concentration. Brilliant wine.

Moueix St-Emilion 1990 16 £D
M&S have been up to their old tricks taming the tannins in
Bordeaux, and the store has come up with a fabulous new
vintage of their own-label St-Emilion 1990 which is a gorgeously soft wine of beautifully rounded fruit with so little
detectable tannin it bursts on to the tongue like soup, then
coats it like chocolate emulsion.

Volnay, Maison Louis Jadot 1989 13 £F
Some faint glimpses of class.

FRENCH WINE – *white and rosé*

Beaujolais Blanc, G. Duboeuf 1992   11   £C

Bordeaux Sauvignon, Yves Pages 1993   14   £B
Grassy overtones, new-worldish but the fruit says it's French
in the finish. Good shellfish wine.

Burgundy, Caves de Lugny 1990   13   £C

Chablis 1992   16   £D
Some nice leafy flavours.

Chablis, Beauroy Premier Cru 1989   14   £F
Delicious and classic.

**Chablis Premier Cru Beauroy, La Chablisienne
1989**   10   £F
Flabby finish but starts superbly.

Chardonnay, Cellier des Samsons   13   £C

Chardonnay de Chardonnay   13   £C
The eponymous village is the origin of this wine, so it's the
most authentic chardonnay you can drink, I suppose.

**Chardonnay 'Domaine de Mandeville', VdP d'Oc
1993**   14   £C
Gently soft and citric. Very good with shellfish. More buttery
richness than the '92. Excellent.

Chardonnay, VdP du Jardin de la France   13   £C

Château de Chamirey, Mercurey 1991   12   £E

Châteauneuf-du-Pape, Les Courversets 1992   14   £E
This is not everybody's cup of wine for it needs food (fish,

chicken). Yet I love its earthy overtones and old-fashioned feel.

Côtes de Gascogne 1993 14 £B
Beautifully tropically fruity and zippy. Great fun.

Cuvée du Chapelain 13 £B

**Domaine l'Argentier, Vin de Pays Terret,
J. Lurton 1993** 13 £C
Falls away at the finish a touch, but the rest of the construction is fine.

Duboeuf Chardonnay, Vin de Pays d'Oc 15 £C
Plump fruit, crisp acidity. Lovely bottle.

French Country 13 £B
Fresh with firm fruit, this is excellent value and great with shellfish dishes.

French Medium White (1 litre) 12 £B

House White Wine, Vin de Table Tresch 12 £B

**Jeunes Vignes de-classified Chablis, La
Chablisienne** 14 £C
Still a good basic Chablis (in fact, if not in name).

Mâcon Villages 1991 12 £D

Mâcon Villages, Rodet 1992 11 £C

Meursault 1990 12 £G

Muscadet, Domaine de Balluettes 1992 15 £C
Under four quid, a bargain. Haven't said that about a muscadet for over a decade or more, it seems to me. But then this delightful specimen harks back to the good old days of mineral acidity and steely melon-edged fruit which was the

hallmark of this classic breed. Drunk with charcoal-grilled sardines, the fish bring out all the wine's most attractive qualities.

Olivier Mandeville Chardonnay, Vin de Pays d'Oc 1992   14   £C
Lush, mellow, buttery fruit: delicious, in a word. Rather New Worldish in its charms.

Petit Chablis 1992   11   £C

Petit Chablis, La Chablisienne 1993   11   £D

Pouilly-Fumé 1993   11   £D

Puligny Montrachet, Domaine Maroslavac-Leger 1991   11   £G

Rosé d'Anjou (1 litre)   12   £C

Rosé de Syrah, Vin de Pays des Coteaux du Libron 1992   11   £B
Delia Smith has a stupendous recipe for salmon steaks with black bean salsa and this wine might have its uses when such a dish is on the table.

Rully Blanc, Les Thivaux 1989   14   £E
Delicious, refined, almost a treat.

Sancerre AC, La Charmette 1993   10   £D
M&S's great and good wine buyer thinks this wine is brilliant, but the store's £2.99 Hungarian Sauvignon Blanc is a better wine, more arousing and much better value.

Selection Blanc, George Duboeuf   14   £B
Excellent value for grilled fish dishes. Stylish, balanced, and most attractive fruit.

Vin de Pays des Côtes de Gascogne, Plaimont
1993   13   £B

Vin de Pays du Gers White, Plaimont 1993   14   £B
Lashings of ripe, rounded fruit with a clean finish. Very good
value.

Vouvray AC, Domaine Pouvraie 1993   14   £C
Nice wine with delicious chenin typicity. 'Pineapples and
guava', says M&S description. Yum yum, say I.

White Burgundy AC, Caves de Lugny 1993   13   £C

GERMAN WINE – *white*

Bereich Nierstein 1991   11   £B

Drohner Hofberger Riesling Kabinett 1989   15   £C
Brilliant, lemony wine.

Hock (1 litre)   11   £C

Liebfraumilch   10   £B

Moselle (1 litre)   11   £C

Piesporter Michelsberg 1992   11   £B

Trittenheiner Apotheke Riesling Spätlese 1986   14   £C

HUNGARIAN WINE – *red*

Hungarian Cabernet Sauvignon 1993   15   £B
Outstanding wine. Lovely rounded fruit yet the lush, flavourful tannins are never far away.

HUNGARIAN WINE – *white*

Hungarian Sauvignon Blanc 1993   15   £B
Brilliant value. Real sauvignon style with controlled herbaceous character and a rich-edged finish.

ISRAELI WINE – *white*

Carmel Valley Colombard 1993   11   £B

ITALIAN WINE – *red*

**Amarone della Valpolicella, Single Vineyard
'I Communi'**   14   £E
Great food wine. Try it with Peking duck.

Barbera d'Asti 1990   14   £B
A roast beef Italian rather than a spag bol merchant.

Barbera del Piemonte, S. Orsola 1993   14   £B
Hugely soft (like a plump cushion) and subtly leathery, with
echoes of mint. Lush with it. Quite startlingly drinkable.

Chianti Classico, Villa Cafaggio 1990   12   £D

Italian Table Red, Girelli   13   £C
Perfectly drinkable, lush sweet fruit.

Italian Table Wine (1 litre)   10   £C

Montepulciano d'Abruzzo, Girelli 1992   15   £B
Sweet, soft, as drinkable as beer. Lovely fruit.

Re Noir, Fratelli Martini 1991   11   £E

**Vino Nobile di Montepulciano DOCG, Girelli
1989**   15   £D
Gamey, sweaty, big, tarry, aromatic, richly fruity, yet finally
dry, this is a lovely wine. Available through mail order only.

ITALIAN WINE – *white*

Bianco Veronese 1991   13   £B
Great value for such firm, clean, fruity drinking.

Chardonnay   13   £C

Chardonnay del Veneto, Tino de Tavola, Girelli 12   £B

Chardonnay, Vino de Tavola del Piemonte 1992   14   £B
Very attractive pear-drop fruity wine with a good fresh shell of
acid. Brill with brill – or even take-away cod and chips.
Excellent value.

Cortese de Piemonte, Vino de Tavola   15   £B
Beautifully presented bottle with beautifully presented fruit, crisp, clean and gently nutty to finish.

Frascati Superiore 1992   13   £C
Attractive light wine to lubricate lubricious light gossip.

**Frascati Superiore DOC, Estate Bottled, Girelli
1993**   13   £C

**Giordano Chardonnay, Chardonnay del
Piemonte 1993**   14   £C
Full, creamy, nutty, very full yet not overblown. Delicious fish wine.

**Italian Chardonnay, Vino de Tavola del
Piemonte 1993**   15   £B
Has rich, lush chardonnay touches to even balancing acidity. Elegant, clean, very good value.

Italian Table Wine, Girelli (1 litre)   15   £C
Has mature tasting fruit, deep flavoured, yet lots of crispness to balance it. Superb thirst-quenching stuff.

Orvieto Superiore 1993   10   £B

**Pinot Grigio delle Tre Venezie, Vino de Tavola,
Girelli**   14   £C
Lots of fruit, flavour and balance.

Soave DOC, Girelli 1993 (1 litre)   13   £C
Basic, fresh.

NEW ZEALAND WINE – *white*

Gisborne Dry White 1993	12	£C
Hawkes Bay Chardonnay 1992	13	£C
Hawkes Bay Chardonnay 1993	11	£C

Kaituna Hills, Gisborne Chardonnay 1993 13 £C
Good but rather indistinct – pleasant, light, inexpressive of the grape. Expensive.

Kaituna Hills, Marlborough Sauvignon Blanc 1993 12 £C
Has the herbaceousness up front but doesn't deliver so balanced a finish. Rather fat here and not typical of the style at this point.

PORTUGUESE WINE – *red*

Dão Garrafeira, Caves Aliança 1989 16 £C
Soft, very opulent fruit, elegant yet ripe and multi-layered. Lovely spicy food wine – try it with curries.

PORTUGUESE WINE – *white*

Vinho Verde 13 £B
A delicious, frivolous little tipple.

SOUTH AFRICAN WINE – *red*

Stellenbosch Cabernet Sauvignon 1993	11	£C

Stellenbosch Merlot/Cabernet 1993   14 £C
Loads of flavour and fruit.

Stellenbosch Merlot/Cabernet Sauvignon 1992 12 £C
This is made by two men from two different winery set-ups,
Neil Ellis and Jan Boland Coetzee, and it seems to fall
between two stools: on one hand it has cellaring potential, on
the other hand it must be said that although that potential may
realize the wine's soft, lush fruit it will lose its freshness and
vivacity. The '93 coming up may solve this problem. Messrs
Ellis and Coetzee, I should point out, are both committed
winemakers of the highest calibre; Ellis making a lot of wine
for the South African Woolworths organization (which is not
like the UK Woolworths – it even sells a range of non-South
African Marks & Spencer wines), Coetzee into the science
and art of barrel maturation and the granting of freehold
property rights to his farm workers.

Stellenbosch Merlot/Cabernet Sauvignon 1993 13 £C

SOUTH AFRICAN WINE – *white*

Cape Country Chenin Blanc 1994	14	£B
Cape Country Colombard 1994	10	£B
Cape Country Colombard, KWV 1993	13	£B
Cape Country Sauvignon Blanc 1994	13	£B

Craig Hall Chardonnay/Sauvignon Blanc 1993   13   £C

Stellenbosch Chardonnay 1992   12   £C
Comes from the Overgaauw Estate and one of the Cape's
most progressive winemakers, Braam van Velden.

Stellenbosch Chardonnay 1993   15   £C
Excellent style of rich flavour and calm acidity. A very well-
made wine.

SPANISH WINE – *red*

Costres del Segre DO, Raimat 1990   18.5   £C
Blended specially for M&S (the merlot in the blend is not
normal) and it is a stupendously perfect marriage (with cabernet sauvignon and tempranillo). Ripe, full, forward yet never
showy, it has beautifully polished fruit and deep rich berry
flavours of huge class. A great modern wine.

**Marqués del Romerol, Grand Reserva Rioja
DOC 1985**   16   £D
Superb vanilla undertones to the fruit. Great style. Lushness
without yukkiness.

Rioja 1990   13   £B
A decent price for a decent Rioja.

Rioja DOC, A G E   14   £B
Modern, light Rioja with gentle vanilla touches.

Valencia Red   16   £B
An enigma. I rated it 11 upon opening, 14 after half an hour,
and 16 after six hours. What begins with the limp handshake
of dilute cherry from a distant planet ends with the firm,

savoury grip of well-textured blackcurrant and dry, burnt cherry. A most remarkable and utterly delicious turnaround and only recommendable to those with the patience to wait one quarter of a day before touching the opened bottle.

Viña Brava, Torres, 1989   13 £C
A cabernet sauvignon, tempranillo blend in a slightly lower key than is usual with Maestro Torres. It's an attractive wine by virtue of its complete lack of defects rather than its positive set of hugely endearing traits. Dry, soft, red, fruity – it's all these things and it costs nigh on a fiver.

SPANISH WINE – *white*

Concha de Barbera Dry White, H Ryman 1993   15   £B
The usual marriage routine as adapted by Ryman: ripe rounded fruit holding the clean acidity in a firm grip and the two putting on a fluid performance.

Moscatel de Valencia DO   15 £C
A Beaumes de Venise clone at nothing like a B-d-V price. Has marmalade aromas but thereafter it's all soft honey.

USA WINE – *red*

California Red 1992   15 £B
How does an aroma of perfumed armpit strike you? Repulsive? Mildly disgusting? Arousing? Perhaps it might help if I added that the perfume is spiced and the armpit gingery. The whole effect is certainly engaging and is perfect to jazz up an

already well-spiced food. This jazzy character is from the San Joaquin Valley in California, a state renowned for quirky exports (from Michael Jackson to Philip K. Dick), and it's a blend of the barbera grape (a native of northern Italy), cabernet sauvignon, and ruby cabernet which is a crossing derived from cabernet sauvignon and carignan. The fruit of this wine has a mildly challenging aspect: complex, plummy, soft, and warmly evocative – evocative of the San Joaquin Valley itself which is such a hot spot that grapes run riot, and it is not unusual to see members of that awesome body of men The Sacramento Police Department out among the vines with their night sticks, teaching errant bunches a lesson.

USA WINE – *white*

California White 1992   14   £B
An interesting and original wine with a toasted aroma and flavour, although no oak has been used to mature the wine. Sunny fruit. Firm finish. Sound value considering it comes from those folks with the highest standard of living in the world (if you call the levels of material wealth enjoyed by Californians a height or even a standard).

SPARKLING WINE/CHAMPAGNE

Asti Spumante DOC Consorzio   11   £D
Usual sweet stuff.

Australian Chardonnay, Blanc de Blancs Bottle Fermented   16   £E

Rich, ripe, melon edge to the fruit yet this fizz is crisp to finish. Hugely appealing.

Australian Sparkling Brut   15   £C

One of the best Aussie bubblies around. Light yet full with good refreshing acidity. 'Taste the sunshine,' said the wine buyer as he offered me a glass and, lo and behold, sunshine flooded all over my tongue the moment I glugged. This is a very fruity sparkler with an attractive peachiness.

Blanc de Blancs Champagne   12   £G

Blenheim Sparkling Wine, New Zealand   14   £D
Austere, lean, clean, fine.

Blush, Frizzante   11   £B

Brut Sparkling Vin Mousseux   13   £C
Has some decent biting freshness.

Cava   14   £D

Made by the excellent Cava house of Freixenet, this does not exhibit that typical earthy undertone of the type but is a livelier and juicier example.

Champagne Chevalier de Melline, Premier Cru Blanc de Blancs   14   £G

Champagne Veuve de Medts   14   £F
Delicious champagne. Stylish, characterful, fresh and hugely approachable.

Crémant de Bourgogne AC   15   £D
Rich touch to the fruit, yet very refined over all.

Desroches Champagne   13   £F

Freixenet Cava, Spain   15   £D
Brilliant fruit and acid. None of the earthy undertones to it,
touch of austerity to the fruit. It's like a great champagne.

Oudinot Brut, France   12   £E
Pleasant but I'd rather drink the M & S Cava – especially at
four quid less.

Oudinot Champagne   10   £D

Oudinot Rosé Brut, France   11   £F

Prosecco, Italy   16   £C
Outstanding, finely balanced, apricot-fruited fizz with superb
balancing acidity.

Rosé Sparkling Vin Mousseux   14   £C
An excellent value rosé with a lilting touch of soft fruit to the
well-formed fresh structure of the whole.

Saumur Ladubay   14   £D
What a little corker! A gorgeous chenin/chardonnay blend of
quite arrogant aplomb.

Sparkling Chardonnay   13   £D

Sparkling Medium Dry   12   £C

Sparkling Rosé   13   £C
An engaging little fizzer.

St-Gall Champagne 1988   11   £G

**Vintage Champagne, St-Gall, Premier Cru Brut
1988**   14   £G
A mature, richly-edged champagne of class and style.

Morrisons

British Rail doesn't carry passengers any more. It serves customers. I'd just settled into my seat on the 8.35 to Leeds when the voice over the tannoy made this fact plain, as indeed similar voices over train tannoys have been doing for some time now, and I was prompted to wonder if Mr Ken Morrison, the store's chairman, hadn't been advising British Rail about how to improve things. For Mr Morrison is a man who believes in customers. Other stores enjoy the patronage of shoppers, but Morrisons has customers. Customers keep you on your toes. Customers need looking after. Shoppers merely require products like mere passengers need only tickets, but customers need serving. Customers come back and keep coming back week in week out. Shoppers buy today, vamoose tomorrow.

I'm always pleased to depart the Smoke for the day and trundle up to Yorkshire to see round a few Morrisons stores and sample some new wines with Stuart Purdie, the store's wine buyer. Stuart, now an honorary village Yorkshireman after moving to the sixty-odd strong store group a couple of years ago from a Peter Dominic store in Cambridgeshire, is finding his feet superbly now he's speaking the language and becoming acclimatized to the food. The magnificent lump of battered haddock I enjoyed for lunch was doorstep thick, took vinegar without wilting, and was correctly fried in dripping. Along with a superbly conditioned pint of Tetley's bitter, it was reason enough to be up there with or without the interesting new wines he's bought for the store.

He's doing Morrisons a power of good. He's encouraging the managers to take more interest in, and develop their

knowledge of, wine. All sixty-five wine and spirit managers
will have sat the Wine and Spirit Education Trust exams by
Christmas, and one or two 'have said they want to sit the
highest exam'. Things are looking up with the wines as well.

'A quarter of the range has changed,' he told me as he
took me round a store wine department so spacious you
could drive a truck through it. 'And not just on the New
World front. We did quite a lot with New World wines in
1993, but in 1994 I've concentrated very much on the traditional areas of Europe, Spain, Italy and France, though not
the traditional wines. We've been taking advantage of some
of the New World winemakers' technology in these European centres.'

Morrisons isn't in the big league (yet) so it hasn't the
resources to initiate new wine developments off its own bat.
It has to take advantage of schemes already in place and
bearing fruit.

'I keep my ear to the ground,' Stuart says. 'I hear what's
happening. I have to work this way because I'm not out there
travelling abroad as often as a lot of my competitors.'

What did he see as the biggest change in customers' view
of the store since he took over the wine department?

'I think people are now treating us as a very serious wine
merchant. Which I think we've always been, we've maybe not
shouted about it enough. We've not done enough to broaden
their interest.'

Does he mean over and above the bargains that people
expect to find at Morrisons?

'Yes. I think people always knew they'd find bargains, and
they still can. We've been adventurous in shipping direct
from places like Australia, for example, to get more competitive prices, but I've also tried to develop more interesting
themes, through different countries. All this has led to more

interest for the customer, ultimately. I still think we offer a fairly large range, which is important as well.'

But better wines?

'We've got better wines and near on 500 lines, but we do offer a very good range of sizes. We've got liebfraumilch in bottle, litre, litre and a half and two litre. We have a very strict policy. The customer has the choice of sizes. You'll find this throughout the whole of Morrisons stores. God help the buyer if the Chairman finds an inconsistency. If the customer wants a bigger size she gets a lower price. The Chairman's belief is that no customer need wander around with a calculator working out whether the large size tin of baked beans is actually cheaper. In Morrisons, it will be.'

But what about branded wines? Surely he can't claim the customer will find the branded wines, like Piat d'Or or Gallo, cheaper at Morrisons?

Stuart smiles a wry smile. 'We're continually being hassled by branded companies because of our prices. Get your prices up, they tell me, get your prices up.'

Interestingly, he believes that the days of the branded bottle of wine are numbered. Nowadays the brand is the supermarket. Why should a store like Morrisons bow to any pressure from branded wine companies? It has an extremely able buyer of its own who can put more individual wines, at smarter prices, in front of its customers day in day out, not just at the six weeks of Christmas when brands like Mateus, Asti Martini, Blue Nun, Black Tower and Piat d'Or achieve, according to Stuart, 80 per cent of their business with the store.

I asked him if Morrisons would move more into own-label wines, making Morrisons more of a brand on certain wines, and I got more or less the answer I expected. Like Waitrose, Morrisons prefers the shippers' labels, or the wineries', and

apart from the big volume lines like liebfraumilch and lambrusco the store will not, in his own words, 'go ridiculously
massive on own-label'.

I was interested to know how wines from the traditional
areas like muscadet, Chablis, Sancerre, Beaujolais, Rioja
fared at Morrisons. It is these areas which have had the
advantage for some years now of being able to represent
themselves as brands in their own right. But even here,
apparently, the customer is not swallowing any old nonsense
just because of the reassurance of perceived excellence.

'Slowly, as more and more people are discovering New
World wines, the more traditional wines are increasingly
under attack. It's down to the producers of these traditional
areas to maintain the quality/value balance. I don't know that
muscadet offers value these days. Or Beaujolais. Rioja does,
though there's a lot of cheap Rioja landing on my desk to try
which isn't doing Rioja any favours'.

Is he seriously telling me his customers are genuinely turning off muscadet, say, for New World equivalents?

'They're still buying muscadet, but it's an area which is
slowly being eroded. It won't disappear completely, but it's
slowly being chipped away and I think in ten years' time it . . .'

He leaves unsaid what was on the tip of his tongue. He
doesn't find it comfortable discussing the possible eclipse of a
wine area which was once a byword for a certain style of steely
excellence. Morrisons customers, however, have no such
qualms, and are voting with their mouths. Wine sales at the
store are 'up dramatically'.

The proof of which is in the pudding which follows.

Strong Dry Cider   15   £A
Superb thirst-quenching tipple of soft appley-fruit but genuinely dry. A real bargain.

ARGENTINIAN WINE – *red*

Trapiche Malbec   13   £C

AUSTRALIAN WINE – *red*

Baileys Victorian Cabernet 1991   15   £C
Its potent richness, potentially richer, make this a good bottle
to squirrel away for Christmas lunch this year, next year, and
for years after that. You can't miss the bottle; it's as subtly
adorned as a potion to enhance biceps.

Barramundi Shiraz/Merlot   14   £C
Sweaty, leathery, soft and fruity. Treat the turkey to it.

Hanwood Estate Cabernet Sauvignon 1991   15   £C
Delicious minty fruit.

Lindemans Bin 45 Cabernet Sauvignon 1992   14   £C
Attractive berry flavours and residual richness.

Lindemans Bin 50 Shiraz 1992   14   £C

**Lindemans St George Vineyard Cabernet
Sauvignon**   16   £E
Elegant, soft and smooth – an immediate fruitiness of quiet
yet decidedly cassis-like concentration.

Penfolds Bin 35 Shiraz/Cabernet 1992   15   £C
Ripe, soft fruit with some development ahead of it. Attractive
berry flavours, well structured and balanced. Very drinkable
now but a 17/18-pointer in 3/4 years.

Woomera Vale　　　　　　　　　　14　£B
Creamy, raisiny and toasty, nutty, slightly figgy. Curious wine,
but immensely drinkable.

Wyndham Bin 444 Cabernet Sauvignon 1992　　14　£C
Very deep and rich – like Pavarotti clearing his throat.

AUSTRALIAN WINE – *white*

Baileys Chardonnay 1993　　　　　　　16　£C
Though the oak influence is noticeable, it's extremely niftily
integrated with the buttery fruit and the pineappley acidity.

Lindemans Bin 65 Chardonnay 1993　　　　16　£C
Deep bruised fruit – lovely and ripe – superb effect on the
tongue.

McWilliams Hanwood Estate Chardonnay 1992　14　£C
Very fine style.

Penfolds Bin 21 Semillon/Chardonnay 1993　　15　£C
Fresh and lively yet a dollop of pineappley melon keeps
intruding. Delicious refreshing wine.

Woomera Vale　　　　　　　　　　14　£B
Some vigour to the fruit, nicely unfussy; unblowsy. Very sanely
priced with deal of attractive ripe melon and peach flavours.

CHILEAN WINE – *red*

Cousino-Macul Cabernet Sauvignon 1988　　14　£C

Cousino-Macul Cabernet Sauvignon 1989   15   £C
Ripe, rounded, dry finished, very perky with fruit without
being over-rich or blowsy. Has hints of woody, wild strawberry. Delicious to enjoy by itself or with food.

Gato Negro Cabernet Sauvignon   12   £B

San Pedro Merlot   14   £C
Dark, rich, with well-developed fruit. A fine roast meat wine.

Santa Carolina Cabernet Sauvignon 1992   15   £C
Lots of berried flavour which continues to be soft, yet the
tannins are agreeably tasty and soft.

Santa Emiliana Andes Peaks Cabernet/Merlot
1992   13   £B
A bin end some bottles of which may still be found tucked
away in the odd Morrisons shelf somewhere.

Santa Emiliana Cabernet Sauvignon, Nancagua
1992   14   £B
Dry with hints of rich, ripe fruitiness glistening through the
gloom. A serious side to this excellent food wine.

CHILEAN WINE – *white*

Andes Peaks Sauvignon Blanc 1993   14   £B
There were good stocks of this bargain bin end (£2.49 a
bottle) and there may be some Morrisons with a few bottles
left. Austere, steely, with nutty fruit, this is a very refreshing
bottle at any price.

Chardonnay Santa Emiliana, Aconcagua 1993   12   £B
This is a bin end but the odd bottle may be lurking.

Gato Blanco Sauvignon Blanc 12 £B

Santa Carolina Sauvignon Blanc 1993 16.5 £C
Superb style of fruit beautifully balanced by the citric acidity.
Huge style for the money.

ENGLISH WINE – *white*

Three Choirs Estates Premium 1992 15 £C
As good an English wine as you can get. Fresh and zippy on
the tongue, backed by a faint echo of honey on the off-dry
finish.

FRENCH WINE – *red*

Beaujolais-Villages, H. Leger 1990 12 £C

Beaujolais-Villages, H. Leger 1993 12 £C

Brouilly, Duboeuf 12 £D
See entry for Regnie.

**Cabernet Sauvignon, Chais Cuxac, Vin de Pays
d'Oc** 14 £C
Deliciously approachable cabernet. Real class yet real drinkability. Soft, rich, fruity, dry. An excellent food wine.

Cellier des Dauphins, Côtes du Rhône 1992 14 £B

Cellier des Dauphins, Côtes du Rhône 1993 12 £B

Cellier la Chouf, Minervois   14   £A
Earthy and soft. Terrific stuff.

Chantovent Prestige Merlot 1993   15   £B
A lush mouthful of ripe, very ripe, cherry/strawberry/plum
fruit. Great bargain.

Chantovent Prestige Merlot, VdP d'Oc 1992   13   £B

Château de Lastours, Corbières 1990   16   £C
Chocolate edges to the rich fruit which is dry and complex. A
balanced, full wine of depth and style, with a delicious length
of flavour.

**Château Léon, Premier Côtes de Bordeaux
1988**   15   £C
Deliciously light yet mature fruit which bristles with berries.
Soft, ripe, perfect with roast foods. Good price for a claret of
this age.

Château St Galier, Graves 1992   14   £C
Dry, rich, mature. Hints at being more terrific than it actually
is. But the fruit is sound and well structured.

Château Tour Camaillac, Côtes de Bourg 1989   13   £C

Comtesse de Lorancy   15   £A
Swirling black cherry flavours, rich, savoury. Terrific value.

**Corbières Château Lastours Arnaud de Berre
1989**   17   £C
A deep, rich, beautifully mature wine of lush fruitiness yet dry
seriousness. It is a bargain for the money.

Corbières, Les Fenouillets 1992   13   £B
Excellent value.

Côtes du Rhône 1993 13 £B

A Rhône from the quiet side of the river – but excellent value.

Côtes du Rhône Villages, Epitalon 17 £B

Another exclusive Morrisons wine which is amazingly cheap yet amazingly tasty. Has true soft earthy fruit, vivid, dry, rich and very complex for the money.

Côtes du Ventoux 1992 14 £B

Firmly fruity, touch of earth.

Domaine du Vieux Lazaret, Châteauneuf-du-Pape 1990 17 £E

Typically rich, deep Châteauneuf-du-Pape with rich burnt coffee and chocolate undertones to the fruit. Superb stuff. I could drink it all day.

Fleurie, Georges Duboeuf 1992 11 £D

Fronton 1989 13 £C

Gamay de Touraine 1992 12 £B

Ginestet Bordeaux 12 £B

Some typical bordeaux austerity detectable here.

La Rose St-Jean, Bordeaux (50 cl) 14 £A

A simple light claret of great interest to solo lunchers in its odd size. Good touch of soft fruit on the woodiness.

Le Piat d'Or 9 £C

No character, little style. Unattractive. Slightly toffee-ish bouquet. Sweet fruit. Dry finish.

Le Vigneron Catalan 13 £B

Can't grumble at this much reasonable fruit for the money. Also in magnums for under a fiver – useful party size.

Louis Fontaine Vin de Pays des Pyrénées Orientales   11   £A

Margaux 1990   12   £E
Declassified Château Palmer but still overpriced.

Médoc La Taste   14   £C
Has some taste, ironically. And the tannins give it backbone and savour.

Merlot, Vin de Pays d'Oc 1993   12   £B

Regnie, Duboeuf   12   £D
Regnie is the newest Beaujolais cru name. It used to be plain Beaujolais-Villages but it's been upgraded. But like seemingly all Beaujolais crus nowadays (Brouilly and Fleurie for example, also at Morrisons), or at least the cru wines which find their way into British supermarkets, the same high 13% of alcohol is offered along with the high price, and though these wines are smooth, sweetly fruity and reliable, and drinkable immediately upon opening (making them restaurant products really), as value for money they are beaten hollow by cheaper reds from all over the world.

Renaissance Buzet 1992   14   £C
Soft and rich. Delicious.

Tradition Coteaux du Languedoc   17   £B
Exclusive to the store, this wine is so soft and chocolatey with overtones of raspberry that it takes your breath away for the money. Brushed silk fruit imprinted with rougher streaks of corduroy tannin. This textured wine is chewy, rich, beautifully rounded and plump in the mouth, with a finish hinting at a cherry liqueur in its concentrated fruitiness. Dry and very far from austere. Even the label is made from pyjama material.

Vin de Pays des Bouches du Rhône 13 £B

You could chill this red and it would serve the same happy
end as a white (if you wore a blindfold as you drank it) but at
average room temperature, whatever that may mean, touches
of baked earth and herbs on the fruit are apparent which make
it the sort of thing you find in Marseille transport cafés as the
vin rouge de maison. As you knock it back you sense the
proximity of mountainous off-white vested Frogmen with oil-
stained fingers and yellow cigarettes dangling from their lips.
Having said that, though, the wine has an interesting soiled
nappy aroma. Not a wine I'd try offering mothers, child-
minders, nannies, paediatricians, or men under seventy-five
years of age. Looks like grandpa's stuck with it then (and he'll
be thrilled with it if he sucks it up through his shag-packed
pipe).

Vin de Pays des Pyrénées Orientales 15 £B

Will the '94, coming on shelf just as this book is published, be
as good as the '93? I thought the wine last year was lovely and
bright, with fruit just gushing out of the bottle, round and
even a touch mellow. Superbly soft and plummy, this southern answer to the ghastly Beaujolais Nouveau is brilliant to
drink and to buy. Utter, natural tasting drinkability.

FRENCH WINE – *white and rosé*

Cépage Muscat, Pyrénées Orientales 1990 13 £B

Chais Cuxac Chardonnay 15 £C

Full and rich and yet balanced. A really fruity wine for the
money.

Château Saint Gallier 1993   15   £C
Delicious ripe fruit, very rounded and lush, with a fresh-ish
finish. Very fleshy stuff.

Comtesse de Lorancy   13   £A
Very fresh and breezy. Good fish wine.

Côtes de Duras Sauvignon Blanc 1992   14   £B
Fine level of fruit, cleanly finished. Something of a bargain.

Côtes de Provence Rosé   8   £B

Côtes de Provence Rosé, François Dulac 1993   12   £B

Côtes du Rhône   12   £B

Côtes du Roussillon Blanc 1993   14   £B
Terrific style for a white from this area.

Domaine de l'Orme, Petit Chablis 1993   10   £D

**Domaine l'Argentier, Vin de Pays Terret,
J. Lurton** 1993   13   £B
Falls away at the finish a touch but the rest of the construction
is fine.

**Domaine le Galoubis, Côtes de Gascogne
1993**   15.5   £B
Brilliant rich fruit, melony and ripe, with gently citric acidity.
Superbly cheering style.

Ginestet, Graves Blanc 1992   8   £C

J. P. Chenet, Cinsaut Rosé 1993   9   £B

La Sablière Muscadet 1993   10   £B

La Piat d'Or   9   £C
Interestingly, hypermarkets in the ferry ports put this on the

foreign wines shelf rather than the French and quite right. In spite of the brilliant lies of the TV commercials, no Frog would be seen dead drinking this wimpish concoction – made for the British market. Morrisons is the only supermarket brave enough to send me a sample of this wine and I'm pleased it did. This wine has no character and little style.

Le Vigneron Catalan	10	£A

Le Vigneron Catalan Rosé 1991   12   £A
Would best show off its charms, I believe, swigged in July under a Côte d'Azur plane tree along with a whopping salade niçoise, but in Britain in winter, however clement, it's hard pushed to rate much more than 12 points with a tuna sandwich for company.

Lurton Sauvignon Blanc VdP d'Oc 1992   12   £B

Mâcon Villages, Domaine Jean-Pierre Teissedre 1992   13   £C
Good stuff – excellent grilled fish wine.

Muscadet, La Sablière 1992   10   £C

Peyres Nobles Corbières 1993   12   £B

Preiss-Zimmer Gewürztraminer, Vin de l'Alsace 1992   10   £C

Preiss-Zimmer Pinot Blanc 1992   14   £C
An excellent, though unusual expression of the grape; dry, balanced, crisp, peachy.

Premières Côtes de Bordeaux   13   £C
Has some style. Good with hard cheese and hard fruit.

Sauvignon de Touraine 1993   15   £B
Brilliant value for brilliant rich fruit undercut by delicate acidity.

Sauvignon Jacques & François Lurton 1993   14   £B
Excellent value. Really zippy fruit.

Vin de Pays des Coteaux de l'Ardèche 1992   11   £A

Vin de Pays des Côtes de Gascogne, Pouy 1992 12   £B
Rather good with live shellfish.

Vin de Pays du Jardin de la France 1992   6   £A

GERMAN WINE – *white*

Bereich Bernkastel Langguth 1992   13   £A
Some richness of fruit – uncomplex.

**Binger St Rochuskapelle Kabinett, Johannes
Egberts**   11   £B

Flonheimer Adelberg 1992   13   £B

Flonheimer Adelberg Kabinett 1992   13   £B
Delicious off-dry fruit aperitif. Better than any liebfraumilch
for the money.

Graacher Himmelreich Kabinett 1991   14   £C
Try this refined lemony wine with grilled fish.

Herxheimer Herrlich Kabinett   13   £B

Klusserather St Michael   10   £B

**Mainzer Domherr Kabinett Berres-Hahner
1992**   14   £B
Elderflowers, with a honey-tinged finish, but not sweet. An
excellent aperitif.

Shellfish Dry   13   £B
Never was a wine as aptly named or priced.

St Johanner Abtey Ortega Spätlese 1992   12   £B
A drier, cheaper, and more complex alternative to lousy liebfraumilch.

Wiltinger Scharzberg Spätlese 1993   13   £B

GREEK WINE – *red*

Mavrodaphne of Patras   10   £B
This is basically stewed prunes made into wine. Probably
rather good with Christmas pudding.

Vin de Crete n.v.   12   £B
So obvious and straightforward it's almost naive. Has fruit,
not a lot, but it's there and so is balance and structure. It's so
thoroughly respectable and quiet; that's the problem. I'd like
to see an interesting rough edge on wine calling itself Vin de
Crete (and maybe read a dirty Greek classical joke on the back
label).

Vin de Crete 1992   13   £B
Some good fruit and balance, good with fish. Only fails to
collect more points because of the finish which fails to live up
to the vigorous approach of everything else about the wine.

HUNGARIAN WINE – *white*

Gyöngyös Sauvignon Blanc 1993   14   £B
Grassy and keen. Varietally the best vintage yet for Gyöngyös
Sauvignon Blanc.

ITALIAN WINE – *red*

Cortenova Montepulciano d'Abruzzo 1992   14   £B
Bright and full of soft juicy fruit. Plummy and delicious.

Gabbia d'Oro   8   £A
Ugh.

Grave del Friuli, Merlot 1993   13   £A

Montepulciano d'Abruzzo   13   £B
Good value. Dry, yet cherryish and cheering.

Nebbiolo d'Alba Ca Blanca 1990   13   £C

Sangiovese di Romagna   13   £B

Valpolicella (Morrisons)   12   £B

**Vigneti Casterna Amarone della Valpolicella
Classico**   15   £D
Cloyingly rich, herby fruit with baked undertones, şeems
hardly to possess any acids so smooth is it. Great with roast
meats with herbs.

ITALIAN WINE – *white*

Chardonnay delle Tre Venezie 1992 14 £B
Attractive nut and creamed melon fruit – not brash, but firm
and well-balanced. Excellent value.

**Chardonnay Teresa Rizzi, Vino da Tavola delle Tre
Venezie** 11 £B

Est! Est!! Est!!! 10 £B

Gabbia d'Oro 7 £A
It tastes like dilute apple juice without the fruit. I've tasted
bottles of this wine a year apart and found my notes almost
word for word the same, so obviously the producer of this
miracle of mediocrity has found a formula and he's sticking to
it, but then the same can be said of a serial killer. Ugly.

Orvieto Classico 1993 10 £C

S. Orsola Frascati Superiore 1993 11 £B

Trebbiano del Veneto 10 £A

MEXICAN WINE – *red*

L.A. Cetto Cabernet Sauvignon 14 £C
Eat your hearts out, minor Bordeaux growths at three times
the price.

MOROCCAN WINE – *red*

Moroccan Red Wine   16   £B
Touches of Colombian coffee for this superbly rich, leather-
touched wine which slips down superbly.

PORTUGUESE WINE – *red*

Borges Bairrada Reserva 1987   14   £B
Good rich mature tone to the fruit without being strident or
brassy. Remarkable value.

Dão Meia Encosta Reserva 1989   15   £B
Bargain dry fruit with hints of spiced plum. Good rich finish.
Delicious food wine.

Soveral Tinto de Mesa   14   £A
Clodfuls of sock and fruit.

PORTUGUESE WINE – *white and rosé*

'M' Portuguese Rosé   13   £B
So much better than Mateus at the price and zippier in the
fruit department.

Portuguese Rosé   12   £B

Vinho Verde   12   £B

ROMANIAN WINE – *red*

Cabernet Sauvignon Reserve 1985 16 £B

For lunch one Sunday I decanted this 16-point wine and served it to a well-heeled American wine buff and he was bowled over by its lovely dry, dusty aroma and fruit and he was touched that I had opened some ancient fifth growth claret specially for him. When I revealed its true provenance and stunning under-three-quid price tag, he admitted he would have been less surprised to learn that Sylvester Stallone was dating Margaret Thatcher.

Romanian Cellarmasters Feteasca Negra and Cabernet 13 £B

Good value for food related orgies.

Romanian Classic Pinot Noir 1988 14 £B

Cuddly old soul just slipping into its dotage.

Special Reserve Merlot, Dealul Region 1990 15 £B

Vigorous, dry, almost biscuity fruit with strawberry overtones. Light to finish but superb with cheeses and meats. Real bargain style.

ROMANIAN WINE – *white*

Romanian Cellarmasters Chardonnay and Feteasca 14 £B

The perfect quaffer at this price and it even has enough fruity oomph to go with food.

Romanian Chardonnay 1993   14   £B
Has nimble balance and good fruit.

Sauvignon Blanc   12   £B

SOUTH AFRICAN WINE – *red*

Cinsault 1992   14   £B
This is so thick, soft and creamy with fruit that it reminds me
of the Cherry Blossom boot polish I used on my school shoes.
A real forwardly fruity number of superb relevance when
tomato-sauced pizzas and pastas are on the table. It literally
hums with velvet berries.

Fair Cape Cinsault 1992   13   £B

Fair Cape Pinotage 1992   14   £B
Better than most Beaujolais and less money.

K.W.V. Shiraz 1990   14   £C

Landema Falls Cape Red   14.5 £B
Interesting cough syrup undertones to the plum fruit. A firm,
dry, perfectly responsible wine with a hint of exotic wild
abandon about it.

SOUTH AFRICAN WINE – *white*

Fair Cape Chenin Blanc 1993   10   £B

Fair Cape Sauvignon Blanc 1993   12   £B

Landema Falls Colombard, Coastal Region　　12　£B

SPANISH WINE – *red*

Campo Viejo Rioja　　13　£C
A reliable dollop of woody fruit. I've only once sent a bottle of
this wine back and it was in a tapas bar in Madrid but the
bottle was twenty years old, had been badly stored, and even
the bloke behind the bar spat it out when he tasted it. He
graciously presented me with a younger bottle – perhaps
catching the sound of quaking English feet in boots amidst the
deathly silence which instantaneously fell on the crowded bar
as I handed the bottle back. But with this bottle, you should
have no complaints – except maybe the price.

Carreras Dry Red, Valencia 1987　　15　£A
A thundering great bargain: dry, fruity, balanced and flavoursome. Excellent pasta and pizza wine.

Domino Tinto　　15　£A
Domino Tinto is a red Iberian wine which looks and sounds
distinctly unpromising and costs so little it seems silly to drink
it. But a bright, fruity, richly-edged wine of such excellence
emerges from the £2.49 bottle as to silence all doubts.

Jaume Serra Tempranillo 1991　　15　£B
Burnt wood overtones to soft fruit. Superbly gluggable stuff.

Las Campañas Rosada 1992　　15　£B
Arguably a bigger bargain than the Domino Tinto, even at
40p more. Utterly delicious, this rosé wine has compelling
fruit, almost crème-de-cassis-like in feel and is comfortably at
home with chicken and fish dishes.

Marqués de Cáceres Rioja   13   £C

Navajas Rioja Reserva 1985   15   £C
Richly flavoured yet light, but a curiously mature yet youthful
wine.

Raimat Abadia 1990   17   £C
A vivaciously chocolatey wine of deliciously crunchy fruit.
Superb wine.

Rioja 1992   16   £B
A splendid wine from the Navajas family. I gave the '90
vintage of this barely-oaked wine 15 points but the '92 rates a
point more, for it is superb stuff for under three quid. It gives
the tempranillo grape free, soft, fruity, chewy-edged rein
rather than smothering it in wood with all its stiflingly harsh
overtones.

Solaña Cencibel 1993   15   £C
Terrific soft fruit, plummy and lushly ripe, with just a touch of
the lovely polished tannins of the grape type.

Torres Sangredetoro Tres Torres 1989   14   £C
This has some pretensions to be much finer than it is (not
helped by the plastic bull dangling like some cornflake packet
giveaway gee-gaw from the neck), for it has satiny fruit of
some depth and class and as a wine for poultry dishes it is
excellent. Under £4 it's also well-priced but somehow the
feeling grows, as does the ullage, as the wine slips down the
throat, that there's passion missing, along with the customary
vividly orchestrated fruit we've come to expect from Señor
Torres.

SPANISH WINE – *white and rosé*

Campañas Rosé 1993   12   £B
Feebler than other vintages.

Inocente Extra Dry Fino   16   £D
Sherry yes, but so dry it puckers your cheeks. Fabulously
satisfying when it's well chilled and taken with grilled prawns.
The mineral, flinty fruit tiptoes on the tongue like a ballet
dancer on shoes spun from cobwebs. Remarkable value.

Jaume Serra Macabeo 1993   13   £B
Some life here.

La Mora, Moscatel de Valencia   15   £B
Great fun! Liquid raisins laced with nougat ice-cream.

Solaña Torrontes Treixadera 1993   13   £C
Highly lemonic aperitif.

Spanish Dry (Morrisons)   13   £A
Great value for large groups.

USA WINE – *red*

Blossom Hill   11   £B
Stale pot pourri aroma, sweet fruit. Might make an interesting
jelly with a game dish.

Glen Ellen Merlot 1992   15   £C
Has raspberry and strawberry overtones and yet maintains a
solid serious dryness. Delicious.

Sutter Home California Zinfandel 1991   14   £C
Spicy, soft, leathery and finishing sweetly on the earthy fruit.
Delicious.

USA WINE – *white and rosé*

Blossom Hill   11   £B

Blossom Hill White Zinfandel   14   £C
A rosé which is a truly delicious aperitif – like a dilute
Dubonnet.

Glen Ellen Chardonnay 1992   16   £C
Oily, woody, fruity – but never too full or blowsy. A really
elegant Californian.

SPARKLING WINE/CHAMPAGNE

Asti Spumante Gianni, Italy   11   £C
Sweet and peachy. Pour it over ice-cream.

Brut de Channay   16   £C
This is an outstanding dry wine for the money (£4.99). It
offers good balanced fruit and acid, neither overblown nor
sharp, and drops down the throat as smoothly as many an
Australian sparkling wine. If it was repackaged and the store
ditched the hypnotically horrendous black and gold label,
which is the only tarty aspect of the wine, it would go like hot
cakes – which, incidentally, the wine will cheerfully accompany. Rock cakes, unsweetened, warm from the oven for

afternoon tea may not be as fashionable as they once were, but this wine is priced handsomely enough to spark a revival.

Cava Cristalino Brut Spain   14   £C
Excellent value.

Moscato Spumante   11   £B
Shaving foam in a glass.

Nicole d'Aurigny Champagne   15   £E
Still one of the most stylish, serious champagnes under £9 around.

Omar Khayyam, India   12   £D

Paul Herard Brut Champagne   13   £F

Paul Herard Demi-Sec   14   £F
Not at all sweet but delicious and maturely fruity.

Seppelt Great Western Brut, Australia   16   £C
Superb bargain. A finer fizzer on sale for under a fiver it's difficult to name. Lemony, zingy, zesty. Great style.

Vouvray (Morrisons)   14   £D
Good value sparkler.

Seaview Brut   15   £D
Stylish, refined, and quite delicious.

Asti Spumante   10   £C
A small glass with banana cake might do.

Safeway

Safeway now has such solid, and unrivalled, eastern European connections the store could apply for diplomatic status. Certainly the dedicated statue erectors of this part of the world, anxious to acknowledge a debt, have the perfect replacement to fill all those bare plinths violently vacated by disgraced communists. Will Elizabeth Robertson of Safeway become the first supermarket wine buyer to be set in stone? The only barrier to fulfilling this idea is Mrs Robertson's infectious smile. This is not considered a statuesque quality in eastern Europe, indeed not so long ago it would have been construed as a criminal offence had it been in evidence on state occasions when it might have proved injurious to viral communism, so we have some time to wait before the region grows out of the emotionally stunting legacies of corrupt politics and re-admits irony and good humour into the public domain. When it does, Safeway above all supermarkets will be all smiles.

Safeway is overflowing with interesting wines from eastern Europe. Not just the wines everyone else flashes, like the new vintage Gyöngyös Estate Sauvignon Blanc which is now showing deeper herbaceous character than before and thus providing greater grape varietal typicity, or the predictable and sound Bulgarian reds. Safeway also has wines made exclusively for the store as a result of its buyers' initiatives. Thus all manner of attractively fruity and attractively priced wines crop up, demonstrating not only a degree of buying skills but also a flair for blending. This combination of strengths is not bettered anywhere.

Established favourites also remain as testimony to how well

the buyers can choose not just one-off stars but wines which will, over the years, become backbones of the range. The new vintage Young Vatted Merlot, for instance, is every bit as polished as the previous vintage. The Young Vatted Cabernet Sauvignon is a touch drier and more austere than last year but it is sure to soften (don't we all?) as it ages.

For Safeway customers, eastern Europe has value for money coming out of its ears. Leaving aside the fact that this clears up the mystery of the waxy taste to be found in some of its less distinguished and, I'm happy to report, non-Safeway whites, bargains lie thick on the shelves. Among these whites, River Duna Sauvignon Blanc 1993, modern, fresh, full of flavour, and River Duna Pinot Gris 1993, crisp yet with a delicious soft centre, both stand out. Both are Hungarians. It is equally no sweat to pick out a trio of fantastically tasty high-scoring reds: Veneka Gamay/Merlot Reserve 1990, a superbly smooth and distinguished dollop of Bulgarian fruit, Romanian Pinot Noir 1989 which is equally brilliant but with gamey undertones, and Romanian Merlot 1990, a rich and classic brew with hugely food-friendly fruit. Another excellent red is Special Reserve Cabernet Sauvignon 1986 from Romania.

Also worth singling out from Moldova is Hincesti Feteasca 1993, made for Penfolds by Hugh Ryman with all the fresh fruit you would expect, and Hincesti Chardonnay. There is also Matra Mountains Chardonnay 1993, brilliantly rich yet fresh-faced from Hungary, and Badger Hill Chardonnay 1993, a well-balanced Hungarian with lots of freshly picked fruit.

Some retail wine buyers turned up their noses at east European wines a few years back but Safeway has hung on in there, upping the quality of the wines without elevating prices, and the rewards are now being reaped by the store as they are undoubtedly being enjoyed by the customers. It has even managed to persuade the Germans to accept a flying wine-maker and the result, St Ursula Ryman Riesling 1993, is terrific. Truly old-style merchant venturing by Mrs Robertson and her team of buyers, and one reason why Safeway is now reckoned, by professional observers of the retail scene, to be up there with Sainsbury and Tesco. Proof that the British genius for retailing is not merely alive but thriving and ingeniously adjusting itself to the post-recession era in which so many of us wish to maintain the trappings of a civilized lifestyle (e.g. regularly opening a bottle of wine), yet do not wish to spend unwisely.

In circumstances like these, it would attract no censure if the store were merely to attempt to emulate its competitors, but the store has ploughed certain furrows which it can fairly claim to be its own even without its eastern European adven-tures. It is heavily into organic wines, not always so success-fully as it is now, in my view, for there was a time when the organic shelves may have testified to the store's heart being in the right place, but for those drinkers whose taste buds were sited elsewhere there was not a lot to slaver over. Now there is even an oak-aged organic French syrah with fruit tasty enough to produce home-sickness in an Aussie, yet with an under £3.50 price tag. It has also stuck out its neck with Moroccan red (Domaine Sapt Inour), now to be seen, once it was evident that Safeway had backed a winner, on the shelves of two competitors (though under different names). And it has stood by Herr Laubenstein's fruity Dornfelder Trocken 1992 when, for the majority of drinkers, the idea of putting a German red wine on their dining table is a riskier proceeding than asking Hannibal Lecter to babysit.

Safeway has also stood by the Old Country. Fourteen English and one Welsh wine feature on the list and if that isn't brave wine buying then nothing is. The store also has a superb range of Aussies (over 40), solid South African and South American ranges, and is only really weak in the USA and when it comes to reds from New Zealand.

The store contradicts the view held by many among the upper echelons of the wine trade that it is only individual wine merchants who are truly individual, and that the large superstores are just mass caterers servicing mass needs with mass-produced wines of little individuality. This is patently not so where Safeway is concerned. Of course the store will not neglect the interests of the twice-a-week liebfraumilch and lambrusco drinker, for these loyalists not only provide income and its attendant profit, but also the means whereby more adventurous palates can be served. It is to these palates that Safeway increasingly panders with attractive, well-priced wines which reflect not only the burgeoning New World wine areas, but also the reborn areas of the old world.

Doesn't it ever strike you that the one place where Britain can truly be said to be the trend-setter of Europe is in one of its leading superstores? And that of all the aisles in that store, the most telling clue to this country's new-found and evolving cosmopolitan appetite is that long stretch of wine shelves?

Safeway is in the forefront of this revolution. No other store is more active in maintaining its momentum, no other store offers more enjoyable and well-priced bottles as its fruits.

ARGENTINIAN WINE – *red*

Carrascal 1985   13 £D
Goodness, what a serious, austere, almost monkish wine was

to be tasted in this bottle in the spring. Now it's winter, perhaps there's a soft smile on its face.

Casa del Campo Syrah 1992	10	£C

Las Alturas Argentine Red, Mendoza   13   £C
Soft cherry/blackcurrant.

ARGENTINIAN WINE – *white*

Las Alturas Argentine Dry White, Mendoza   13   £C

AUSTRALIAN WINE – *red*

Bowman Reserve Tawny, Arrowfield   11   £D
Useful for making sauces to accompany game (especially grilled wild duck breasts).

Cabernet Sauvignon 1992   14   £B
What a blackcurrant smoothie! With a glug of it in one cheek and a morsel of roast lamb or beef in the other you'll be seriously satisfied.

Eileen Hardy Shiraz, South Australia 1990   15   £E
Hugely elegant and stylish. Deeply disturbing fruit.

**Hardy's Barossa Valley Cabernet Sauvignon
1992**   15   £D
Impossibly soft. Ridiculously easy to drink.

Hardy's Barossa Valley Shiraz 1991   16   £D
A good fiver's worth of savoury fruit. Great to drink by itself.
Soft, full, deep and rich.

Hardy's Nottage Hill Cabernet Sauvignon 1990   15   £C
Brilliant value. Teeth-coatingly rich and delicious fruit of
elegance and power.

Hardy's Stamp Series Dry Red 1993   13   £C

Jacob's Creek Dry Red 1991   12   £C

Moondah Brook Cabernet Sauvignon 1991   14   £D

Orlando RF Cabernet Sauvignon 1990   12   £C

Penfolds Bin 2 Shiraz/Mataro 1992   13   £C

Penfolds Bin 35 Shiraz/Cabernet 1992   15   £C
Ripe, soft fruit with some development ahead of it. Attractive
berry flavours, well-structured and balanced. Very drinkable
now but a 17/18-pointer in 3/4 years.

Penfolds Coonawarra Cabernet Sauvignon
1990   17   £E
The colour of crushed blackberries, subtle eucalyptus/leather
aroma, sheer satiny acids and velvet-textured fruit touches –
lovely tannicky finish.

Penfolds Koonunga Hill Shiraz/Cabernet 1992   15   £C
Getting pricey at over a fiver, this wine. Has lush sweet-
finishing fruit but not a lot of complexity.

Shiraz (Safeway)   14   £C
One of Safeway's competitors tried to hoodwink me into
buying the idea that this soft, modern, eminently gluggable
wine, which travels in bulk from Australia to France to be
bottled and bagged-in-box before crossing the channel to fill

Safeway's shelves, wasn't good enough for *his* store.
Poppycock. Pure jealousy. This is a smashing little wine at a
smashing little price and who gives a kookaburra's fart if it
makes corkscrews redundant?

Taltarni Cabernet Sauvignon 1989   13   £E
I'd open this wine in 2005. And then the men in white coats
can cart me away and chisel on my tombstone: *He led a full,
rich life.*

The Magill Estate, South Australia 1988   13   £F

**Tyrrells Old Winery Pinot Noir, New South
Wales 1991**   11   £D

**Wildflower Ridge Shiraz, Western Australia
1992**   16   £C
Dark summer fruits and dry plums and cassis. Brilliant fruity
wine.

Windy Peak Victoria Cabernet/Merlot 1991   13   £D

**Wolf Blass Yellow Label Cabernet Sauvignon
1992**   15.5 £D
Ripe fruit, very giving, with minty undertones. Very opulent.
Incredibly soft and velvety.

Wynns Cabernet/Shiraz, Coonawarra 1989   14   £D
Rich and saucy.

AUSTRALIAN WINE – *white*

**Arrowfield Reserve Semillon, Hunter Valley
1989**   14   £D
Rich and flavourful.

**Australian Chardonnay, New South Wales
1993**   14   £C
Good firm fruit, good acidity. Very approachable.

**Evans & Tate Two Vineyards Chardonnay,
Western Australia 1992**   10   £E

Hardy's Barossa Valley Chardonnay 1993   15   £D
A grassy shroud for the rich fruit. Hugely drinkable fish wine.

**Hardy's Barossa Valley Chardonnay/Sauvignon,
Clare Valley Vineyard 1993**   16   £D
Great with grilled chicken. Big bruising beautiful. Bagsful of rich fruit. A powerful Barossan.

Hardy's Nottage Hill Chardonnay 1993   15   £C
Getting expensive now it's over £4? A touch. But it's still a lovely rich chardonnay of real style.

Hunter Valley Chardonnay 1993   17   £C
Huge fruit (rounded, ripe, brilliant), great balance, class, style and price. Utterly delicious – a wine to love!!

Jacob's Creek Semillon/Chardonnay 1993   13   £C

Lindemans Bin 65 Chardonnay 1993   16   £C
Deep-bruised fruit – lovely and ripe – superb effect on the tongue.

Orlando RF Chardonnay 1991   12   £C

Penfolds Koonunga Hill Chardonnay 1992   14   £C
Full lush fruit plus a ticklish dollop of lemon zest. Delicious,
but getting pricey near a fiver.

**Penfolds Organic Chardonnay/Sauvignon Blanc
1993**   16   £D
A happy marriage. Fine rich fruit plus gentle rolling acidity
make for a perfect balance of flavours from start to finish. Has
a very sophisticated feel to it.

Penfolds South Australia Chardonnay 1992 16   £D
Lovely polished, lush, woody fruit with touches of lemon,
beautifully balanced. Elegant – a real alternative, at a far lower
price, to fine burgundy.

Rosemount Roxburgh Chardonnay 1988   15   £E

Rosemount Show Reserve Chardonnay 1991   13   £E

Semillon (Safeway)   12   £B

**Semillon/Chardonnay, SE Australia 1993
(Safeway)**   13   £C

Wakefield 'White Clare', Clare Valley 1989 16   £C
A wine so full of flavour it dazes the taste buds. Marvellous
brash stuff.

AUSTRIAN WINE – *white*

Lenz Moser Pinot Blanc 1992   14   £C

Seewinkler Impressionen Ausbruch 1991 (half) 13   £D
A burnt-honey edge to the fruit which is aromatically

attractive. Has some botrytis character (i.e. the true noble rot fungus has set into the grapes thus dehydrating them and enriching the fruit), but this is not hugely concentrated and you pay through the nose for it.

BULGARIAN WINE – *red*

Cabernet Sauvignon 1988　　　　　　　　　15　£B
Remarkable price for a five-year-old and delicious stuff it is. Wonderful woody perfume, but not a trace of arthritic fruit, just supple, cherry-cheeked, figgy richness.

Cabernet Sauvignon Suhindol (Safeway)
(3 litres)　　　　　　　　　　　　　　　13　£F

Krazen Vineyards Cabernet Sauvignon 1992　16　£B
This has a gorgeously soft, ripe, yet vigorous style with the blackcurrant fruit having a cherry razzmatazz finish to it. This provides a decidedly brash side to the normally sombre cabernet fruit and gives the wine enough flavour, style, and persistence to go with a dish like pheasant with madeira sauce which is exactly what it did. That it is this fruity is the result of the *macération carbonique* method of fermentation the grapes undergo similar to the technique used in Beaujolais. The winemaker also claims to employ near-organic working methods in the vineyard and to use no sulphur dioxide prior to bottling. Certainly this 16-point wine causes no headaches at its price.

Mavrud 1992　　　　　　　　　　　　　　13　£B

Merlot Reserve 1987   14   £B
Scrumptuous wine of lush plum and blackberry fruit.
Balanced, dry, very well made.

Venenka Gamay/Merlot Reserve 1990   16   £B
Smooth and very distinguished. Remarkable price.

Young Vatted Cabernet Sauvignon 1993
(Safeway)   14   £B
Drier and a touch more austere than the '92 but still one heck
of a good cabernet sauvignon for the money. Better in six
months.

Young Vatted Merlot 1993   15   £B
Deliciously chewy fruit. As brilliant as the '92 – polished and
waxy, a delightfully drinkable wine.

BULGARIAN WINE – *white*

Bulgarian Country Wine (Safeway)   11   £B

CHILEAN WINE – *red*

San Pedro Cabernet Sauvignon 1992   14   £B
Soft, attractive, plummy fruit – leathery undertones. Delicious
and very good value.

Santa Rita Medalla Real 1989   15   £D
Not cheap but a gorgeous, dry wine with blackcurrant fruit
and a sweet rich finish. Soft, sustaining – and of huge appeal
to meat stew eaters.

Villa Montes Cabernet Sauvignon 1990 13 £C
Very attractive pasta plonk.

CHILEAN WINE – *white*

Caliterra Sauvignon Blanc 1993 16 £C
Elegant, slightly lemon fruit, classy, demure, not tough.
Lovely clear aperitif wine. Excellent structure.

**Santa Carolina Special Reserve
Chardonnay 1992** 16 £D
Superb fruit balance, cool, unfussy. An excellent bottle.

CZECH WINE – *white*

Czech Pinot Blanc 1993 13 £B

ENGLISH WINE – *white and rosé*

Denbies Optima/Pinot Blanc 1990 10 £C
Odd. Cloying as crab-apple jelly.

Elmham Park 1991 10 £D

Estate Selection Dry, Sharpham 1990 13 £C
Reasonable delivery of fresh fruit, sane and balanced.

Lymington Medium Dry 1991 10 £C

Pilton Manor Dry Reserve 1991   12 £D
A bit muddy on the front and a bit short on the finish. Rather
expensive for the fruit on offer.

Sharpham Estate Selection 1992   12 £D
Gingery nose and fruit which has some richness.

Stanlake, Thames Valley Vineyards 1992   12 £C
Pleasant melon bouquet. Good finish, firm structure. Well
made. Crisp finish. Melon style. Attractive aperitif, good but
not great.

Surrey Gold 1991   12 £D

Sussex Reserve 1990   12 £C
Someone farts in the glass just as you take in the bouquet, but
this is a minor niggle. Probably excellent with shellfish.

Three Choirs Seyval/Reichensteiner 1990   13 £C
Apple-bright fruit, developed and attractive, wrapped in wet
wool, i.e. that musty feral aroma given off by a sodden sweater
drying in front of the fire.

Valley Vineyards Regatta 1991   13 £C
Keen, fresh, dry – a grilled sardine wine.

Sussex Sunset Hidden Springs Rosé 1993   10 £D
Overpriced cosmetic production with cheap cherry drop fruit.
Expensive wine for a Barbie doll collection with a garish label to
match (and a back label which says 'Hi!'). Yuk! Hungarian
Cabernet Sauvignon Rosé is three times better at half the price.

Valley Vineyards Fumé Blanc 1992   15 £E
Great wood and fruit integration. Better than most Sancerres
and Chablis for the money.

FRENCH WINE – *red*

Abbaye de Tholomies, Minervois 1991	14	£C

Dry, very dry, yet very, very undemanding. Lots of flavour here. Good with food.

Abbaye de Tholomies, Minervois 1992	14	£C
Beaujolais (Safeway)	11	£C
Beaujolais-Villages 1992 **(Safeway)**	11	£C
Beaune Luc Javelot 1989 **(Safeway)**	12	£E
Bourgogne Rouge 1991, **Aged in Oak (Safeway)**	11	£C
Brouilly, Duboeuf 1992	11	£D
Cavalier du Roi, Vin de Pays des Côtes de Gascogne	13	£C

You could do a lot worse for a picnic.

Chambole Musigny C. Masy-Perier 1991	11	£F
Ch. Beychevelle, Cru Classe St-Julien 1991	11	£F
Ch. Laroze, Grand Cru St-Emilion 1989	11	£F
Ch. Les Ormes de Pez, St-Estephe 1991	12	£E

Lay down.

Ch. Malescot de St-Exupéry, Cru Classe Margaux 1988	11	£F
Château Canteloup, Cru Bourgeois Médoc 1990 **(Safeway)**	12	£D

Château Castera, Bordeaux 1993   15   £C
A bargain Bordeaux. Friendly, easy-to-like fruit with a
plummy centre. Dry, stylish.

Château de Belesta, Côtes de Roussillon 1992   13   £B

Château de Caraguilhes, Corbières 1992   13   £C

Château Joanny, Côtes du Rhône 1993   12   £C

Château La Forêt 1993   13   £B

**Châteauneuf-du-Pape, La Source Aux Nymphes
1991**   14   £E
Deep, rich, stratified, stylish.

Claret Oak-Aged 1990 (Safeway)   14   £C
Superb, mature, woody fruit aromas and flavours. Good fruit
and another claret lovers' bargain.

Corbières (Safeway)   11   £B

Côtes de Duras 1992   13   £B

Côtes du Roussillon Villages 1988 (Safeway)   15   £B
Hairy fruit slicked back smoothly. Great stuff for the money.
Lovely rustic wiry roughness.

Côtes du Ventoux 1993 (Safeway)   14   £B
A bargain bottle of rich, dry fruit.

**Domaine Anthéa, Merlot, Vin de Pays d'Oc
1991**   13   £B
An organic merlot of extraordinary good value for money: dry
and softly earthy. And it improves quickly in bottle. Indeed, it
comes out of the vat unworldly and semi-literate and after a
year in bottle it's trilingual and an expert on cosmic strings.

Domaine La Tuque Bel-Air, Côtes de Castillon
1990   15   £D
Well-built, slightly husky wine with a wonderful long finish of
coffee fruit.

Domaine Richeaume Cabernet Sauvignon,
Côtes de Provence 1991   17   £E
Powerful, forward, dry and complex. Blackcurrants brushed
with dry tannins, yet smooth and full. This is a lovely bottle of
wine.

Fortant de France Cabernet Sauvignon, Vin de
Pays d'Oc 1992   14   £C
Good class of wine.

French Organic Vin de Table (Safeway)   11   £B

La Cuvée Mythique, Vin de Pays d'Oc 1991   15   £C
Well-balanced, well-styled fruit made of plums. Full, rich and
lengthy.

Les Trois Moulins de Cantemerle, Haut-
Médoc – Second wine of Ch. Cantemerle 1990   13   £E

Margaux, Barton & Guestier 1989   11   £E

Médoc, Oak-Aged 1992   13   £C

Merlot, Vin de Pays des Coteaux de
l'Ardèche 1993   13   £B

Michel Lynch Bordeaux Rouge 1990   13   £D
An overrated wine of some charm in the middle but little
effective structure either side. Very expensive for the paucity
of style on offer.

Minervois (Safeway)   12   £A

| St-Emilion Gabriel Corcol 1992 | 13 | £C |

| St-Julien, Barton & Guestier 1990 | 11 | £E |

**Vegetarian Red Wine, Oak-Aged Claret,
Bordeaux Supérieur 1992**   13   £C
Still and dry, faintly charred fruit (cabernet franc grapes?).
Excellent with food like pizzas.

| Vin de Pays de l'Ardèche 1993 (Safeway) | 11 | £A |

| Vin de Pays de Vaucluse 1992 | 12 | £B |

| Vin Rouge, Vin de Pays Catalan (Safeway) | 10 | £B |

FRENCH WINE – *white and rosé*

**Aged in Oak Chardonnay, VdP des Coteaux de
l'Ardèche 1992 (Safeway)**   14   £C
A solid structure of well-mannered fruit.

Bergerac Sauvignon 1993 (Safeway)   13   £B
Impossible to grumble at this construction. Especially with
shellfish.

| Blanc de Bordeaux, Oak-Aged 1992 | 13 | £C |

| Blaye Blanc 1993 | 13 | £B |

| Bordeaux Blanc Demi-Sec (Safeway) | 11 | £B |

| Bourgogne Blanc, Oak-Aged 1993 (Safeway) | 9 | £D |

| Cabernet d'Anjou Rosé | 11 | £B |

Cavalier du Roi, Vin de Pays des Côtes de
Gascogne 13 £C

Ch. de Berbec, Premier Côtes de Bordeaux 1989
(half) 13 £B
Good with pud.

Ch. Voigny, Sauternes 1992 12 £F

Chablis 1993 (Safeway) 14 £D
Classy, correct, expensive.

Chablis Premier Cru Fourchaume, L. Javelot
1990 (Safeway) 11 £E

Chardonnay, Vin de Pays du Jardin de la France
1993 14 £B

Chardonnay, Vin de Pays des Coteaux de
l'Ardèche 1993 (Safeway) 13 £C

Château de la Botinière, Muscadet Sur Lie
1991 13 £C

Château de Plantier, Entre Deux Mers 1993 13 £C

Château Joanny Rosé 1993 13 £B

Château Le Pesquey, Bordeaux Sec 1993 14 £C
Elegant fruit, stylish and bold.

Château Prieure de Villepreux Rosé 1993 13 £C

Corbières Blanc de Blancs 1993 (Safeway) 11 £B

Côte de Beaune, C. Masy-Perier 1992 10 £D

Côtes du Luberon 1993 (Safeway) 14 £B
Excellent structure and fruit.

Côtes du Luberon Rosé 1993   14   £B
Great rosé for the summer. Everything a rosé should be.

**Dom. de l'Ecu, Muscadet de Sèvres et Maine
Sur Lie, Guy Bossard 1992**   12   £C

Domaine Brial Muscat de Rivesaltes 1992 (half) 15   £B
Expensive but glorious, floral, waxy, honeyed fruit. Complex
and compelling.

Domaine de la Tuilerie Chardonnay, VdP d'Oc 12   £C

**Domaine de Malardeau, Côtes de Duras,
H Ryman 1993**   15   £C
Delicious, undercutting, subtle grassiness to rich-edged
freshness. Great shellfish wine or for solo drinking pleasure.

Domaine de Petits Perriers, Sancèrre 1993   13   £E
Expensive but very decent.

**Domaine de Rivoyre Chardonnay, Vin de Pays
d'Oc, Ryman 1993**   12   £C

**Domaine du Bosc, Vin de Pays des Coteaux
d'Enserune 1992**   14   £C
Rich, fresh, peachy wine of zest and kick.

**Domaine du Rey, Vegetarian White Wine, VdP
des Côtes de Gascogne 1993**   13   £C
Layers of fruit.

Domaine Sainte-Marie, Côtes du Rhône, 1993   11   £C

**Fortant de France, Syrah Rosé, Vin de Pays d'Oc
1993**   13   £C

Gaillac 1993   13   £C

Gewürztraminer d'Alsace, Turckheim 1992   14   £C
Rosy fruit with a touch of soft spice.

J & F Lurton Sauvignon, Vin de Pays d'Oc 1993   13   £C

La Coume de Peyre, Vin de Pays des Côtes de Gascogne 1993   15   £B
Masses of swirling, tropical fruits and acids. Lovely wine.

Le Vigneron Ardèchois, VdP des Coteaux de l'Ardèche, Syrah rosé 1993   14   £B
Close your eyes and you're drinking delicious white wine.

Mâcon Villages 1993 (Safeway)   14   £C
Unusually assertive fruit here.

Muscadet de Sèvre et Maine (Safeway)   10   £B

Muscat, Cuvée José Sala   16   £C
Honeyed nougat on sweet raisin toast. Offensively fruity.

Organic White Vin de Pays des Bouches du Rhône   12   £B

Pinot Blanc d'Alsace, Turckheim 1993   14   £C
Soft apricot touches to the fruit. Delightful drinking.

Premières Côtes de Bordeaux (Safeway)   12   £C

Touraine Sauvignon 'Les Silleries' 1993   14   £B
Delicious grassy aroma and flavour undercutting the fruit.

Vin Blanc (Safeway) (1 litre)   10   £B

Vin de Pays d'Oc Sur Lie 1993   13   £B
Ripe, earthy fruit. Good glug.

Vin de Pays de Vaucluse 1993   11   £A

Viognier, Vin de Pays de l'Ardèche 1993   14   £C
Classy.

Vouvray Demi-Sec   10   £C

GERMAN WINE – *red*

Dornfelder Trocken, Rheinhessen 1992
(Safeway)   15   £C
A well-fruited wine with such softness it caresses the tongue
like taffeta.

GERMAN WINE – *white*

Auslese, Pfalz 1992 (Safeway)   14   £C
Delicious, sweet, honeyed, peachy fruit which is light enough
to tickle any palate. Or drink it with grapes and hard cheese.

Bereich Bernkastel, Mosel-Saar-Ruwer
(Safeway)   12   £B

Dienheimer Tafelstein Kabinett, Rheinhessen
Organic 1993   13   £C
Try it as a different aperitif. Yes, it is off-dry but it's
wonderfully mellow and orchard-ripe.

Gewürztraminer Rheinpfalz (Safeway)   13   £C
A model and inexpensive introduction to the grape but
experienced gewürtzophiles may find it too undemanding.

Goldener Oktober Red Orange 15 £A
Great but not wine. Really vivid fruit fun for near-teetotallers.

Hock Deutscher Tafelwein (Safeway) 10 £A

Kabinett, Pfalz 1993 (Safeway) 13 £B
Summery and pleasing as an aperitif. It has a sweet finish.

Morio Muskat, St Ursula 1993 11 £B

**Rudesheimer Rosengarten, Nahe 1993
(Safeway)** 11 £B

Rulander Kabinett, Ihringer Winklerborg 1992 12 £C
An off-dry, very fruity introduction for those being weaned off
liebfraumilch.

**Ruppertsberger Nussbein Riesling Kabinett
1990/92** 13 £C

Spätlese 1990 (Safeway) 12 £B

St Ursula Pinot Blanc 1991 10 £D

St Ursula/Ryman Riesling, Pfalz 1993 15 £B
A very interesting German riesling. It has a lot of approachable fruit yet it's dry. Excellent – great Oriental food plonk.

**St Ursula/Ryman Scheurebe/Rivaner, Pfalz
1993** 13 £B

GREEK WINE – *red*

Xinomavro Naoussis 1990 14 £C
A tongue twister. But with its dry blackcurrant and raspberry
it's also a palate smoother and that's all that matters.

HUNGARIAN WINE – *red*

Cabernet Sauvignon Villany 1993 (Safeway)	12	£B

Great Plain Kekfrancos 1993   15 £B
Soft, slightly spicy, rounded fruit. A terrific bargain to drink
like Beaujolais.

Hungarian Country Wine Kiskoros Region
1993   16 £B
All the gorgeous, savoury-edged fruit of the kekfrancos
grape – better than gamay at freshness and yummy fruit
flavour. A layered cake of a wine with a bitter cheery and
almond fruit combo underpinned by the bit of balancing
acidity.

Merlot, Villany Region 1993 (Safeway)   12 £A

HUNGARIAN WINE – *white and rosé*

Badger Hill Chardonnay 1993   14 £C
Fruit and freshness equally balanced.

Cabernet Sauvignon Rosé 1993   14 £B

Dry Muscat Nagyrede (Safeway)   14 £B
Bit of a sharp finish cuts across the terrific muscat smell and
taste and sure-footed dryness, but for all that great value for
money. A first-rate aperitif.

Gyöngyös Chardonnay 1993   14 £B

Gyöngyös Sauvignon Blanc 1993 14 £B
Some attractive herbaceous fruit. More characteristic of the grape than the '92.

Hungarian Chardonnay 1993 (Safeway) 14 £B
Fresh and young, a touch of apple or pear-drop and acid-drop fruit. Sounds like a kid's sweet but it isn't. It's dry with a streak of seriousness that makes it a bargain.

Hungarian Country Wine 1993 (Safeway) 15 £B
Lemons, pears and melons and a touch of zesty slightly orange acidity. What a brilliant little fruit salad of a wine for a silly price.

Matra Mountains Chardonnay 1993 15 £B
Brilliant rich fruit. Quite delicious and forward, yet fresh-faced.

Nagyrede Sauvignon Blanc Reserve 1993 13 £C

River Duna Pinot Gris 1993 15 £B
Typical soft-centred pinot gris. Lovely touch of fruit.

River Duna Sauvignon Blanc 1993 14 £B
Ripe fruit-drop flavours underpinning the freshness.

ISRAELI WINE – *red*

Carmel Cabernet Sauvignon 12 £C
An interesting curiosity; dry and respectably clothed in fruit.

ISRAELI WINE – *white*

Carmel Dry Muscat 1993	9	£B
Yarden Chardonnay, Golan Heights 1992	11	£E

ITALIAN WINE – *red*

Bardolino (Safeway)	13	£B
Chianti 1992 (Safeway)	12	£B
Chianti Classico, Rocca delle Macie 1990 (Safeway)	13	£C
Don Giovanni 1991	13	£B

Lambrusco, Tenuta Generale Cialdini 1992   15   £B
Overshadowed by those millions of anonymous, sweet, fizzy
bottles of feeble Italian blandness, could there lie a fresh, dry,
pétillant *genuine* lambrusco with an amazingly nutty fruitiness
allied to a superbly swashbuckling acidity, together producing
a 10.5 per cent wine of great flavour and unique deliciousness? Yes, and here it is. This lambrusco oozes panache
and style and it is worth any adventurous wine drinker's time
and money. Drink the wine chilled, drink it with rich fish
dishes, on its own, with a salad, or drink it with cold meats and
salamis. But *drink it!!!!*

Le Monferrine Dolcetto d'Asti 1993	11	£C
Le Trulle Country Cellars Puglian Red	14	£B

Cheeky and flavourful.

Montepulciano d'Abruzzo 1992	13	£B

Sicilian (Safeway) — 14 £B
Terrific little plonk at a terrific little price.

Salice Salentino Riserva 1988	11	£C

'Salvanza' Sangiovese di Toscana 1990	12	£C

Tenuta San Vito Chianti 1991	13	£C

Teroldego Rotagliano 1990 — 13 £C
From Trentino in northern Italy, this wine, like the teroldego grapes which make it, is peculiar to the area. Has some pleasant chewy fruit but I suspect it's asleep and will wake up with a roar in a while.

Valpolicella 1993 (Safeway) — 12 £B
Sweet fruit touches.

Villa Pagello Merlot, Breganza 1991	10	£B

Villa Pagello Merlot, Breganza 1992 — 14 £B
Bright, very soft fruit finishing sweetly.

ITALIAN WINE – *white*

Chardonnay del Triveneto 1993 (Safeway)	12	£B

Frascati 1993 — 13 £B
Fresh and crisp. Attractive light style. Improvement on the '92.

Grave del Fruili Pinot Grio 1993 — 15 £C
Such ripe fruit it could be poured over ice-cream. Delicious.

| I Frari, Bianco di Custoza, Santi 1992 | 13 | £C |

| Le Monferrine, Chardonnay del Piemonte 1993 | 12 | £C |

| Le Monferrine, Moscato d'Asti 1993 | 13 | £B |

Lugana 1993   14   £C
Full of melony fruit yet balanced. Superb.

| Orvieto Classico Secco 1993 (Safeway) | 13 | £C |

| Pinot Grigio del Triveneto 1993 (Safeway) | 11 | £B |

| Riva Trebbiano di Romagna 1993 | 13 | £B |

| Sicilian Dry | 11 | £B |

Soave 1993 (Safeway)   11   £B
Some zip here.

MOLDOVAN WINE – *white*

| Hincesti Chardonnay 1993 | 14 | £B |

| Hincesti Feteasca, Moldova 1993 | 14 | £B |

MOROCCAN WINE – *red*

| Domaine Sapt Inour | 11 | £B |

NEW ZEALAND WINE – *red*

Matua Valley Cabernet Sauvignon 1990   14   £E
Delicious with rare roast beef.

NEW ZEALAND WINE – *white*

Millton Vineyard Chardonnay 1992   13   £E
Attractive aperitif.

Millton Vineyard Semillon/Chardonnay 1993   14   £C
Interesting asparagus and honey hints.

Montana Chardonnay 1992   13   £C

Montana Sauvignon Blanc, Marlborough 1993   15   £C
Outstanding herbaceousness on the nose, great fruit on the palate.

Taura Valley 1993   14   £B

Wairu River Sauvignon Blanc, Marlborough 1993   10   £E

PORTUGUESE WINE – *red*

Bairrada 1990/91 (Safeway)   13   £C

Duque de Viseu, Dão 1990   14   £C
Soft yet dry and serious . . . lovely stuff.

Dow's Crusted, bottled in 1987   14   £F
Excellent quality port. A brilliant bargain.

Fine Vintage Character Port   11   £D

Grahams LBV 1986   13   £F
Delicious blue cheese port.

LBV 1987 (Safeway)   12   £D

Tawny (Safeway)   11   £D

Taylors LBV 1987   12   £F

Tinto da Anfora 1990   12   £D

PORTUGUESE WINE – *white*

Bairrada 'Bical', Aliança 1992   13   £C
Good structure, light fruit, not overblown.

Botricised Late Harvest White 1988 (half)   11   £D

Falcoaria, Almeirim 1991   15   £C
Delicious, elegant, tinged with rich fruit almond finish. Lovely.

João Pires Dry Muscat, Terras do Sado 1991   14   £C
A very assertive label disguises a delicious fish wine or aperitif.

João Pires Muscat 1992/93   13   £C

Lezíria   15   £A
This is a lovely, fresh wine at a terrific price. It has more
attractive hay-like fruit than many a white burgundy of the
small-mortgage variety. I enjoy it as an aperitif, but grilled fish
is fine with it.

Lezíria Medium Dry White, Almeirim 14 £B

Sogrape Bairrada Reserva 1991 12 £D
Wood, wood, wood. You could build a tree house from the wood in this wine.

Terre de Lobos, Vinho Regionale Ribatejo 1992 14 £B
Simple, straightforward glugging fish wine. Very fresh, clean and restrained.

ROMANIAN WINE – *red*

Special Reserve Merlot 1990 13 £B
Delicious lightly chilled.

Romanian Merlot 1990 (Safeway) 16 £B
A magnificent merlot for the money: almost classic.

Romanian Pinot Noir 1989 (Safeway) 16 £B
Brilliant, just brilliant.

**Special Reserve Cabernet Sauvignon 1986
(Safeway)** 14 £B
Great with spicy foods.

SLOVENIAN WINE – *white*

Laski Rizling (Safeway) (1 litre) 10 £C

SOUTH AFRICAN WINE – *red*

**Hamilton Russell Vineyards Pinot Noir, Walker
Bay 1991**   11   £E

Kanonkop Kadette 1991   15   £D
Sounds like the republic's first home-produced motor car
instead of a vehicle for a load of tasty, fresh-faced fruit. A soft,
aromatic wine, tinged by a suede-like dryness, which is just
superb with roast meats.

Kleindal Pinotage 1992   15   £B
Great food wine and a brilliant bargain. Delicious, whizzbang
firecracker fruit, dry, and a nutty finish.

Simonsvlei Pinotage, Paarl, Ryman 1993   13   £C

SOUTH AFRICAN WINE – *white*

Bateleur Chardonnay 1993   14   £E

Culemhof Colombard 1993   11   £B

**Danie de Wet Chardonnay Sur Lie, Robertson
1993**   15   £D
Excellent style, elegance and restrained power. Citrus butter
fruit. Well structured.

Landskroom Pinot Blanc 1992   13   £D
Some elegant, delicious touches here.

Namaqua (Wine in a Box, 3 litres)   15   £F
Modern style, full of ripe fruit. Terrific freshness, too, so it's
good for thirsts as well as being good for fish.

Sauvignon Blanc, Vredendal 1994　　　15　£B

Every bit as brilliant as last year's superb wine. A very attractive tipple at a knock-down price.

Swartland Stern 1993　　　13　£B

Van Loveren Special Late Harvest
Gewürztraminer 1993　　　16　£C

This is one of those bottles which adds to the delight of
skipping through Elmore Leonard's latest improbability; a
bottle so expressive of its fruit that it can even help ease one's
way through those soggy serpentine lumps of untrimmed
turgidity Iris Murdoch is pleased to call prose. Having slept
under maker Wynand Retief's roof, even, by God, jogged
through grower Nico Retief's vines and sampled Penny
Retief's big breakfast, I can personally testify to the delights to
be found at this South African estate. Vinously, its gewürztraminer is the most hedonistic of these delights, for it reeks
of rose petals, tastes of mango and peach with a sort of nutty
undertone (a fat greasy nut like a macadamia), and, yes, it is
sweet, but it drips with flavour and if you can't tackle a whole
bottle by yourself without food then enjoy it with soft goat's
cheese and fresh fruit. But it is delightful drunk alone with
literature.

SPANISH WINE – *red*

Agramont Tempranillo/Cabernet, Navarra
1989　　　14　£C

Lovely smooth fruit.

Agramont Tempranillo/Cabernet, Navarra 1990   15   £C
Little beauty.

Alentejo, Vinho Regional 1992   15   £B
Excellent value, rich and chocolatey and quite lovely; dry,
well-defined fruit.

Berberana Oak-Aged Tempranillo, Rioja 1992   15   £C
Lovely vanillary fruit without a hard note in its makeup.
Effortless, soft and quaffable.

Cariñena 1988 (Safeway)   12   £B

Casa de la Viña Cencibel 1992   14   £B
Good tasty savoury honeyed fruit within a very dry cloak.

Castilla de Sierra Rioja Crianza 1990 (Safeway)   13   £C

Don Darias   14   £B
You know how sometimes you meet an upfront fruity person
whose ribald sense of humour almost makes you blush but
you can't help yourself falling completely under his or her
spell? So it is with this wine.

Qunita do Vale de Raposa, Douro 1992   13   £C

Raimat Tempranillo 1990   15   £C
The '89 vintage of this was pleasing but this newly released
vintage is deeper and more complex and an altogether more
charismatic bottle. It exhibits velvety berried fruits with a
lovely balancing acidity and has delightfully soft fruit tannins
and integrated wood tannins. It will age with great grace this
wine, and I see no reason, though it is delicious now, not to
expect it to improve and lengthen its fruit over the next half
decade and more – should anyone possess the saintly strength
of will to keep from quaffing it. It rates 15 points now and with
a few years' bottle age may well be knocking on 17's door.

Ribatejo, Vinho Regionale (Safeway) 14 £B
Excellent value.

Rioja Crianza 1989 (Safeway) 13 £C

**Señorio de Nava Crianza, Ribera del Duero
1987** 14 £D
Delicious.

Valdepeñas 1987 (Safeway) 13 £B

Vino de Valencia (Safeway) 13 £B
Good, sound, dry fruity stuff.

Young Vatted Tempranillo, La Mancha 1993 17 £B
Out-Beaujolais Beaujolais's raspberry-soft aromatic fruit of
massive quaffability. Makes the taste buds hum with pleasure
and the pocket smile with delight.

SPANISH WINE – *white*

La Mancha 1993 (Safeway) 13 £B

Moscatel de Valencia (Safeway) 16 £B
Still brilliant value. Glorious, subtly marmalade and honey
fruit.

The Cream of Cream Sherry, Pedro Ximenez 15 £E
A brilliant sticky wine of quite glorious unguency. The ultimate hedonism.

Valencia, Aged in Oak 1993 (Safeway) 15 £B

Viña Ardanza, Rioja Reserva 1989 10 £D
Amazing old-fashioned woody Rioja.

Viñas del Vero Chardonnay, Barrel Fermented,
Somontano 1991   13   £D
Good wood integration with the fruit. Mucky finish.

Vino de Valencia Dry (Safeway)   14   £A

USA WINE – *red*

Fetzer Zinfandel 1991   15   £C

USA WINE – *white*

Californian White (Safeway)   15   £B
Brilliant sunny fruit and biting acid. Full of flavour yet
refreshing.

WELSH WINE – *white*

Cariad Gwin da o Gymru 1991   11   £D

SPARKLING WINE/CHAMPAGNE

Albert Etienne Brut (Safeway)   12   £G

Albert Etienne Rosé (Safeway)   16   £F
Truly a beautifully balanced, delicious rosé worth every penny.

Albert Etienne (Safeway) 13 £F

Angas Brut Rosé, Australia 15 £D

Australian Sparkling (Safeway) 14 £D
Excellent.

Blanquette de Limoux, Bernard Delmas 13 £D
An organic sparkler full of delicious peachy/nutty fruit.

Bollinger Special Cuvée Brut 12 £H
Over twenty quid: is it worth it? I wish I could provide a wholehearted yes, in spite of Bollinger's very particular dry charms.

Cava (Safeway) 13 £F
Buy it for the style and the big fat magnum.

Chardonnay Spumante (Safeway) 13 £D
Very pleasant champagne substitute.

Chartogne-Taillet Champagne Brut 13 £G

Crémant d'Alsace Brut (J. Keller) 13 £D

**Crémant de Bourgogne Blanc de Blancs
(Safeway)** 13 £D

Crémant de Bourgogne Brut (Safeway) 13 £D

Cuvée Napa, USA 14 £E
Compares to a classic brut champagne in style.

Freixenet Cordon Negro Brut Cava 13 £D

Heritage English Sparkling 12 £E
Not a bad stab at making an Australian bubbly.

**'Le Baron de Monceny' Chardonnay Brut, Blanc
de Blancs** 12 £D

Le Grand Pavillion de Boschendale, Cuvée Brut
Blanc de Blancs, South Africa   16   £D
Refreshing, stylish, and tastes like a grand marques champagne at three times the price. Brilliant sparkler with which to
mystify your wine buff acquaintances.

Lindauer Brut, New Zealand   13   £D

Lionel Derens Champagne   15   £E
A dry but fruity champagne, without the intimidating acidity
of the classic brut examples, this is a very satisfying tipple and
under £9 a good price.

Maison la Motte Chardonnay 1992   14   £E
Lovely peachy touch to acids.

Seppelt Pinot Rosé Cuvée Brut Sparkling
(Australia)   15   £D
Delicious. Real fruit here, justifying the colour. Available in
selected branches only.

Seppelt Premier Cuvée Brut, Australia   15   £D
Good fruit and balanced. Great style for the money.

Seppelts Salinger Sparkling Wine, Australia 15   £F
Mature yet fresh finishing. Some elegance. Dry.

Seppelts Sparkling Shiraz 1990   16   £E
Fabulous roaring fruit.

Sainsbury's

To the bafflement of ordinary mortals, Sainsbury's has done it again. Number one supermarket wine retailer in most wine journalists' estimation a few years back, it moved the man who ran the department over to fruit and veg. The store then spent time reorganizing the department, weathering wide journalistic scorn, and over the past year it's come right back in favour again with the critics who recognize a superb range of wines. And what does Sainsbury's do then? That's right. They move the bloke who helped sort the department out over to screws and light bulbs.

True, Mike Connolly, the director of wine buying, has stayed in place all this time, an authoritative *éminence grise* behind the department's more flamboyant manager, Simon Blower, now at Homebase after his stint in wine, but such changes of personnel has other retailers, especially the high street wine boys who daily battle to keep up with Sainsbury, puzzled and astonished. But the fact is that in this executive volatility lies Sainsbury's strength. A buyer is a buyer, the store reckons. If you can buy beans you can buy beaujolais. What's the difference?

There is no difference. All the matters is that the customer is asked to pay the right price for a better than acceptable product. To be sure, the new chap who's come over from the fresh meat & deli department, Mr Robin Tapper, to take over from Simon, obviously can't be a teetotaller or have religious objections to alcohol, but nothing else stands in his way. He'll get the support of experienced buyers and wine-tasters as he finds his feet and susses out the scene, but the most important skill he possesses he has already demonstrated in his previous department. That skill is a buying skill.

No skill is rated more highly at Sainsbury. It spreads to all departments as a result of the store's flexible managerial career path and it is available to anyone with the ambition and drive to pursue it (for many of the store's wine buyers will, by their own choice and narrowness of interest, remain wine buyers). Its supreme virtue, to my way of thinking, is two-fold. It constantly permits new blood to be transfused within the organization rather than seeking it outside. This in turn prevents hardening of the arteries and inspires, rather than inhibits, innovation at the very managerial level in which the retail trade has traditionally been found wanting when compared to other industries.

It certainly pays off for the store. It now flogs over 1.8 million bottles of wine a week and if any supermarket's wine-buying department, along with Tesco's and Safeway's, can feel a sense of personal pride in the figures published earlier this year which showed that white wine had at last ousted beer as Britain's favourite tipple, then this is the one. A Gallup research survey, published in the spring, revealed in a survey of 1,000 drinkers that 42 per cent preferred white wine, 32 per cent lager, 22 per cent bitter and 21 per cent red wine. Over the past ten years our average consumption of wine per head (mouth?) of population has gone from fifteen bottles a year to twenty-two, whilst beer drinking has dipped from an average of 190 pints a year to 180.

There is no doubt that the supermarkets' drive to make decent, inexpensive wines widely available has succeeded beyond their most sanguine expectations. A crucial aspect of this success has been that these wines are obtainable without customers having to enter the hallowed portals of the traditional wine merchant. As the barriers have come down, sales have gone up. As per usual where matters of taste are concerned, this is a revolution led by women.

I make no apology for discussing these matters, or for indulging in so many statistics, in an introduction about Sainsbury's. There can be no doubt of this supermarket's pre-eminence as the nation's major wine retailer (probably the world's), or the part it has played over the past decade in spearheading the revolution in the British drinker's changing tastes. Only Tesco and Safeway have had the stamina and the resources to keep up alongside.

Of the £4,100-plus million spent on wine in this country, Sainsbury's has the largest slice. The recession did nothing to blunt the upward trend of its wine sales and I fully expect that its sales reflect the overall rise in the size of the market which is worth, in my estimation, getting on towards 45 per cent more than it was when I first started my Superplonk column in *Weekend Guardian* five years ago, and maybe more. Price rises account for much of this expansion in the value of the market but not all of it. Prices have risen as a result of the fall in the value of the pound against the French franc in particular, but New World producers, too, have increased prices, though for different reasons – their quality has gone up. The value of the market has also increased because there has been, as the survey results quoted above show, an increase in the number of people buying and drinking wine *because wine is better value and better made (at the lower level) than it has ever been*. It is also seen to be a healthier choice and a more sophisticated one.

It's instructive to look at how prices have risen, and which ones, at Sainsbury's over the past five years. The store's own-label Muscadet cost £2.35 a bottle in 1989. In 1994 it costs £2.95. Is a price rise of 25 per cent in half a decade reasonable? It depends on the reasons for the rise. The British government must take blame for much of that increase since its management of the pound sterling caused it to fall in value against the French franc. Add this to French inflation and increases in production costs and the rise seems almost unreasonably low. The Bulgarians, however, have been model suppliers. In 1989 Khan Krum Chardonnay was £2.79. Today, it's £2.99 – an easy to swallow rise of 7 per cent. But why should we pay 42 per cent more for the Australian Shiraz/Cabernet (£2.45 in '89, £3.49 in '94)? The answer is easy. The rise in the cost of Australian living. The grapes cost more, the production process is more expensive, and Australian wineries are as pleased to make money as the next business. And the fact is that the big boys in Oz are making sparkling profits.

This is perhaps not the place to go into this in detail, but I would say that with the likelihood of 200 million bottles of Australian wine being that country's annual sales to this country in the not too distant future, I would have thought it imperative to nurture this growth by swallowing costs which will lead to further intemperate price hikes. Maybe the Aussies reckon the Scandinavians will be the buoyant market for them in the future, but with South Africa, South America, and increasingly eastern Europe keeping prices steady and quality high with their wine exports to the UK then Australia cannot rest on its laurels at the lower end of the market. Retailers like Sainsbury's will not tolerate price rises which deflate the impact on consumers of a country's wines, however well-established it is, and will simply turn elsewhere for supplies and put more effort into alternative bottles.

Isn't Italy already cooking up a dandy shiraz? So watch it, Oz. You thought Blower was a tricky enough negotiator, but Tapper won't even board the plane if the prices don't make sense.

ARGENTINIAN WINE – *red*

Argentinian Malbec/Cabernet (Sainsbury's)   14   £B
Remarkable richness of style and class for the money.

Bright Brothers Malbec, Las Palmas 1992   16   £D
A big, rich, soupy wine with lots of berried fruit flavour.
Out-Cahors Cahors. Very impressive and broad-shouldered.

Cavas de Weinet, Mendoza 1985   17   £D
This has improved immeasurably over the past year in bottle.
It is still soft and quaffable but it now slips beautifully into
leathery middle age and the layers of fruit on offer are deep
and thought-provoking.

Malbec/Cabernet Red Mendoza (Sainsbury's)   15   £B
Malbec/Cabernet Sauvignon Mendoza from the Argentine is
a curious beast in its own way. It has the aroma of a freshly-
peeled Cox's orange pippin, but when the fruit wallops the
palate English hard fruit is the last thing it is reminiscent of;
assertive, chewy, excellent, balanced with a dark fruit centre,
it's one of those generous red wines to be poured into a big
jug and left to savoury-stew eaters to help themselves. A
bargain bottle.

Trapiche Oak Cask Cabernet Sauvignon 1990   13   £C

ARGENTINIAN WINE – *white*

Torrontes (Sainsbury's)   14   £B
Delicious aroma, taste and overall balance. Lots of fruit, good
length. Excellent value. Excellent fish wine.

Trapiche Oak Cask Chardonnay 1992   15 £D

AUSTRALIAN WINE – *red*

Arrowfield Pinot Noir, NSW 1990   14 £C
Deliciously gamey aroma leading to well-put-together soft
fruit. Surprisingly varietal class.

Baileys Shiraz 1992   15 £D
This leathery, furry-fruited wine may well be descended from
the one which sozzled Ned Kelly, for it was in the Victorian
hamlet of Glenrowan, where Baileys built their winery in
1870, that the law finally caught up with the drunken bandit.
Baileys Shiraz grabs the drinker by the throat every bit as
effectively, though somewhat more affectionately, as the
noose from which the rogue finally swung. Linctus-like texture offering layered fruits, blackcurrants to plums, with
touches of tobacco and coffee. Superb, even if available in
only seven Sainsbury's stores.

Bright Brothers McLaren Vale Shiraz, 1992   15 £C
Impressive, soft, subtle, spicy wine.

Church Hill Cabernet/Shiraz, Mildara Blass
1992   15 £C
Lovely texture to the blackcurrant-dominant fruit. Savoury
edge is very attractive.

Church Hill Shiraz/Cabernet, Mildara Blass
1991   14 £C
Mature, dry, comfortably well-fruited.

**Cockatoo Ridge Cabernet Sauvignon/Merlot,
Yalumba** 1993   14   £C
Savoury fruit well matched by the excellent acid balance. Not
huge but very tasty.

Devil's Lair Cabernet Sauvignon, Margaret River
1991   14   £E
Has the most imaginative label of any Australian wine but not
quite the most imaginative fruit. Delicious but pricey.

**Hardy's Stamp Series Shiraz/Cabernet
Sauvignon** 1993   12   £C

**Lindemans Limestone Ridge Vineyard Shiraz/
Cabernet, Coonawarra** 1990   14   £E
Intriguing eucalyptus hints to unspeakably soft and luxurious
fruit.

Lindemans Pyrus 1990   14   £E
A four-grape blend; the usual Bordeaux varieties combine to
produce very rich, softly tannic fruit which will, I feel, develop
further over the next 2/3 years.

**McWilliams Mount Pleasant Philip Shiraz,
Hunter Valley** 1988   13   £D
Reminds me, aromatically, of the first great wine I ever drank:
Château Margaux 1947. The fruit is not so vibrant or huge,
however, or anywhere near so complex. Like seeing Brian
Lara out for a duck.

Mount Hurtle Grenache Shiraz 1992   15   £C
Softly leathery, blackberry and strawberry cream–cassis notes.
Gorgeous.

Mount Hurtle Shiraz, McLaren Vale 1992   16.5   £C
Gorgeous, soft, minty, beautiful.

Murrumbidgee Estate Shiraz Grenache, South Eastern Australia 14 £B

Soft and easy. Cherry-relation, savoury edge. Very light but lightly purchaseable.

Nottage Hill Cabernet Sauvignon 1992 15 £C

Still sporting a day-old growth of beard to the smooth fruit (courtesy of the tannins). Lovely performer – one of the best-made cabernet sauvignons around for the money.

Penfolds Bin 389 Cabernet/Shiraz 1990 14 £E

Penfolds Coonawarra Cabernet Sauvignon 1990 17 £E

The colour of crushed blackberries, subtle eucalyptus/leather aroma, sheer satiny acids and velvet-textured fruit – plus a lovely tannicky finish. Ripe squashed prunes and ripe plums with a quite brilliant texture of silk and suede.

Penfolds Koonunga Hill Shiraz/Cabernet 1992 14 £D

Getting pricey at over a fiver, this branded wine. Has lush sweet finishing fruit but not a lot of complexity.

Peter Lehmann, Clancy's Barossa Valley Australian Red, South Australia 1990 15 £D

Delicious, sweetly-finishing fruit, fine and full yet fresh and vigorous. Delicious, striking.

Peter Lehmann, Vine Vale Shiraz 1992 15 £C

Delightful fruit with hints of plum and blackberry. Has some soft spice. Good with fried sausages.

Rosemount Cabernet/Shiraz 1992 15 £C

Rosemount Estate Shiraz 1992 16 £C

A concentration of dry rich fruit of almost cassis-like proportions.

**Ryecroft Peppertree Cabernet/Shiraz Merlot,
McLaren Vale, South Australia 1991**   15   £D
Good nutty nose (typical). Lovely rich deep fruit with a ripe
fruit finish. Very attractive.

**SE Australia Cabernet Sauvignon Bin 937,
Wyndham Estate 1992**   13   £C

**SE Australia Shiraz Bin 822, Wyndham Estate
1992 (Sainsbury's)**   14   £C

Shiraz/Cabernet (Sainsbury's)   15   £B
Rich and meaty, savoury and velvety – this is an outstanding
roast fowl wine. Has gusto and guts. Sheer gustatory delight.

St-Hallett Cabernet Merlot 1991   14   £D

**The Menzies Coonawarra Cabernet Sauvignon,
South Australia 1990**   13   £D

**Tim Knappstein Cabernet Merlot, Clare Valley
1991**   16   £D
Lovely chocolatey finish on this soft, rich, fruity wine. Has
complexity, flavour and forceful style.

**Wynns John Riddoch Cabernet Sauvignon,
Penfolds Coonawarra 1988**   16   £E
Such great flavour and smoothness it's actually a £10 wine.

**Yarra Ridge Cabernet Sauvignon, Mildara Blass
1992**   14   £E
Good, very drinkable, but is it as complex as it might be for
£8?

AUSTRALIAN WINE – *white and rosé*

Australian Chardonnay, Riverina (Sainsbury's) 15 £C
Lush fruit, pineappley and melony, with lemony acidity. Great
style for the money. An oaky, deliciously fruity wine which is
brilliant value under four quid. It has so much balance and
style, it's difficult to think of any winemaker making tastier
chardonnay for the money.

**Barramundi SE Australian Semillon/
Chardonnay**   15 £C
Rich, fruit-salad nose. Lots of pineapple acidity and great,
swinging melon-mango fruit. Smashing wine to let the heart
soar.

Berri Estates Wood-aged Chardonnay 1991   13 £D

Dalfarras Marsanne, Tahbilk 1993   14 £C
Interesting. Fresher than the usual Marsanne.

Geoff Merrill Chardonnay, McLaren Vale 1990 15 £E
Weighty fruit of stylishly balanced flavour and texture. A great
grilled chicken wine.

**Hunter Valley Chardonnay, Denman Estate 1993
(Sainsbury's)**   13 £C

Jacob's Creek Semillon/Chardonnay 1993   12 £C

Jacob's Creek Chardonnay 1993   14 £C

Jacob's Creek Riesling, South Australia 1992 12 £C

Krondorf Show Reserve Chardonnay 1992   13 £E

**Leeuwin Estate Chardonnay, Margaret River, W
Australia 1989**   13   £G
Delicious. Expensive. Wood not entirely integrated with the
fruit and acid. This is a minor niggle but at £15 this has a
major wine price tag.

**Lily Farm Vineyard Muscat, Grant Burge,
Barossa Valley 1993**   16   £C
Delightful! Fragrantly expressive fruit, dry yet honey-
finished, make this a superb aperitif. Better than ever now
honey/citric undertones mingle with the ripe muscat fruit.

Lindemans Bin 65 Chardonnay 1993   16   £C
Deep bruised fruit – lovely and ripe – superb effect on the
tongue.

**McWilliams Mount Pleasant Elizabeth Semillon,
Hunter Valley 1988**   13   £D

**Mitchelton Goulburn Valley Reserve Marsanne
1991**   14   £D
The rich chicken or savoury fish stew wine par excellence!
Deeply rewarding fruit.

Mitchelton Semillon 1988   14   £D
Very rich and offering enough fruit to wallow in.

Moondah Brook Estate Chenin Blanc 1993   14   £C

**Mount Hurtle Grenache Rosé, Geoff Merrill
1993**   14.5 £C
Expensive but verging on the complex (an unheard of attribute for a rosé).

Mount Hurtle Sauvignon Blanc, Geoff Merrill
1993   14   £C
More forward than most sauvignon blancs, this is good wine
for grilled chicken.

Mount Hurtle Sauvignon Blanc, McLaren Vale,
South Australia 1992   12   £C
Deep grassy nose, earthy fruit.

Mount Hurtle Sauvignon Blanc, McLaren Vale
1993   15   £C
A softer, slightly spicier style of sauvignon blanc, both delicious and different. Good Oriental food wine.

Penfolds Koonunga Hill Chardonnay 1993   13   £C

Peter Lehmann Semillon, Barossa Valley, South
Australia 1992   15   £C
Outstanding wood and fruit integration and an overall classy
style of rich and well-achieved fruit at that make this an
interesting chicken and fish wine.

Peter Lehmann Semillon, McLaren Vale 1993   15   £C
Ripe yet not floridly so. Lush and keen at the same time. A
lovely bottle to enjoy by itself.

Richmond Grove Verdelho, Cowra Vineyard,
New South Wales 1993   13   £D

Rosemount Estate Chardonnay/Semillon 1993   13   £C

Rosemount Estate Diamond Label Chardonnay,
Hunter Valley 1993   17   £D
Excellently priced fine wine. Has dashing acidity counterpointed by tumbling soft fruit all held together by a toasty
undertone. Beautiful.

Rowan Chardonnay, Rothbury 1993   14   £C
Tasty and ripe.

Tasmanian Wine Company Chardonnay 1993   13   £E

**The Rothbury Estate Chardonnay, Cowra
Vineyard** 1993   15   £D
Quietly impressive. Elegant and finely tuned.

Tyrrells Old Winery Chardonnay 1992   12   £D
Not a lot of fruit here for the money.

Yarra Ridge Chardonnay, SE Australia 1993   16.5   £E
Toothsome beyond compare at a price which though not low
is considerably lower than the Chassagne-Montrachet it
knocks into a cocked hat.

Yarra Ridge Sauvignon Blanc, SE Australia   15   £D
Lush gooseberry acids pushing up against the ripe fruit in a
lush and appealing mouthful.

BULGARIAN WINE – *red*

**Bulgarian Cabernet Sauvignon, Oak-Aged,
Russe Region** 1993 (Sainsbury's)   15   £B
Oodles of tastebud-lashing soft fruit. A pasta wine and a huge
bargain.

Bulgarian Merlot, Oak-Aged, Liubimetz Region
1993 (Sainsbury's)   16   £B
Seriously dry finishing fruit (plummy and soft). Terrific
flavour and class for the money.

**Bulgarian Reserve Gamza, Lovico Suhindol
Region 1990** 15 £B
Soft plums, rich and drily edged.

**Country Wine Russe Cabernet Sauvignon/Cinsault
(Sainsbury's)** 13 £B

**Country Wine Suhindol Merlot/Gamza
(Sainsbury's)** 12 £B

**Lovico Suhindol Cabernet Sauvignon Reserve
1988** 13 £B
Excellent dry style.

Lovico Suhindol Merlot Reserve 1989 14 £B
Delicious soft plummy wine with a faint hint of liquorice and
mint.

**Stambolovo Merlot Special Reserve, Haskovo
Region 1987** 16 £C
Damsons and blackcurrants, touch of chocolate. Serious yet
hugely quaffable. Brilliant with roast foods; soothing with a
thriller to hand.

**Vintage Blend Oriachovitza Merlot and Cabernet
Sauvignon Reserve 1989** 16 £B
Lovely vanillary fruit, soft and very attractive. Polished, very
polished, soft and highly attractive. A wine to enjoy for the
sheer joy of drinking cheap drinking, stylish wine.

**Zlatovrach Reserve Mavrud, Assenovgrad
Region 1990** 17 £B
Superb fruit, multi-layered and rich. Has flavour, style and
satisfactory depth for relative peanuts.

BULGARIAN WINE – *white*

**Bulgarian Chardonnay, Lyaskovets
(Sainsbury's)**   15   £B
Terrific value. Lots of rich fruit and style. Superb fish wine
which is classier than many a feeble Chablis.

**Bulgarian Country Wine Muskat and Ugni Blanc
(Sainsbury's)**   13   £A
Very attractive, powder-compact soft fruit undercut by a
tingling freshness. Good value.

Khan Krum Chardonnay Reserve 1990   13   £B
Excellent value chardonnay of some varietal strength.

**Vintage Blend Khan Krum Chardonnay and
Sauvignon Blanc Reserve 1990**   14   £B
Nice, toasty, nutty, fruity example of a blend of grapes which
is rarely outstanding. This one beats the odds – at a great
price.

CHILEAN WINE – *red*

Caliterra Cabernet/Merlot, Chile 1991   14   £C
Classy fruit style, well structured and firm.

**Chilean Merlot, San Fernando 1993
(Sainsbury's)**   16   £C
A soft touch to this ripely, richly-berried wine. Delicious
enough to be tackled solo; weighty enough to handle food.

**Santa Carolina Cabernet Sauvignon, Gran
Reserva Cinqo Estrellas Maipo Valley 1989**   13   £E

**Santa Carolina Cabernet Sauvignon, Special
Reserve, Maipo Valley 1988**   15   £C
Delicious fruity woody wine with great style and class. Terrific
by itself or with roast lamb or beef and handsome enough to
stand alongside either. Superbly mature, classy blackberry
fruit. Very biscuity, dry-edged. Not big, Chilean wines aren't,
but softly proud – like a whisper from a voice of authority.

CHILEAN WINE – *white*

**Casablanca Valley Chardonnay, Santa Isabel
Estate 1992**   18   £E
Such melony, nutty fruit, with a soft creamy undertone, which
is pulled back from the brink of blowsiness by superbly well-
balanced subtly citric acidity. A daring, wonderful wine of
massive style.

**Chilean Sauvignon Blanc, Maipo Valley 1993
(Sainsbury's)**   16   £B
Smashing wine! Impactful and stylish, just made for any white
fish dish or scallops, it has demure fruit, quiet elegance and
great unfleshy style. Brilliant value for such cool class.

Villa Montes Sauvignon Blanc 1993   12   £C
Interesting bouquet of cheap eau-de-cologne and guava.
Muted soft fruit limps home a bit after this.

**Villa Montes Sauvignon Blanc, Cuvée Ryman,
Curico, Chile 1993**   13   £C

ENGLISH WINE – *white*

Denbies Estate English Table Wine, 1992   13 £C

Hastings, Carr Taylor   14 £B
One of my favourite English wines, for it has a lot of decent
fruit and a keen sense of balance. Plus it's less expensive than
last year.

Lamberhurst   14 £B
One of the better English wines which prompts the thought
that if they were all this tasty, and under £3, muscadet makers
would have to think of turning to apple growing to make a
living.

Three Choirs English Table Wine 1992   14 £C
Has a fat touch of off-dryness that I'm less convinced about
than I was.

Three Choirs Seyval Reichensteiner 1992   12 £C

Wootton Trinity West Country Table Wine   14 £C
Attractive woody aroma, ripe fruit clearly and freshly
presented, not fully dry but extremely well balanced. A very
attractive wine which will surprise many a drinker.

FRENCH WINE – *red*

Beaujolais (Sainsbury's)   11 £B

Beaujolais-Villages, Les Roches Grillées 1992   14   £C
One of the more respectably decent Beaujolais on sale.

Bergerac Rouge (Sainsbury's)   12   £B

Bergerie de l'Arbous, Coteaux du Languedoc, 1990   13   £C

Cabernet Sauvignon, Vin de Pays d'Oc (Sainsbury's, 3 litres)   12   £F

Cahors (Sainsbury's)   14   £B
Bargain price for a rich dark wine which is brilliant with grilled food. Chewy like coal, but a lot, lot softer to swallow. Excellent.

Chais Baumière Cabernet Sauvignon, Vin de Pays d'Oc 1992   13   £C

Chais Baumière Merlot 1992   14   £C
This seems far too drinkable for a young merlot from this area. A rating of 14 seems churlish when it was so pleasing, but it isn't especially complex or demanding, for it is lighter and less mellow than previous vintages. Yet the wine is soft and cherry-ripe.

Château Barreyres, Haut-Médoc 1990   13   £D

Château Beaumont, Haut-Médoc, Cru Bourgeois 1990   13   £E

Château Blaignan, Médoc, Cru Bourgeois 1989 (1.5 litres)   14   £G
A real dark chewy claret of depth and power. Great roast beef wine!

Château Calon-Segur, St-Estephe 1989   15   £G
Always one of my favourite St-Estephes, this is a rich wine of

considerable class. It will benefit from 5 years more ageing. Available from the Cromwell Road store only.

Château Carsin, Premières Côtes de Bordeaux
1991   13   £D
Good but will be better as it ages.

Château Carsin, Premières Côtes de Bordeaux
1992   14   £D
There is more complexity and satisfying flavour here. And I think it will develop further. This will be available in stores once the 1991 has been exhausted.

Château Chasse-Spleen, Moulis en Médoc
1990   14   £G
At only six stores, this wine will be superb in 6–8 years. It is impressive, with its herby, cherry-plum fruit, but very expensive.

Château Clos Delord, Bordeaux 1991   13   £C
Good Bordeaux style, with dry soft tannins. An ideal partner for roast meat.

Château Clos Fourtet, St-Emilion 1985   13   £G
Available from the Cromwell Road store only.

Château Cos-Labory, St-Estephe 1990   14   £G
Powerful, dry, deep tannins rolling around nicely with the rich fruit give it a compelling, brushed suede quality. Available from the Cromwell Road store only.

Château Coufran Haut-Médoc, Cru Bourgeois
1986   13   £E
Soft and very attractive.

Château d'Aigueville, Côtes du Rhône 1992   12   £C

Château de Fontgraves Pic St-Loup, Coteaux du Languedoc 1992   14   £B

A simple but not inelegant wine of soft, gently earthy, plummy fruit. Excellent with a plain roast chicken with garlic cloves. Nicely mannered tannins – will age well over 2 years.

Château de Gourgazaud, Minervois 1992   14   £C

Château de Jonquières 1992 (Sainsbury's)   15   £B

Great bouquet of old leather, soft fruit and baked herbs. Rich, mouth-filling fruit, soft and ripe. Very lush, very dry to finish. Superb style and flavour.

Château de Roquetaillade la Grange, Graves 1988   16   £D

Serious stuff – leathery, rich, concentrated. Dry, textured, perfect with a steak au poivre.

Château de Rully Rouge 1990   10   £E

Not that there is anything remotely undrinkable about this wine. Goodness me, no. What is wrong is that it is unthink-able. Unthinkably dull. It is rather like paying good money to see a play only to discover the cast has failed to turn up. To be sure, you are able to report, you had a unique experience at the theatre but it somehow lacked something. This wine, sporting soi-disant pedigree and reputation, has been shrewdly purchased and priced, but the prudent drinker will surely wonder why he has spent so much money for so little effect. France 0 – Bulgaria 10.

Château de Turegand Pecharment Bergerac 1992   13   £D

Château du Peyrat, Premières Côtes de Bordeaux 1989   16   £C

Brilliant fruit beautifully packed: dry yet sweet and rich with a blackcurrant finish. Elegant, decisive and very well priced. A lovely fruity Bordeaux which competes with and beats many Aussies.

Château Grand Bourdieu, Bordeaux Supérieure
1992   12   £C
Pleasant soft savoury tannins to the fruit.

Château Haut-Batailley, Pauillac 1985   12   £G
Available from the Cromwell Road store only.

Château Hauterive le Haut, Corbières 1990   15   £C
Rich, tasty, handsome.

Château l'Espau, Bordeaux 1992   14   £C
Some layered, rich fruit here, well constructed and rolled out. Good cheese wine.

Château La Graverie, Côtes de Bourg, 1990   13   £C

Château La Gurgue, Margaux 1990   12   £E

Château La Mission Haut-Brion, Graves 1984   13   £G
Available from the Cromwell Road store only.

Château La Rose Coulon, Bordeaux 1990   14   £D
Excellent, dry, soundly constructed fruit. Has spiciness, style and some depth.

Château La Rose Maréchal, Haut-Médoc, Cru
Bourgeois 1989   11   £E

Château La Vieille Cure, Fronsac 1989   14   £E
Brilliant, but keep for 2–3 years more and it'll be even smoother and richer.

Château La Voulte Gasparets, Corbières 1990
(Sainsbury's)
17.5 £C

Soft, coal-edged fruit of great smokey flavoursomeness. Lovely beef wine (roast, casseroled or grilled). Has developed gloriously in bottle to open up superbly rich, complex fruit.

Château Lalande d'Auvion, Médoc 1989
15 £D

Very rich and meaty. A dry, full wine of outstanding depth of flavour.

Château Lamothe Bergeron, Haut-Médoc, Cru Bourgeois 1989 (1.5 litres)
14 £G

Excellent style. Good fruit, good structure and depth. Very tasty.

Château Le Bon Pasteur, Pomerol 1988
15 £G

Wonderful tannins here. Enjoy them now, and feel their impact on the teeth for minutes afterwards, or stick them away in bottle for 3/4 years. Available from the Cromwell Road store only.

Château Le Boscq, 'Vieilles Vignes', Médoc, Cru Bourgeois 1989
11 £E

Château Liversan, Haut-Médoc 1990
11 £E

Château Lynch Bages, Pauillac 1990
13 £H

Powerful and tannic. Put down for 10 years or more. It will achieve 18 points at its best. Available from the Cromwell Road store only.

Château Maucaillou, Moulis 1989
13 £F

Château Moisson Bel-Air, Bordeaux Rouge 1990
13 £C

Plum-sweet introduction to Bordeaux for beginners.

Château Moulin du Breuil, Haut-Médoc 1989   15   £D
Lovely brambley fruit and teeth-clenching tannic softness.
Will get even fancier over the next 2–3 years.

**Château Pontet Clauzure, St-Emilion, Grand
Cru 1990 (1.5 litres)   14   £G**
Very tasty, like the Château Lamothe Bergeron.

**Château Poujeaux Cru Bourgeois, Moulis-en-
Médoc 1990   14   £G**
Although it is perfectly delicious now it will, I fancy, improve
spectacularly over 4/5 years and justify its price.

Château Rolland, Bordeaux 1992   14   £C
Has fruit and flavour and real Bordeaux style for not a lot of
money. Superb roast food wine.

**Château Segonzac, Premières Côtes de Blaye,
Cuvée Barrique 1991   15   £C**
Structured, tannic (yet soft), lots of purposeful fruit. Excellent
fruit wine (and cheese). Lush yet savoury edge. Good value
from Bordeaux!

**Château Tour Prignac, Médoc Cru Bourgeois
1990   14   £D**
Lovely roast food wine. Highly approachable, soft yet serious
claret.

**Château Vermeil, Costières de Nîmes 1992
(Sainsbury's)   15   £B**
Excellent value for such flavoursome, dry, berried fruit.

Châteauneuf-du-Pape, Les Galets Blancs 1991   13   £D
In a light and less bloody vein.

Chinon, Domaine du Colombier 1992   12   £D

Claret Bordeaux (Sainsbury's) 13 £B

**Côtes du Frontonnais, Château Bellevue la Forêt
1992** 13 £C

Côtes du Luberon (Sainsbury's) 11 £B

Côtes du Rhône (Sainsbury's) 14 £B
Outstanding value for a soft, earthy fruit wine of some character.

Côtes du Rhône Villages, Beaumes de Venise 13 £C

**Côtes du Rhône Villages, St Gervais, Laurent
Charles Brotte 1990** 14 £C
Fruity, soft, simple.

**Côtes du Roussillon Villages, St Vincent 1990
(Sainsbury's)** 14 £B
Very dark rich fruit on display here with an admirably balanced overall style. Dry, full, very good with roasts and grills. Almost vies with Australia for softness and depth of colour. Not a drink for the faint hearted, needs food etc.

Crozes-Hermitage 13 £C
Bit of an acquired taste this one (also a touch pricey). Like chewing light bulbs and rich plums. I don't dislike this sort of mouthful. I enjoyed this wine with herb-drenched, char-grilled lamb chops.

Domaine de Serres-Mazard 1991 (Sainsbury's) 15 £B
More complexity here (and ageing potential). Vivid fruit. Has a vigorous fruit style with some acidity.

**Domaine du Révérend, Corbières, 1990
(Sainsbury's)** 15 £C
Soft and delicious. Has a serious side but not enough to overpower the wine's quaffing qualities.

Domaine Ste Anne, St-Chinian 1992   11   £B

**Domaine Serres-Mazard, Cuvée St-Damien,
Corbières** 1991   15   £B
Soft, simple but hints of serious fruit can't help showing
through.

Domaine St-Marc, Syrah, VdP d'Oc 1993   14   £B
Interesting and immediately arresting soft tannins which
nevertheless are firm on the teeth. Great roast food wine.

Faugères   14   £B
A healthy fruity red wine from southern France, perfect with
sausage and mash. Some excellent on-form fruit here.

Fitou, Les Guèches 1991   12   £B

Fleurie, La Madone, 1992   11   £D

**Fortant Collection Cabernet Sauvignon,
Vin de Pays d'Oc** 1991   12   £D

Fournas Bernadotte, Haut-Médoc Cru Bourgeois
1990   13   £D
Sound fruit but limps a bit at the finish.

**Gamay, VdP des Coteaux des Baronnies, Les
Ramerottes (Sainsbury's)**   15   £B

Gevrey Chambertin 1983   10   £F
Tries hard, has maturity and some semblance of style but is
hugely overpriced.

Gevrey Chambertin, Maurice Chenu 1990   10   £F
Some attractive sweet fruit but not worth the money.

Gigondas Tour du Queyron 1990 15 £E
Expensive but expansive. Big, hearty, huge, smokey fruit.
Concentrated soft centre. Lovely wine.

Graves Selection Sainsbury's, Louis Vialard 13 £C
Good, soft fruit.

**Hautes Côtes de Nuits, Les Dames Huguettes
1990** 12 £E

Les Forts de Latour, Pauillac 1987 12 £G
Please see the entry for the 1985 vintage of this wine Waitrose
(p. 328).

Madiran, Château de Crouseilles 1988 14 £D
Stylish dry beauty with lots of soft berried fruit.

**Mercurey, Domaine Jean Marechal Premier Cru
1991** 13 £E

Moulin à Vent, Cave Kuhnel 1991 10 £D

Nuits St-Georges, Paul Dugenais 1991 13 £E
Not a bad interpretation of pinot noir but a little weak with the
left hand.

**Peter Sichel Selection, Oak-Aged Bordeaux
1990** 14.5 £C
Truly deep structure and weight of fruit. Dry rich tannins and
blackcurrant edginess. Solidly built and well priced.

Red Burgundy Pinot Noir (Sainsbury's) 11 £D

Sainsbury's Bourgueil 1992 14 £C
Wild, delicious raspberry fruit. Will improve over the next year.

**Santenay Gravières, Château de la Maltroye
Premier Cru 1988** 14 £E
Attractive gamey, raspberry fruit. Expensive but authentic.

Saumur Champigny   13   £D
Coal-edged, chewy fruit and has some lovable characteristics
but overall it's expensive for the final effect it produces.

Savigny-les-Beaune, Jean Marc Pavelot 1989   13   £F
Stale cauliflowers and dry strawberries. Burgundy freaks con-
sider this a marriage made in heaven.

Touraine Gamay 1993 (Sainsbury's)   16   £B
Brilliant cherry-ripe fruit, great chilled. Soft yet with a delicious bristle to its savoury edge, this is a tastier, more complex, more deliciously constructed wine than scores of
Beaujolais.

Vacqueyras, Paul Jaboulet-Isnard 1990   13   £E
Has delicious texture but it's somewhat expensive.

Vieux Château Gaubert, Graves 1990 (1.5 litres) 12   £G

**Vin de Pays de la Cité de Carcassonne Merlot
1993 (Sainsbury's)**   11   £B

Vosne Romanée, Georges Noellat 1987   12   £F
Attractively fruity but unattractively pricey.

FRENCH WINE – *white and rosé*

Alsace Gewürztraminer (Sainsbury's)   12   £D

Alsace Pinot Blanc (Sainsbury's)   13   £C

Bergerac Blanc (Sainsbury's)   13   £B

Bordeaux Sauvignon Blanc (Sainsbury's)   13   £B
Solid.

**Chablis, Cuvée Pargues, Brocard 1992
(Sainsbury's)** 14 £D
Rich and well-turned out.

**Chablis Grand Cru, Preuses, Jeanne Paule
Filippi 1990** 15 £G
More in the Mersault style than pure Chablis.

**Chablis Premier Cru, Montmains, Brocard
1992** 16.5 £E
Expensive but very satisfying: complex, finely balanced,
stylish.

**Chais Baumière Chardonnay, Vin de
Pays d'Oc 1992** 14 £C

**Chais Baumière Sauvignon Blanc, Vin de Pays d'Oc
1992** 15 £C
Excellent balance, fruit and acid in nice harmony. Classy and
stylish. Great aperitif or with fish and shellfish.

Chardonnay, Vin de Pays d'Oc Ryman 1993 15 £C
Delicate but assertive. Has buttery rich fruit and finely tuned
acidity.

Château Bastor-Lamontagne, Sauternes 1989 15 £E
Huge, mouth-filling Sauternes with the unctuousness and
liquid smoothness of a Disraeli. A pudding in itself.

Château Carsin, Bordeaux Blanc 1992 16 £D
Elegant haute couture act. Impress the prospective father-in-
law with this one.

Château Carsin, Bordeaux Blanc 1993 16 £D
As good as the '92 vintage.

Château de Davenay, Montagny Premier Cru
1991   11   £D

Château de Rully Blanc, 1990   10   £E
See the entry for this château in the red wines.

Château de Ste Hélène, Sauternes 1990 (half)   15   £E
Burnt, waxy honey. Hugely rich and deep. A very potent pud
wine.

Château l'Ortolan, Entre-deux-Mers, Hugh
Ryman 1993   14   £C
Plumply rounded fruit of great appeal.

Château Les Bouhets, Bordeaux Blanc Sec
1993   15   £C
A fruity, well-balanced wine in the white Graves mould.
Classy and not expensive.

Château Mayne des Carmes, Sauternes 1990
(half)   14   £E

Château Suduiraut, Premier Cru Classe 1990
(half)   13   £F
Available from the Cromwell Road store only.

Châteauneuf-du-Pape André Brunel 1992   14   £E
If you like your wine this soft, seductive and purring like a
pussy-cat, your money's well spent.

Clos St-Georges, Graves Supérieures 1990/91   15   £E
Try this as an aperitif. It's wonderful even though it's honeyed
and toffeed.

Corbières Blanc (Sainsbury's)   12   £B

**Domaine de Grandchamp Sauvignon Blanc,
Bergerac** 1993   13   £D
Brilliant gooseberry fruit with a mineral undercut. Superb
balance, style, class.

**Domaine de la Tuilerie, Merlot Rosé, Hugh
Ryman** 1993   15   £C
Firm and delicious. Depth of fruit and flavour surprising in a
rosé.

Domaine des Blancs, Côtes du Luberon Rosé
1993   13   £C
Good basic stuff. Better than most.

**Fortant Collection Chardonnay, Vin de Pays
d'Oc** 1992   13   £D

Gentil 'Hugel', Alsace 1992   14   £C
Typical: quiet, reserved. A TV wine.

Gustave Lorentz Riesling Reserve, Alsace 1991   13   £D
Light, delicious, expensive. Will dazzle if cellared five years.

Jurançon Sec (Sainsbury's)   14   £C
Not quite back to the splendid '88 vintage (£2.75). But very
nice.

Les Longes Rousses, Chardonnay, VdP d'Oc
1992   17   £B
Staggeringly good value chardonnay of true, rich varietal
character and complexity. Bold, explicit, exciting.

Mâcon Blanc Villages, Domaine les Chenevières
1992   13   £C
Very good style. A true minor burgundy at a good price.

**Mâcon Chardonnay, Domaines les Ecuyers
1992**   12   £D

Menetou Salon, Domaine Henri Pelle 1992   14   £D
Sancerre ringer. Good old-fashioned likeness, too.

Mouton Cadet 1992   9   £C

Muscadet de Sèvres-et-Maine (Sainsbury's)   13   £B
A lot of fruit for a muscadet.

**Muscadet de Sèvres-et-Maine Sur Lie, Château
de la Dimerie 1992**   13   £C
Attractive fruity specimen.

**Muscadet de Sèvres-et-Maine Sur Lie, Première Jean
Drouillard 1990**   13   £D

Muscat de St-Jean de Minervois (half)   14   £B
Sweet satin.

**Oak-Aged Chablis, Madeleine Matthieu 1993
(Sainsbury's)**   15   £D
Lots of flavoursome woody fruit. Class act.

Pouilly-Fumé le Bouchaud, Fouassier 1992   13   £E

Premières Côtes de Bordeaux N.V.   11   £C

**Puligny Montrachet, Domaine Gérard Chavy
1992**   14   £F
Difficult to rate. It is fine, solid, well made, even a touch
classy, but at three times the price of other French chardonnays at Sainsbury's is it even twice as good? It is only 50%
better.

Sainsbury's Blush Wine   14   £B
A truly feebly-coloured wine which has gently rousing fruit.

Sancerre Les Beaux Regards 1992   14 £E
Still one of the best supermarket Sancerres on sale.

Sancerre Les Celliers de Ceres 1993   16 £C
A miracle! Sound Sancerre under a fiver! Indeed, it's better than sound, it's terrific. Only a few bottles left.

Saumur Blanc, Domaine des Hauts de Sanziers 1991   12 £C
Lip-puckering curiosity of interest to live shellfish eaters.

Sauvignon Blanc, Domaine de la Done, VdP d'Oc 1993   13 £B

Sauvignon, Vin de Pays d'Oc, Domaine St-Francois 1992 (Sainsbury's)   14 £B
Elegant, modern, fruity. Excellent aperitif or for salad and light soups.

Selection Peter Sichel, Bordeaux Oak-Aged White 1993   13 £C
A lean wine with some pretensions to elegance. Some fruit too.

Tokay Pinot Gris, Cave de Ribeauville 1989   16 £E
Brilliant apricot aroma. Captivating fruit of great concentration of flavour and complexity and firmness of finish. A superb bottle of wine.

Touraine Sauvignon Blanc (Sainsbury's)   15 £B
Superb value. Varietally pure (so it's steely and fresh), fruity (it's full of flavour) and it's very well balanced. Great glug.

Vin de Pays d'Oc Chardonnay (3 litres)   12 £G

Vin de Pays d'Oc (Sainsbury's)   13 £B
Good value clean wine.

**Vin de Pays d'Oc Sauvignon Blanc,
Domaine St-Marc** 1993   13   £C

Vin de Pays de Gascogne, Domaine Bordes
1993   13   £B

**Vin de Pays des Côtes de Gascogne
(Sainsbury's)**   14   £B
One of the most attractive white Gascons on sale: lush fruit,
fresh and flint-edged. Lovely style for the money.

Vin de Pays du Gers (Sainsbury's)   14   £B
A lush refreshing mouthful. Terrific price for this quality of
fruit and structure.

Viognier Resplandy, Vin de Pays d'Oc 1992 16.5 £C
Superb banana fruit with a nutty undertone. Complex, light,
fresh and drinkable, this is an excellent example of the grape
at a knockdown price. Odd bottle still around.

**Viognier, Vin de Pays des Coteaux de l'Ardèche,
Cévenne Ardèchoise** 1993   13   £C

Vouvray Demi-Sec (Sainsbury's)   12   £C
Delicious aperitif if you can take the toffee sweetness.

White Burgundy Chardonnay (Sainsbury's)   15.5 £C
I guess this is a bargain under a fiver because it tastes like a
first class Côtes Châlonnaises.

GERMAN WINE – *white*

Baden Dry (Sainsbury's)   14   £B
Subtly spicy and fruity and excellent value.

Binger St Rochuskapelle Spätlese, QmP 1992	10	£B
Kabinett Sainsbury's, Dalsheimer Burg Rodenstein 1992	12	£B
Morio Muskat St Georg	11	£B
Niersteiner Gutes Domtal (Sainsbury's)	12	£A

Ockfener Bockstein, Riesling Spätlese, Mosel-Saar-Ruwer QmP, Rudolf Müller 1989   10   £C
Pure kerosene.

Oppenheimer Krotenbrunnen Kabinett, QmP 1992   10   £B

Reichsgraf von Kesselstatt, Riesling, QbA 1989   16   £C
As brilliant as before. Gorgeous, elegant, lemonic style.

Spätlese Mosel-Saar-Ruwer, Bernkasteler Kurfurstlay 1992 (Sainsbury's)   11   £C

Trocken Rheinhessen (Sainsbury's)   11   £B

Wiltinger Scharzberg Kabinett 1992 (Sainsbury's)   11   £B
Too sweet to be attractive.

GREEK WINE – *white*

Retsina   13   £B
Resinated and fruity, but also clean to finish, and at under £3 I find this wine both a bargain and excellent with grilled fish as well as, of course, Greek starters.

HUNGARIAN WINE – *white and rosé*

Chapel Hill Chardonnay, Balaton Boglar, Barrique
Fermented 1993   15.5 £C
This is a superb wine which will benefit from a year's further
ageing to reach even greater heights. An elegant, well-made
wine which shows the huge potential of Hungary and fine
wine, and the French should be scared witless.

Chapel Hill Chardonnay, Balaton Boglar
1993   15.5 £B
A fine helping of fruit, true to the grape, nicely balanced by
the acids. Fantastic value.

Chapel Hill Irsai Oliver, Balaton Boglar 1993   15 £B
Lovely melon and muscat aperitif with subtle smokey
undertones.

Chapel Hill Sauvignon Blanc, Balaton Boglar
1993   13 £B

Chardonnay, The Gyöngyös Estate, Ryman
1992   14 £B
Rich, well-rounded. Attractive fruit, attractive price.

Country White Wine (Sainsbury's)   14 £B
Can't argue with this level of Old World fruit and New World
acidity. Fantastic value.

Gyöngyös Estate Chardonnay 1993   13 £B

Gyöngyös Esztergom Country White Wine,
Ryman 1992   12 £B
Bit ho-hum for Ryman, who usually gives a full symphony.

Hungarian Cabernet Sauvignon Rosé, Nagyrede
Region, (Sainsbury's)   16   £B
The best rosé for the money I've tasted in ages. Apple cheeked, raspberry/cherry fruit, soft yet fresh – it's brilliant.

Hungarian Country Wine, Balaton Boglar
(Sainsbury's)   14   £B
Fresh and fruity and full of value. Good with grilled foods. Tasty with *Coronation Street*.

Hungarian Pinot Gris, Nagyrede Region
(Sainsbury's)   13   £B

ITALIAN WINE – *red*

Bardolino Classico (Sainsbury's)   13   £B
Cherries and white chocolate.

Barolo, Giordano 1988   14   £E
Expensive but possessing great length of flavour (which is fruity and of a soft-berried nature enhanced by a faint liquorice echo).

Barrique Aged Cabernet Sauvignon, Atesino
1993   16   £C
Brilliant, soft, warm fruit with hints of liquorice and eucalyptus. Superb roast food wine. Brilliant.

Cabernet Sauvignon delle Tre Venezie
(Sainsbury's)   16   £C
Needs months to soften and develop. Sweet fruit finish. Sensationally good.

Cabernet Sauvignon Grave del Friuli, Roncaccio
1991   13   £C
Attractive, soft.

Castello di San Polo in Rosso, Chianti Classico
1989   14   £E

Cecchi, Chianti 1990   15   £C
(Villa Cecchi de-classified.) Dry, earthy, stylish – lots of soft,
beautifully berried fruit. Very classy.

Chianti Classico, Briante 1990   16   £C
Full, dry, savoury, gently earthly. A wonderful Chianti for
posh roast food.

Chianti Rufina Riserva, Galiga 1982   14.5   £C
Maturity and sweet fruit at a surprising price.

Chianti (Sainsbury's)   14   £B

Collavini, Campo Olivo Merlot, Grave del Friuli
1991   12   £C

Copertino Riserva 1990   16   £C
Has less of the tobacco dryness of previous vintages but riper,
sweeter fruit. Lovely wine at a lovely price.

San Lorenzo Rosso Conero, Umani Ronchi
1990   14   £D
Delicious as usual, like the last vintage.

Sicilian Red (Sainsbury's)   14   £B
Brilliant pasta-eaters' bargain. Soft, touch of sunny earth –
good finish. Excellent stuff for the money.

Teroldego Rotaliano (Sainsbury's)   14   £C
Soft and very supple. Damsons, spicy and soft. Probably OK
with pasta. Delicious.

Valpolicella Classico, Negarine 1991
(Sainsbury's)   13   £B
13 points at time of tasting but the '89 and '90 are terrific
15/16 pointers and I see no reason to disbelieve this '91 won't
be up here by Xmas '94 and beyond.

Valpolicella Classico Amarone, Sartori 1988   14   £D
Serious, complex, deep. Serve it to serious guests whose
boring anecdotes need fruity enlivening.

Valpolicella Classico (Sainsbury's)   12   £B

Vino Nobile di Montepulciano, Fattoria di Casale
1989   12   £D

ITALIAN WINE – *white*

Barrique Aged Chardonnay Atesino 1993   14   £C
14 now, 16 in 2/3 months time (i.e. Christmas 1994) when
the wood and creamy fruit notes will have integrated fully.
Will be very fine in a while.

Bianco di Custoza 1993 (Sainsbury's)   14   £B
Balanced, rich fruit cut with freshness.

Chardonnay delle Tre Venezie (Sainsbury's)   15   £C
A lemony elegant chardonnay of reserve and class. Not hugely
fruity or dynamic but quietly impressive. Lovely balanced
fruit, freshness and finish. Exceptional value.

Collavini Chardonnay, Grave del Friuli 1992   13   £C

Frascati Secco Superiore 1993 (Sainsbury's)   15   £C
Pots of melony fruit with a hint of cream and nuts. Superb.

Frascati Superiore, Cantine San Marco 1993   16   £C
Stupendously tasty Frascati. Complex fruit, fine balance.
Quite delicious.

Gavi, Bersano 1992   12   £D

Grechetto dell'Umbria (Sainsbury's)   13   £C

Lugana San Benedetto, Zenato 1992   14   £C
Classy, stylish – quite superb.

Orvieto Classico (Sainsbury's)   10   £C
Dull.

Pinot Grigio Atesino (Sainsbury's)   14   £B
At last, a pinot grigio which nods firmly in the direction of
the p.g. of Alsace with its rich fruit and nutty overtone.
Smashing aperitif.

Sauvignon Blanc delle Tre Venezie, 1993   15   £C
Intensely fruity, concentrated but surrounded by lots of freshness and modern-style zippiness. Good price.

Sicilian White (Sainsbury's)   14   £B
Not a lean mean Sicilian but a full-flavoured, even meaty,
wine yet clean and fresh to finish. Great value.

Soave Classico Costalunga Pasqua 1992
(Sainsbury's)   13   £C
Delicious, fruity Soave which goes some way to restoring the
reputation of this often bland dull wine.

Tocai del Veneto (3 litres)   11   £E

Trebbiano di Romagna (Sainsbury's) (1.5 litres) 13   £C

Vernaccia di San Gimignano, San Quirico 1992   12   £C

LEBANESE WINE – *red*

Château Musar 1987   15   £E

MOLDOVAN WINE – *red*

Moldova Cabernet Sauvignon   8   £B
Thin as ink and just about as attractive to drink.

Moldova Codru, Cabernet and Merlot   14   £B
Simple cherry fruit finishing sweetly.

Moldova Pinot Noir, Cricova   14   £B
Light, supple, fruity. Good chilled.

MOLDOVAN WINE – *white*

Moldova Hincesti Chardonnay 1992   15   £B
Delicious, richly fruity, well-balanced, firmly structured. A
bargain flavouring to pour over your tongue.

MORAVIAN WINE – *white*

Moravian Grüner Veltliner 1993 (Sainsbury's)   14   £B
Fresh, but not overly so – fruity, but not too fat! A perfect
quaffing bottle.

NEW ZEALAND WINE – *red*

Cook's Cabernet Merlot 1991   12   £C

**Corbans Cabernet Merlot Private Bin,
Marlborough 1991**   15   £E
One of the most impressively complex NZ reds I've tasted.
Lots of flavour and style, masses of deeply appealing fruit.

**Montana Cabernet Sauvignon, Marlborough
1992**   14   £C
Uncooked vegetable undertones to rich fruit which has some
depth. Must be drunk with rich food, with which it shines.

NEW ZEALAND WINE – *white*

**Jackson Estate Sauvignon Blanc, Marlborough
1993**   16   £E
Not huge grassiness here, just gentle soothing fruit and
balanced stylishness. One of the most elegantly purposeful of
sauvignon blancs around. Will repay cellaring for 2/3 years.
Very fine.

Matua Valley Sauvignon Blanc 1993   12   £D

Montana Sauvignon Blanc, Marlborough 1993   15   £C
Has the honey edge to the ripe gooseberry fruit typical of
several 1993 sauvignon blancs from New Zealand. Lovely
shellfish wine.

Nobilo Chardonnay, Poverty Bay 1992   14   £C
Peachy fruit, delicious and refreshing. Lovely wine.

Nobilo White Cloud 1993 15 £C
Best year yet for this Müller-Thurgau/sauvignon blanc blend.
Lots of balanced fruit, fresh and flavoursome.

**Villa Maria Private Bin Sauvignon Blanc,
Marlborough 1993** 15 £D
Typical '93. Impressively full fruited and the herbaceousness
is more controlled and less grassy.

PORTUGUESE WINE – *red*

Alentejo 1989 15 £B
This Alentejo, so named from its area of growth which is
vying with certain parts of eastern Europe to be the hot spot to
watch, is dry, dusty, yet has lots of richness and freshness,
typically Portuguese in many respects yet also very 1990s, and
with its chunky meaty fruit would be excellent with stews and
roasts. A terrific little wine for well under £3.50.

Arruda (Sainsbury's) 14 £B
Burly fruit, yet balanced and dry. One of this book's long-
term favourite reds which is now beginning to be a little
overshadowed by the rest of the JS Portuguese red range.

Bairrada Terra Franca, Sogrape 1990 14 £B
Nice balance of components (fruit, acid, tannin). Good to
drink with cold meats.

Bright Brothers Cabernet Sauvignon 1993 14 £C
Rich, dry blackberries.

Bright Brothers Merlot 1993 15 £C
Impressively integrated fruit/acid. Lovely polished fruit.

Do Campo Tinto (Sainsbury's)   14   £B
Dry and more complex than before. Subtle black cherry
touches.

Douro 1992 (Sainsbury's)   15   £B
Typical Douro ripe red with character and earthy plum/
cherry fruit. Aromatically a bit old socks but impressively solid
thereafter. Has richness and depth but neither is reflected in
the price.

Fonseca Guimaraens Vintage Port 1978   17   £G
Rich spiced plums plus a cassis-like concentration and
ripeness of fruit which is always, magically, dry.

Herdade de Santa Marta 1991   14   £C
Great style at a great price. The distinctive sweetness, in an
essentially dry wine, is genuine and fresh-fruity and makes the
wine perfect with all manner of well-flavoured foods from
spicy sausages to chilli con carne.

Noval Colheita Tawny Port 1976 (half)   16   £E
Sheer bliss: nutty finish, sweet, fruit-cake, glace-cherry fruit
with figs and cream. Splendid wine for cheese.

Quinta da Bacalhoa 1991 (1.5 litres)   16   £G
Potentially the most exciting of the trio. Great now, in 3/4
years brilliant.

Quinta da Bacalhoa, Palmela 1989 (1.5 litres) 15   £G
As the 1990 vintage, but becoming more polished and softer
in the mouth. Tannins sorting themselves out.

Quinta da Bacalhao, Palmela 1990   15   £D
A dusty warhorse of a wine with lots of rich fruit finishing with
a sweet blackcurrant note.

10-Year-Old Tawny Port (Sainsbury's)16£F
Magnificent, raisiny fruit which starts basso profundo and finishes mezzo soprano. Great cheese wine and also worth trying with fruit cake.

PORTUGUESE WINE – *white*

Bright Brothers Chardonnay 199314£C
Soft, melon fruit. Good style. Tropical fruit undertones.

Bright Brothers Sauvignon Blanc 199314£B
Gentle, herbaceous fruit and acid, very clean and fresh. Great shellfish wine.

Chello Vinho Verde, Seco Sogrape13£B

Do Campo Branco15£B
A Peter Bright special for Sainsbury's (see *tinto* version also). A delightfully fresh and fruity wine in the modern manner, with an extended lush melony middle (prior to the wine gushing down the throat and showing its lovely acidic zip which refreshes the palate for further glasses), a result of Mr Bright allowing the wine to spend time resting on its lees – that is, all the bits and bobs from the crushed grapes – an acquaintanceship with which gives wine character and fullness. It is an excellent bottle to enjoy by itself or with shellfish or grilled fish.

Do Campo Rosado, Peter Bright (Sainsbury's)14£B
Fleshy and flavoursome.

João Pires, Terras do Sado 199214£C
Delicious muscat elegance. Lovely aperitif or with complex and saucy fish dishes.

Santa Sara 1993   15   £C
Fresh and nutty. Lovely style of balanced fruit.

ROMANIAN WINE – *red*

Romanian Pinot Noir   16   £B
Shrewd boozers appreciate the absurdity of forking out under
three quid for a pinot noir which has spent between three and
four years in barrel and emerged rich, aromatic, and quite
stunningly concentrated (and better endowed than many a red
burgundy costing five times as much). If the store redesigned
the off-putting pseudo-KGB label it would sell twice as well as
it does. (N.B. to JS Director of Label Design – I have a
cracking idea for this label which would help sell *three times* as
many bottles but this idea is only available for (1) a lifetime's
supply of this wine or (2) the money to buy a small vineyard in the
Côte d'Or. Thinking about it, however, I think I'll take the first
option.)

ROMANIAN WINE – *white*

Burgund Mare 1986   14   £B
This is a dry, perfectly perky nonagenarian (in wine terms) and
it has very tasty raspberry-flavoured fruit. It's not a rich wine or
a complex one but it's a treat with grilled meat and vegetables
and excellent with poached chicken. This wine can hardly
expect a long shelf life but I have been told the stock situation is
ample. Whether this amplitude is proof against Volvo estate
drivers with vast boots and thirsts to match, however, I doubt.

SLOVENIAN WINE – *white*

Chardonnay Vinakoper, Labor Koprski Region
1992 14 £C
Delicious, attractive wine of style and fruity purpose. Good
with grilled fish – excellent with poached.

SOUTH AFRICAN WINE – *red*

Fairview Shiraz Merlot, Paarl 1992 14 £C
Delicious – rich, savoury, dry, faintly spicy, blackcurranty
fruit.

Kanonkop, Paul Sauer, Stellenbosch 1990 14 £E
A rich and very potently berried wine.

Pinotage, Coastal Region (Sainsbury's) 15 £B
A brilliant alternative to overpriced Beaujolais. Just as soft and
fruity, but with a lovely dry edge.

SOUTH AFRICAN WINE – *white*

Chardonnay Vergelegen 1993 14 £C
What a pity the somewhat muted finish lets down an otherwise
splendid performance, which, at this price, is a bargain.

Chardonnay, Western Cape (Sainsbury's) 15 £B
Elegance and concentration. Superb! No vintage on the label
but it's a '92 all right and it's remarkable stuff for the money,

with a delicious touch of exotic fruit to the subtle butteriness
and fresh, lemony finish. It cries out to be drunk with rich
crustaceous dishes. Smashing wine for just over £3.

Chenin Blanc (Sainsbury's)   15   £B
Gets to be a fruitier bargain every vintage. Pear-drops and
sticky toffee to finish – oodles of fruit and great with fish and
chips.

Danie de Wet, Grey Label Chardonnay 1993   16   £C
Wonderful style, beautiful elegant woody fruit, citrus finish.
Fabulous, fabulous wine for the money.

Fairview Estate Sauvignon Blanc and Semillon
1993   13   £C
Nice touch of ripeness from the semillon.

Fairview Sauvignon Semillon, Paarl 1993   13   £C
Modern, light and lots of candied fruit, fresh.

Hamilton Russell Chardonnay, Walker Bay
1992   15   £D
Drinking elegantly and well – it's a quiet, gentle wine with an
undertone of oily richness not fully realized. It whispers rather
than shouts, but there is no denying the voice that's there and
it's eloquent. I just feel I wish it was more pushy. Fruit and
wood integration is good.

Les Enfants Chardonnay, Vergelegen 1992   13   £C
Subtle, woody and rather restrained.

Les Enfants Chardonnay, Vergelegen 1993   14   £C
Healthy wood-tinged fresh fruit with a soapy finish undercut
with subtle bitterness.

Les Enfants Sauvignon Blanc, Vergelegen 1992　14　£C
Keen herbaceous style of fruit and a nuttiness to the finish.
Has to be drunk with shellfish.

Les Enfants Sauvignon Blanc, Vergelegen 1993　13　£C
Grassy scents plus rich-edged fruit. Simple style.

**Sauvignon Blanc, Olifants River (Sainsbury's)
1992　　　　　　　　　　　　　　14　£B**
Delicious. Grilled fish – meet thy maker!

**Spes Bona Chardonnay, Van Loveren 1993,
Robertson　　　　　　　　　　　14　£C**
Delicious, stylish, fruity and well-crafted. Good fruit, not
over-rich or gawky. Nice balance. Touch of mint perhaps, but
this passes for elegance.

SPANISH WINE – *red*

El Conde Vino de Mesa (Sainsbury's)　15　£B
Declassified Rioja. Interesting wine (and at this price, ridiculous) which has been used to season new barrels, for three to
six months, for grander wines which will spend years in them.
So: can't be sold as Rioja but can be sold as wine. It has the
vanilla aroma and delightful soft fruit but not the hefty finish.
Remarkable value for Rioja lovers and perfect with a leaf salad
topped with flash-grilled slices of chorizo.

Jumilla Altos de Pio 1989　　　　　　12　£B
'Big' says someone or other on the label.

La Mancha, Castillo de Alhambra (Sainsbury's)
1992   15   £B
Spain's answer to Beaujolais (but without Beaujolais' price
and acidic freshness). Beautiful, bright, supple fruit, very drily
finished. Terrific value.

Marqués de Cáceres Rioja 1989 (1.5 litres)   13   £E

Navarra (Sainsbury's)   11   £B

Navarra Tempranillo/Cabernet Sauvignon 1991
(Sainsbury's)   15   £C
Quieter than before but still has soft yet chewy fruit.

Rioja Crianza, Bodegas Olarra 1989
(Sainsbury's)   14   £C

Rioja Crianza Torrealba 1985   15   £B
This uses the tempranillo grape of course but in a very light
style with the distinctive touch of vanilla. Sainsbury's has
bought a massive job lot of the wine and is flogging it off at
£2.75. I rate this wine highly, for it is formidably cheap for the
fruit on offer, but it is not as heavy or as deep as you might
expect and its distinctiveness will disappear under rich food.

Rioja (Sainsbury's)   15   £B
Bargain fruit and flavour. Light, unwoody, very fresh and
delicious yet with hints of depth.

Torres Gran Coronas Reserva 1988   13   £E

Valencia Red (Sainsbury's)   13   £B
Excellent value for pizzas.

Viña Herminia Reserve Rioja, Bodegas Lagunilla
1985   14   £D
Lush, raunchy stuff – delicious cheese wine.

Viño de la Tierra Tinto (Sainsbury's) 15 £B
Plummy and soft with a lovely dry chewy finish. Great to drink
by itself.

SPANISH WINE – *white and rosé*

Altos de Pio 1989 15 £B
Elusive aromatically but some pleasant burnt fruit emerges
which is soft, naturally tannic and dry – and with a subtle and
very attractive edge of savoury plums. The name translates as
'the heights of piety'.

Castillo de Alhambra Rosé 1993 13 £B

La Mancha Rosado, Castillo de Alhambra 1993 15 £B
Terrific value rosé. Lots of rosy fruit (in flavour as well as hue)
and tons of style.

Moscatel de Valencia (Sainsbury's) 16 £B
Brilliant honeyed wine with a finish like marmalade. Superb
pudding wine for a song.

**Navarra Barrel-Fermented Viura-Chardonnay
1993 (Sainsbury's)** 15 £C
Has woody overtones to the ripe finish. Delicious and has
pretensions to true class.

Rioja Blanco (Sainsbury's) 13 £B
Milky, coconutty, but also fresh and light. Good salad wine.

Rueda, Hermanos Lurton 14 £B
Soft, slightly spicy melon fruit. Clean and fresh on the tongue
to finish. Very pretty aperitif.

Rueda Sauvignon Blanc 1993   15 £C
Gorgeous, aromatic, floral aperitif. Lovely ripe fruit well
matched by the citric fruited acidity. Deliciously unstoppable
(i.e. you can't leave the bottle half empty to finish tomorrow).

**Santara Dry White, Conca de Barbera, Hugh
Ryman**   15 £B
Peachy and fresh, light and gluggable, with a touch of banana.
Drink it while the flavours are this assertive and fresh. Has a
curious echo of turps in it on the finish.

**Viño de la Tierra Blanco, Extremadura, Peter
Bright (Sainsbury's)**   15 £B
Modern, ripe, very rich-edged fruit, yet fresh to finish. Deli-
cious. A terrific aperitif.

URUGUAYAN WINE – *red*

Carte Pujol Tannat 1988   16 £C
A most unlikely new wine from Uruguay – a country many
people could not even find on a map let alone expect to
discover on a wine shelf. Castel Pujol is chewy and dry, with
suggestions of black cherry and raspberry to the fruit, and the
leathery, softly spicy feel to it suggests an oddball Australian
shiraz. Tannat is the name of the grape by the way and this
translates as tannic, so get plenty of air into the wine for
twenty minutes or so before sinking your teeth into it.

USA WINE – *red*

Beaulieu Vineyards Beautour Cabernet Sauvignon
1990   12   £D

USA WINE – *white*

Firestone Chardonnay, Santa Ynez 1992   14   £E

Sauvignon Blanc, Firestone 1992 (Sainsbury's)   10   £C

Stratford Oak-Aged Pinot Noir 1991   12   £C

Stratford Oak Chardonnay 1992   14   £C
A very attractive, well-fruited but well-controlled (almost
stiffly so) wine. Has style and elegance but, anxiously for a
Californian, is not outdoor and all-embracing but indoor and
bookish.

SPARKLING WINE/CHAMPAGNE

Australian Sparkling Wine (Sainsbury's)   14   £C
Excellent stuff for cheap wedding givers.

Blanc de Noirs Champagne (Sainsbury's)   17   £F
If you must buy champagne then why not spend less than £12
to acquire this classic.

Cava (Sainsbury's)   16   £C
Has lost its earthiness and replaced it with more fruit. Yet it

still has freshness and elegance. Better than many a
champagne.

Champagne Extra Dry (Sainsbury's)   14   £F
Good at the price; lovely biscuity fruit and dry with it. So
much better than the famous marques for so much less
money.

Champagne Rosé (Sainsbury's)   13   £F

Cuvée Napa, Mumm California   13   £E
Quiet, not explosive, and rather like a reasonably made
champagne.

**Green Point Vineyard Domaine Chandon,
Australia 1991**   12   £F

Madeba Brut, Robertson, South Africa   14   £D
This smartly packaged bottle from South Africa is excellent
value. The fruit is creamy and gently nutty and the acidity
comes clean with every prickly bubble. Its price, style and
sheer cheek is further depressing news for the Champenois.

Mercier Champagne   11   £G

Sainsbury's Sparkling Chardonnay   15   £D
Has deliciously controlled fruit. Flavour *and* freshness.

Salinger Brut 1990   13   £E

Saumur (Sainsbury's)   14   £D
Bargain. Pleasant dry fruit of some distinction for the price.

Seppelts Salinger Sparkling Wine, Australia 15   £F
Mature yet fresh finishing. Some elegance. Dry.

**Vintage Champagne Blanc de Blancs 1989
(Sainsbury's)**   13   £G

Vouvray (Sainsbury's) 14 £D

Yalumba Pinot Noir/Chardonnay, Australia 16 £E
Absolute stunner for the money: rich and biscuity, great balancing acidity and an overall style hinting refinement and class. Rheims quakes in its Gucci boots!

Somerfield

This retailer is in an evolutionary stage. Its right hand doesn't always know what its left hand is doing. This is a passably amusing fault in a jazz pianist but in a juggler, the sort of juggler the company aspires to be, it is a crippling insufficiency requiring urgent surgery. Gateway would like to keep as many balls in the air as Tesco, that is to develop superstores as well as keeping crucial inner city and small town sites, but it will not do this unless it has customers' loyalty. Earlier this year, it demonstrated how uncoordinated it was when readers of the Superplonk column drove down a blind alley when they attempted to buy certain Gateway wines I enthused about. I quote from two of these: 'I drove ten miles to my nearest Gateway, to be told by the manager that he was aware three weeks before that the wines were a special offer, had ordered therefore six cases, and had received none.' And: 're. the special offer on the two wines . . . we met a delightful lady who stocks the wine shelves, who said she knew nothing about any of it.'

I wrote to the store asking for an explanation, and I also wrote the following in my *Guardian* column: 'I am extremely irritated with this cack-handed organization on behalf of those readers who were told by certain branches that two of the cut-price wines I recommended a few weeks back were cut-price no longer. I have been told by Gateway's head office that someone in the organization took it upon himself to suddenly foreshorten the offer. I have been assured that the culprit will be flogged and mistakes like this will never again occur. This column is supposed to celebrate the affordable joys of life, not record its frustrations. Any reader who was inconvenienced by this store's bungling should write to me. I have already received a couple of letters and I also know a Mr Selwood telephoned the *Guardian*, and one other reader who left no name.'

The pity is that this store has a terrific chief wine buyer, a woman surrounded by eunuchs, who regularly offers bargains. When the letters started pouring in, she wrote to me saying, among other things, the following:

> I was dismayed, embarrassed and ultimately very frustrated to receive copies of the letters from your rightly disgruntled readers. I am enclosing copies of my replies.
>
> I am acutely aware of how great a readership and reader/consumer level your Superplonk column has, and how vital it is that the information I give you is 100 per cent accurate. I am also extremely grateful for the many kind and positive words you have written about me and our wine range over the past few years . . .
>
> I am treating your letter with great seriousness and have taken the matter up with our Operations Director, since I want a full explanation from each store concerned. Somerfield and Gateway now have an excellent product range, and sales are extremely buoyant. Our number one priority has to be the customer, and to ensure that he or she is satisfied, and that the product is always available . . .
>
> The strategy at Gateway (or Somerfield Holdings Ltd as we shall be from 1 May) is that all decisions regarding product selection, distribution, pricing, what goes where on shelf etc. is determined at Head Office, in this case, by myself and my department. You will appreciate that many of our smaller stores do not have the space to carry the full range; however, in this case the wines in question should all have been in the stores mentioned. We determine the range by size of store fixture and stores are sent planograms

telling them which wines to order and where to site them on shelf. Whereas years ago this was slightly left to the manager's discretion, it is now mandatory for stores to obey these plans ... Where wines on promotion are in limited distribution, I shall always let you know; this situation is hugely embarrassing for me as I always give you my assurance that the stock is widely available in the belief that our stores are doing as they are told – that is why I have taken this issue up and will get in touch as soon as I have received a reply from Operations ...

As Buying Controller I am angry and appalled, but ultimately I must accept responsibility, as an employee of the company, for the embarrassment and irritation caused to yourselves and your readers and offer my profound apologies. I shall provide you with a full explanation as soon as possible.

I can fully understand your reluctance to recommend Gateway wines in the future, but would be very sorry if you had to take this course of action. I hope that by making a major issue of your letter I can prevent the ridiculous comments being made again; with last year's change of senior management, disciplines are now being imposed on stores and I foresee huge improvements in stores adhering to the plans they are given.

Please don't stop writing about us – if you are concerned, please ring me and I will forewarn stores of any recommendations you are about to make – then we can ensure that all stores order stock. I'm about to launch about thirty new wines (details of press tasting to follow) and would hate you not to tell your readers about them.

This is a very revealing letter and I was pleased to receive it. I was also pleased to receive letters from several of the original complainants, telling me that Angela Mount had gone to great lengths to put matters right with them. To wit:

'A complimentary bottle of each of the two wines has just been delivered to the above address.' And: '. . . restitution has now been made by a conciliatory letter from the Wine Buying Controller, Angela Mount, closely followed by a special delivery of the wines in question . . .' And (most fulsome of all, from a reader in Belton in Rutland): 'Credit where credit's due. Gateway have come up trumps in response to your efforts on readers' behalf. I received a letter of apology and, subsequently, two nice bottles of plonk. Today, I'm happy to report I was able to buy two cases of the £1.99 V. de P. d'Oc and am just about to take a sip.'

I reproduce these letters because they provide, I hope, reassurance. There is no doubt that the store has one of the most able wine buyers around, and the listing which follows demonstrates the breadth of the range, the depth of the quality, and the appetizing nature of the prices. Angela, young fruit, I'll carry on rooting for you all the way.

AUSTRALIAN WINE – *red*

Australian Cabernet Sauvignon (Somerfield)   **15** **£C**
Always sound, always delicious, always lovely and subtly minty.

Cabernet Sauvignon, SE Australia   **15** **£C**
I was dragged in front of a TV set to watch the BBC's *Middlemarch* just as I'd opened a bottle and I must say I found the wine a more compelling interest than the costume drama. It is free of any hard edges, ladles a rich helping of

leathery, soft, brilliant, blackcurrant fruit on the tongue, is dry yet full of lingering flavour, and roast meat and veg would be much better company for it than George Eliot.

Château Reynella Cabernet Sauvignon 1988	13	£D

Koonunga Hill Shiraz/Cabernet 1992	13	£C

Mount Hurtle Cabernet Sauvignon/Merlot	11	£D

Nottage Hill Cabernet Sauvignon 1992   15   £C
Still sporting a day-old growth of beard to the smooth fruit (courtesy of the tannins). Lovely performer – one of the best-made cabernet sauvignons around for the money. Not stocked in the majority of Somerfield stores.

Penfolds Bin 35 Shiraz/Cabernet 1992   15   £C
Ripe, soft fruit with some development ahead of it. Attractive berry flavours, well structured and balanced. Very drinkable now but a 17/18-pointer in 3/4 years.

Penfolds Bin 389 Cabernet/Shiraz   13   £E
Excellent stuff.

Somerfield Australian Red   14   £B
A very unlikely but nevertheless very attractive Australian. Terrific soft fruit and terrific value.

Somerfield Shiraz 1990   14   £C
Excellent. Not as spicy as some, but luscious soft fruit.

Somerfield Shiraz/Cabernet 1991   15   £C
Under four quid this is a brilliant wine, absolutely knock-out stuff.

AUSTRALIAN WINE – *white*

Berri Estates Unwooded Chardonnay 1993   15 £C
Has a depth of flavour to the freshness rather like the fruit
centre in a confectionery product. But this wine is no kid's
sweet. It is adult and very attractive. Not stocked in the
majority of Somerfield stores.

Chardonnay (Somerfield)   13 £C

Koonunga Hill Chardonnay   14 £C
Excellent. Delightful rich fruit well kitted out with flashes of
acidity and one of the most consistently endearing Aussie
chardies on sale under a fiver.

Nottage Hill Chardonnay 1993   15 £C
Lovely stuff. Has firmness of fruit, delicacy of acidity and
decisiveness of structure – without being blowsy or offensively
overripe.

Penfolds Bin 21 Semillon Chardonnay 1993   15 £C
Fresh and lively yet a dollop of pineappley melon keeps
intruding. Delicious refreshing wine.

Penfolds Padthaway Chardonnay 1990   14 £E
Amazing bucket of fruit.

Somerfield Australian Dry White   15 £B
Delicious, not shrieking with fruit but definitely announcing it
clearly and cleanly. Fantastic value.

BULGARIAN WINE – *red*

Melnik Cabernet Sauvignon   14   £B
Great value, great style. Dry, plush fruit of plummy almost
biscuity fullness. Very clean, balanced red.

Sliven Country Red Wine, Merlot/Pinot Noir   14   £B
Very bright and breezy. Soft fruit, smashingly allied to apple-
skin fresh acidity. 11.5%. Superb value for light dishes (cold
meats) or drinking any time.

Stambolovo Merlot Reserve 1988   15   £B
Intriguing, tarry bouquet leading to dry, perhaps too dry,
raspberry/blackcurrant fruit – delightfully mature and devastatingly effective with roast meat and vegetables.

BULGARIAN WINE – *white*

Country White Wine Russe Riesling/Misket   10   £B

Sliven Chardonnay 1992   12   £B

CHILEAN WINE – *red*

Cabernet Sauvignon, Segu Olle 1993
(Somerfield)   15   £B
Lovely ripe plum fruit held back from sweetness and squash-
iness by tannins. Elegant, dry, very profound. A bargain for
under £3.50.

Santa Rita Reserve Cabernet Sauvignon 14 £C
Delightful plum fruit, quite soft yet dry, well balanced. An attractive wine.

CHILEAN WINE – *white*

**Chilean Sauvignon Blanc, Canepa 1993
(Somerfield)** 14 £B
Herby, mineralized edge encircling the fruit. Tasty.

Sauvignon Blanc 12 £B

ENGLISH WINE – *white*

Denbies English Table Wine 12 £C

Lamberhurst Sovereign 13 £B
Appley and sweet melon fruit. Some freshness. Good aperitif and garden party wine.

FRENCH WINE – *red*

Beaujolais-Villages, Duboeuf 12 £C

Beaune 1989 11 £E

Brouilly, Duboeuf 12 £C

**Cabernet Sauvignon, Vin de Pays d'Oc, Val
d'Orbieu 1992 (Somerfield)**   15   £B
Somewhat austere aromatically but soft and smooth and
untroubled by roast foods. Given 45 minutes to breathe this
wine opens up blackcurrant soft, hugely drinkable, uncomplex and marvellous value.

Château de Caraguilhes, Corbières   13   £C

Château de la Liquière, Faugères 1991   13   £C
Very individual wine: chewy with dry-edged fruit, it will come
alive with roast meat and vegetables.

**Château La Chappelle Baradis, Côtes de
Castillon 1990**   10   £C

**Château La Rocheraie, Bordeaux Supérieur
1989**   10   £C

Château Le Clariot, Bordeaux 1992   15   £C
A superb introduction to the classic Bordeaux blend of cabernet sauvignon, cabernet franc and merlot. It is soft and
friendly with just a faint bristle of the punk haircut of the
tannic franc showing through the smoothly berried fruit (some
lovely touches here) and though a dry wine it is rounded to
finish. If Bordeaux could turn out more wines like this unpre-
tentiously drinkable bottle for these sorts of prices then the
Australians would have nightmares.

Château St-Robert, Graves 1987   13   £C
Nice style, nice price. Dry and fruity with a distant hint of the
cedarwood aroma of fine Graves.

Château Talence 1987   12   £D

Châteauneuf-du-Pape, La Solitude   13   £E

Claret NV, Eschenauer (Somerfield) 12 £B

Corbières, Val d'Orbieu 1992 (Somerfield) 14 £B
Lovely soft wine of such easy-going style. Balanced and well polished.

Coteaux de Tricastin (Somerfield) 13 £B
Very pleasant. Not a rough edge in sight.

Côtes de Duras 13 £B
You can pick up some attractive fruit here for not a lot of money.

Côtes de Gascogne Red, Yvon Mau 1992 (Somerfield) 13 £A
Hugely drinkable and cheap. No complexity but very approachable.

Côtes de Roussillon, Jean Jean (Somerfield) 13 £B
Soft, with an echo of burnt fruit to it. Excellent food wine.

Côtes de Roussillon Villages 12 £B

Côtes du Marmandais, Côtes du Rhône 12 £B

Côtes du Rhône, Velliers de l'Enclave des Papes (Somerfield) 13 £B
Very soft and likeable – a teddy bear of a wine. Very sweet to finish. A beginner's Côtes du Rhône.

Côtes du Ventoux (Somerfield) 12 £B

Domaine de Bonserine, Côte-Rotie 1989 11 £F

Domaine de la Solitude, Côtes du Rhône 1992 10 £C

**Domaine de St-Julien, Vin de Pays de l'Hérault,
les Chais Beaucairois**   14   £B
Delicious fruit, most engaging. A good price for a Vin de Pays
de l'Hérault.

**Domaine des Salaises, Saumur Remy Pannier
1992**   13   £C
A cabernet franc/cabernet sauvignon blend (85%/15%)
which is lightly drinkable but comes apart a touch at the
finish. Drink chilled with grilled sausages and roast vegetables. Not stocked in the majority of Somerfield stores.

Hautes Côtes de Beaune 1991   10   £D

La Pelissière, Cahors 1992   11   £C

La Solitude, Châteauneuf-du-Pape   13   £E

Mâcon Rouge, G Desire 1991   12   £C

Médoc   10   £C

Merlot, Domaine de la Magdelaine 1993   12   £B

Minervois, Jean Jean 1992 (Somerfield)   14   £B
Lovely soft wine of such easy-going style. Balanced and well
polished.

**Red Burgundy, Caves de Buxy 1990
(Somerfield)**   11   £C

St-Chinian 1992   12   £B

St-Joseph 1990   14   £E

**St-Tropez Côtes de Provence, Les Caves de
Provence 1993**   14   £C
Chewy, brambly fruit. Very attractive flavours – fun for picnics
and barbecues. Not stocked in the majority of Somerfield stores.

Somerfield Beaujolais 11 £B

Somerfield Bergerac 13 £B

Somerfield Claret 12 £B

Somerfield Claret, Eschenauer 12 £B
Soft and approachable.

Somerfield Oak-Aged Claret, Eschenauer 13 £C
Very attractive proposition for steak and chips.

St-Chinian, Caves de Cucumont 1991 12 £B

**Syrah, Vin de Pays d'Oc, Jean Jean 1993
(Somerfield)** 16 £B
Lovely tannins here, making a soft, dry wine with mulberry/
cassis undertones to its rich berried fruits. Brilliant value. A
benchmark vin de pays for the money. Fruit right. Price right.
Competes seriously with New World wines. Not stocked in
the majority of Somerfield stores.

Vacqueyras Vieux Clocher 1991 15 £C
Cough linctus depth with burnt berried fruit. Delicious –
great with *boeuf bourguignon*.

VdP des Coteaux de l'Ardèche Rouge 1992 14 £B
Excellent, simple plonk for salads and vegetable soups and
hard cheese.

FRENCH WINE – *white and rosé*

Bordeaux Blanc Sec 1992 (Somerfield) 13 £B
Can't complain at this with oysters. Good style fruit/acid
balance.

Chardonnay, Vin de Pays de l'Hérault 1993   12   £C

Château Bastor-Lamontagne 1989 (half)   13   £E

Château Tour de Montredon, Corbières 1993   13   £B

Domaine de la Bouletière Rosé 1993   13   £C

**Domaine de la Tuilerie Chardonnay, Hugh
Ryman 1993**   14   £C
A lot has been said by the wine press on behalf of this wine.
14 says it all for me.

Domaine de Montjoui, Côtes de Thau 1993   12   £B

Domaines Grassa 1993 (Somerfield)   12   £B

Hautes Côtes de Beaune 1992   11   £D

Oak-Aged Bordeaux Blanc, Eschenauer   12   £C

Sancerre, Domaine Brock 1993   13   £D
Better, the '93 vintage, than before. Sancerre is stirring, but
still has to fully awake to the under-£5 New World wines
which compete with it and offer better value.

Somerfield Bordeaux Sauvignon Blanc   12   £B

Somerfield Chablis 1993   12   £D

Vin de Pays des Coteaux de l'Ardèche Blanc   13   £B
Terrific value. Very clean. Good with shellfish.

White Burgundy, G Desire 1992 (Somerfield)   14   £C
Wooded and richly fruited. Loosely integrated only on the
finish, but otherwise a sound food wine (grilled chicken).

GERMAN WINE – *red*

Dornfelder Trocken St Ursula   13   £C

GERMAN WINE – *white*

Baden Dry (Somerfield)   12   £B
This has been an excellent blend in the past, but this batch
lacks a zip on the finish which was always this wine's high
note.

**Bodenheimer Burgweg Juwel Beerenauslese
1989 (half)**   14   £D
With a slice of fruit tart or an apple and a hunk of cheese this
wine is a jewel indeed. Alas, it's over a fiver for that half bottle
which is an angelic size for such a wine but a devilish price
tag, though it is beautifully stratified sipping, with layers of
herby honey-tinged fruit wound around subtle orange and
lime peel flavouring.

Morio Muskat, St Ursula 1992   14   £B
Lovely, face-powdery elderberry fruit on the nose and eau-
de-cologne fruit. Great style for those drinkers who don't
immediately turn up their noses at flowery fruit with a fructose
polish.

**Mosel Riesling Halbtrocken, Rheinberg Kellerei
(Somerfield)**   13   £B
Very attractive, some lemonic cut but not a lot, and a soft fruit.

Niersteiner Spiegelberg 1991   12   £B

Oberemmeler Rosenberg Riesling 1989	10	£E
Pinot Blanc Gallerei	11	£B
Somerfield Trocken	13	£B
St Johanner Abtei Kabinett	12	£B
St Ursula Weinkellerei Bingen Morio Muskat	10	£B
St Ursula Weinkellerei Bingen Rheingau Riesling	11	£B

Trocken G. Bauer (Somerfield)   14   £B
Excellent fruit style to this Baden Dry type wine. Very aromatic and attractive.

HUNGARIAN WINE – *red*

Bull's Blood   13   £B

HUNGARIAN WINE – *white*

Chardonnay (Somerfield)   13   £B
Good fruit up front but not hugely effectively round right to the finish. But for all that very attractive and excellent value.

Chardonnay Villany 1992   11   £B

Gyöngyös Estate Sauvignon Blanc 1993   14   £B
Very ripe pear bouquet with a touch of wet grass – delicious fruit which falls a mite short at the finish, but this is a niggling drawback of little consequence when the wine is drunk with fish.

Gyöngyös Estate Dry Muscat 1992 13 £A
Pleasant aperitif, and less expensive than last year.

ITALIAN WINE – *red*

Bardolino, Fratelli Pasqua 1992 (Somerfield) 12 £B
Light and frivolous. Rather attractive.

Barolo, Castiglione Faletto 1988 11 £D

Cabernet Sauvignon del Veneto 1993 14 £B
Soft, dry-edged cherries.

Caldeo Rosso Vina da Tavola del Veneto, Cielo 12 £A

Chianti Classico Montecchio 1991 13 £C
Sweet finish to the baked, earthy fruit. Not stocked in the
majority of Somerfield stores.

Chianti, Conti Serristori 13 £B

Copertino 1990 14 £C
Mature, rich, raisiny, figgy, with strawberry undertones. A
food wine without a shadow of doubt. Try it with pasta, grilled
meats, mushroom risotto.

Cortenova Grande Friuli Merlot 1992 14 £B
Squashy fruit, very black cherry-like and plummy. Excellent
style, very drinkable.

Lazio Rosso, Casale San Giglio 1993 13 £B
A hairy wine. Bristles on the tongue. Not stocked in the
majority of Somerfield stores.

Librandi Ciro 1990 12 £C

Montereale	13	£B
Riserva di Fizzano, Chianti Classico	13	£E
Rosso de Braganze 1991	13	£C
Salice Salentino 1986 Rich, mature, figgy fruit.	13	£C
Sangiovese di Romagna, Fabbiano 1992 Slightly ham-sandwich nose. Fruitful and very attractive.	14	£B
Valpolicella, Fratelli Pasqua 1992 (Somerfield) Very soft and approachable. Very attractive.	13	£B
Vignetti Casterna Valpolicella Classico 1990	13	£B

ITALIAN WINE – *white*

Caldeo Bianco Vino da Tavola del 1992, Cielo	12	£A
Chardonnay del Piemonte 1993 (Somerfield) Delicious, full-fruited wine. Has balance, style, modernity (without brashness) and lots of flavour and freshness.	15	£C
Colli Lanuvini Vino da Tavola 1992 (**Somerfield**)	11	£B
Lazio Bianco, Pallavicini 1993 Gentle lemon fruit. Excellent value.	14	£B
Montereale 1993	12	£B
Pinot Bianco del Veneto	12	£B

**Pinot Bianco del Veneto, Fratelli Pasqua 1992
(Somerfield)** 13 £B
Creamy fruit/fresh acid – good balance – rather an overall
muted wine – shellfish. Excellent price.

Pinot Grigio del Veneto 12 £B

Soave, Fratelli Pasqua 1992 (Somerfield) 11 £B

Somerfield Frascati, Principe Pallavicini 12 £C

LEBANESE WINE – *red*

Château Musar 1985 15 £E
This wine is in the luxury class as a mouthful of volatile, spicy,
velvety fruit, quite superb with a richly stuffed festival fowl,
and, alas, it is now touching the luxury class in price.

MOLDOVAN WINE – *white*

**Hincesti Moldovan Chardonnay, Hugh Ryman
1993** 15 £B
Great value glug. Lots of fruit and freshness. Tastes of sour
melons and gooseberries. Not stocked in the majority of
Somerfield stores.

NEW ZEALAND WINE – *white*

Nobilo White Cloud 1993   15   £C
Best year yet for this Müller-Thurgau/Sauvignon Blanc
blend. Lots of balanced fruit, fresh and flavoursome. Not
stocked in the majority of Somerfield stores.

PORTUGUESE WINE – *red*

Caves Velhas Garrafeira 1990   13   £D

Dão Reserva 1987   14   £B
Oooh . . . lashings of lovely baked fruit at a give-away price.

Lezíria Tinto, Co-op da Almeirim 1993   15   £B
Raspberry flavours turning dry. Terrific value for a terrific
chunk of fruit.

Quinta da Pancas 1990   13   £D
This is an attractive wine, made by an immensely attractive
man who lives in a fabulously attractive house with wooden
ceilings. His family have been making wine at their *quinta* for
500 years, so he merits our respect – but I do wish this red of
his was at least £1.50 cheaper than it is.

Terras del Rei, Alentejo 1992   14   £B

Terras del Rei, Co-op da Reguengos 1993   14   £B
Herbs, baked earth and plum fruit. Good with food. Not
stocked in the majority of Somerfield stores.

PORTUGUESE WINE – *white and rosé*

Bairrada Branco, Caves Aliança (Somerfield)   15   £B
Echoes of yoghurt to fruit which is also Brazil-nutty. Great
fish wine.

Bairrada Rosé 1992   13   £B
A pleasant summery rosé with an aroma of particular appeal,
appropriately, to rose growers. Excellent price.

SOUTH AFRICAN WINE – *red*

Cape Selection Pinotage 1992   12   £B

SOUTH AFRICAN WINE – *white*

Simonsvlei Chenin Blanc 1993   13   £B
Modern, pear-drop fruit. Might work with fish and chips.

SPANISH WINE – *red*

Berberana Tempranillo, Rioja 1991   15   £C
Lovely vanillary fruit. Light yet full, rich yet very far from
filling.

Don Hugo Tinto NV, Bodegas Vitorianas   14   £B
Great teasing vanilla fruit. Great fun for parties.

Moscatel de Valencia, J Gandia (Somerfield)   16   £B
Great stuff for the money. Honeyed with soft marmalade
undertones.

Navarra Tinto   15   £A
Grown in Spain and bottled in France, this is brilliant value,
full of ripe sunny fruit, plummy and fresh.

Rioja Alemenar 1990   15   £C
The price isn't a lot nowadays for wine of this downright
delicious sort which isn't so hefty and hyped-up with wood
that it begs for food; this Rioja is most enjoyable by itself,
having lightly oaked savoury fruit of a very soft variety (but be
damned if I can tell you which), and I would guess that there's
a good deal of the garnacha grape variety (Spanish grenache)
along with the tempranillo. This makes for a very smooth
landing on the tongue.

Señorio de Agos, Rioja Reserva 1987   12   £C

Señorio de Val 1988   14   £C
Beautiful vanilla, coconut, and banana woodiness and lengthy
blackcurrant fruit. For all that, a dry wine and quite delicious.
But more expensive than last year.

Viña Albali Gran Reserva 1984   13   £C
It's creamy, vanillary, blackcurranty, and rather forceful.
Drink with dishes equally characterful.

Viña Ardanza Rioja Reserva 1985   12   £D

SPANISH WINE – *white*

**Castillo Imperial, Vino da la Tierra Valle de
Monterey 1992**   14   £A
Not a huge amount of fruit but what there is is attractive, it's
fresh and it strikes the palate very pleasantly and crisply with
no clamour or complexity and hits the pocket not at all.
Excellent with salads, fish and parties because it's light and
you can drink lots. Nothing over-baked or half-baked about it.

Don Hugo Blanco NV, Bodegas Vitorianas   15   £B
Banana, vanilla, coconut – terrific breezy fruit just packed
with flavour. Great with fish curries!

Rioja Blanco Mariscol 1988   13   £C

Valencia Dry White   13   £B
Good value for money.

USA WINE – *red*

Glen Ellen Cabernet Sauvignon 1988   13   £C

Glen Ellen Merlot 1991   13   £C
Not yet in the class of '90 which rated 16.

Sebastiani Zinfandel   14   £C
Delicious savoury mélange of dry berries.

Somerfield Californian red   13   £B
Very good value.

USA WINE – *white*

Sebastiani Chardonnay   13   £C

YUGOSLAVIAN WINE – *red*

Pinot Noir, Slovenijavino 1989   14   £B
Very pleasant, dry, chewy wine of no complex fruit or varietal
character, but it's cheering and cherryish and smooth.

SPARKLING WINE/CHAMPAGNE

Chardonnay Brut, Varichon (France)   15   £C
A cool, elegant alternative to champagne. Not stocked in the
majority of Somerfield stores.

Crémant de Bourgogne, Cave de Lugny   13   £D
Excellent structure. Good balance. Very good value.

Lindauer Brut   13   £E
What a pity it's a touch over £7! Still, it's a delicious lemon
sparkler for all that.

Moscato Fizz   13   £A

Prince William Blanc de Blancs   13   £G

Prince William Brut Reserve Champagne   13   £F

Prince William Brut Rosé Champagne   13   £G
Not a bad rosé, as rosés go.

Seppelt Great Western Brut, Australia 16 £C

Superb bargain. A finer fizzer on sale for under a fiver it's difficult to name. Lemony, zingy, zesty. Great style.

Somerfield Cava, Conde de Caralt 15 £C

One of the best value sparklers for under a fiver in Britain. Terrific wine and knocks many a witless champagne speechless.

Touraine Rosé 15 £D

A richly aromatic wine, with a mature, elegantly fruity feel balanced by an assertive acidity (as a good sparkler must be to be refreshing and second-glass inviting), and it is a serious champagne sub: classy, distinguished and extremely good value for money.

Tesco

Tesco has permanent curvature of the spine. It comes from bending over backwards to please customers. Other supermarkets are stiffer backed *and* upper-lipped but Tesco strives uncommonly hard to make its customers' needs the true focus of its activities and it is uncommonly frank when it comes to talking about its business aims. No other supermarket chain, at time of writing, has stores which offer extra-wide car parking spaces set aside for mothers with young children. No other offers a Club card with discounts for frequent shoppers. No other gives customers, disappointed at finding out of stock an item on special offer, the opportunity to buy it at the special offer price when the item is restocked. No supermarket monitors more closely its customers' problems and acts so swiftly to solve them (as when it moved the confectionery shelves away from the checkouts to please parents happy to see temptation taken out of tiny hands), and Tesco has been the first among the big three to move back into the high street after the furious expansion into out of town superstores. These smart new Metro stores don't have car parks, they hardly need them, but they lack for nothing else and even the Tesco management must be surprised at how successful the concept has become.

For the wine buyer, a new aspect of shopping at Tesco is to discover full-time wine advisers patrolling some of the booze shelves – ready, willing, and, most important of all, *able* to help people not just with general wine advice but also ideas on what wine might go with which food. These gentlemen, and they are all just men at the moment (and then only in a few, very large stores), have a background in wine and can conduct

on-the-spot tastings, offer instant advice, and even arrange
the hire of glasses and delivery of cases of wine for parties.
Why should a supermarket go to this trouble? Why should it
incur these extra overheads?

It isn't altruism. It's a simple recognition that making shopping less of a chore encourages customers to spend more time
on the company's premises. And the more time spent, the
more money. Tesco is as acutely sensitive to these basic
principles of exchange trading (i.e. I give you goods, you give
me money) as is a seismograph to an earth tremor. It revels in
making itself meet customers' needs as it revels in making
money. This is something of a tarnished concept these days
after the repulsive excesses of the 1980s but profit on turnover
is oxygen. The manager of a Tesco superstore is a busi-
nessman or woman running a little empire with a £60 million
turnover. The wines this shop sells make money for the store
over and above the incentive they supply in themselves for
people to decide to do their shopping there.

In this respect, Tesco is a brand. It sold, for example,
20,000 cases of their own-label Californian red and white
wine in four weeks last year. Gallo, the most successful and
most sophisticated wine-marketing machine on earth, sold
around 5,000 cases, I would guess, of its various California
wines through Tesco during the same period. From these
statistics arises the thought that no matter how many millions
spent on advertising, no wine importer and marketer – even
Gallo, who spend more than anyone else in their field – can
compete with a brand as powerful as Tesco.

The basis of this brand has changed over the years. The
dirt in *dirt cheap* has been sifted, polished and refined. *Pile it
high sell it cheap* is a slogan the company made its own during
past decades, but in the consumer-conscious 1990s Tesco has
changed to *Pile it where the customer can best reach it and make it*

good value. As part of this change of culture, the store made 800 people redundant this year and I was told that 'A managerial interface had to go. Some people spent a lot of energy trying to prove Head Office wrong. Now we're all trying to shoot in the same direction.' These changes, as far as I can understand them, involve a change from a conveyor-belt mentality, where the individual had a set task, to one of collective responsibility and teamwork, where a group is involved with a set of tasks. I suppose this bears comparison to the new working practices in the car industry which have resulted in more reliable cars being built by less disgruntled workers.

The wine department, however, knows all about teamwork because that's the way manager Stephen Clarke runs it. His team is down-to-earth, resilient and in perfect tune with the contemporary needs of its customers as well as being alert to the possibilities of their future moods. Tesco was the first supermarket to sort itself out over South African wine when Nelson Mandela was freed and apartheid crumbled; it has persisted with the flying winemaker concept over a wide range of wines and continues to invest in this area and, best of all, to produce increasingly tasty and good value wines as a result; and it has developed its mail-order side to good business effect. I was especially pleased by this latter operation because many of the wines on offer represent small parcels of an insufficient case quantity to go into store. This not only allows the wine department to have more fun doing its job, it also allows it to develop wider business relationships; of most relevance to drinkers, of course, is that wines which would otherwise be overlooked, or sold only by the odd specialist wine merchant, can be made available. The store has several outstanding red Corbières from small producers which fall into this category.

But its biggest success, in my view, is in its own-label range.

It is simply the best of any supermarket, with hardly a weakness anywhere. Undoubtedly, huge effort has been exercised by the wine department to concentrate on this area, and it has paid off. Tesco wine customers, more than those of any other retailer, are buying the ultimate in own-label wines across the whole board and the value is outstanding. When wine buyer Janet Lee presented this range to me, over several weeks and several wine-tastings, she made clear how much effort is put into the own-label wines. 'Tuesday morning is the nightmare morning,' she told me. 'A team of six of us taste randomly picked samples of all the own-label wines. We don't take phone calls. We hope we never have to make one.' What happens if a wine doesn't come up to scratch? 'We put an immediate freeze on its distribution. We taste again from another case of the wine and if there is an overall fault, however minor, all the wine is sent straight back to the supplier.' I shudder to think of all those scores of Tesco suppliers who must pray they never get a phone call from one of the store's wine buyers on a Tuesday. I bet they put a ring round Tuesdays on the calendar and try to be out among the vines where they can't be reached.

Tesco's wine department is also acutely conscious of gaps. It shudders worse than an American orthodontist at the thought of gaps. These gaps in a range of wines need not be very large but they must be filled. Take the store's Italian range. No one has a more comprehensive one with the Chiantis, Barolos, Amarone della Valpolicellas, sparkling wines, etc, on sale, but without question there was no Recioto de Soave wine among them. Now a recioto wine is hardly everybody's cup of tea. It is made from specially selected grapes (not just hand-picked but finger-picked), grapes which are then allowed after picking to dry out to near-raisins, which produce concentrated juice of a greatly ripened sweetness, which is

fermented over months and barrel-aged. But a gap is a gap
and so Tesco filled it with an excellent little bottle of perfect
proportions (50cl), perfectly formed sweet fruit, and perfectly
formed price.

For the wine drinker, then, Tesco is heartening news. For
the wine drinker with a car Tesco is often the best news of all.
The company has its own gas stations, its own tanker fleet,
and those of its stores which boast a forecourt are almost
always able also to boast that no one in the vicinity has lower
prices, not even Shell or Esso.

That Tesco customers buy their wines from the country's
largest independent petrol retailer drives yet one more nail
into the coffin of the peculiarly British concept of wine as a
highly specialized and expertly appreciated indulgence available only to the privileged few, rather than a cheap and
delicious everyday joy open to everyone. Tesco is practised at
wielding the hammer which forces these nails home and when
the day comes, as come it will, when alongside all those Tesco
petrol tankers is a fleet of wine tankers delivering cheap but
hugely drinkable *vin ordinaire* or *vino da tavola* to the stores'
wine pumps, from which customers can fill their own con-
tainers at 70 pence a litre red or white (excise duty by this time
having been drastically cut), that coffin will finally be laid to
rest. I will be the first to shovel over the dirt.

ARGENTINIAN WINE – *red*

Uvas del Sol Argentinian Red   13   £B
Hairy and well-muscled with fruit so mouth-filling you need
food to help you chew your way through it.

Uvas del Sol Malbec/Cabernet Sauvignon 1992   13   £B
Good rich fruit.

ARGENTINIAN WINE – *white*

Argentinian White 1991 (Tesco)   11   £A

Uvas del Sol 1992   12   £B

Uvas del Sol Chardonnay 1993   13   £C
Rich, forward fruit. Needs fish soup.

Uvas del Sol Torrontes   15   £C
Floral and fragrant; has body and flavour, also has a freshness.
A lovely aperitif wine.

Uvas del Sol Torrontes 1992   12   £C
Rich aperitif.

AUSTRALIAN WINE – *red*

**Australian Cabernet Sauvignon, SE Australia
(Tesco)**   15   £C
Leathery, slightly exotic aroma. Full, soft, caressing fruit of a
degree of complexity which is surprising at the price.

Australian Shiraz, McLaren Vale (Tesco)   16   £C
Exceptionally, compulsively drinkable bottle. Has vivid fruit,
velvety and rich, and a weightiness which makes it a great
partner for cheese and rich foods.

Barramundi Shiraz/Merlot   14 £C
Vibrant, spicy, fun.

Bin 707 Cabernet Sauvignon, Penfolds 1989   15 £G
You need to be well-heeled to enjoy this wine's embrace and
well-lipped to survive it. Will age beautifully.

Cabernet Sauvignon (Tesco)   13 £C
Lovely cuddly soft fruit. Very tongue-huggable.

Chapel Hill Shiraz 1990   16 £E
A dry-edged, firmly fruited beauty from the McLaren Vale.
Slightly minted fruit, plummy wine, soft tannins, good finish.
Excellent food companion.

Chapel Hill Shiraz 1991   14 £E
Expensive, rich, full, flavoursome.

Coonawarra Cabernet Sauvignon 1992 (Tesco)   16 £D

Delatite Cabernet Merlot, Devil's River 1991   15 £D
Mentholated fruit on the nose leads to perfectly poised fruit
on the tongue. Delicious.

Hardy's Nottage Hill Cabernet Sauvignon 1991   15 £C
Delicious chocolate-coated berried fruit yet young and
spritely in style. Lovely wine.

McLaren Vale Merlot, Ryecroft 1992   16 £D
Brilliantly soft brambly fruit which is never less than seriously
constructed, but equally is very entertaining. Plummy, dry,
brilliant.

Mitchelton Cabernet/Shiraz 1992   14 £C
The fruit plays hide and seek with the acidity to pleasing
effect.

Orlando RF Cabernet Sauvignon 1991   13 £C

**Penfolds Australian Red, Shiraz/Cabernet
Sauvignon, South Australian (Tesco)** 14 £B
A ripe example of vivacious fruit. Brilliant value.

Penfolds Bin 35 Shiraz/Cabernet 1992 15 £C
Ripe, soft fruit with some development ahead of it. Smooth
and palate hugging. Delightful. Attractive berry flavours, well-
structured and balanced. Very drinkable now but a 17/18-
pointer in 3/4 years.

Penfolds Bin 128 Shiraz, Coonawarra 1990 14 £D
Very immediate soft fruit. Delicious with grilled sausages and
meats.

**Penfolds Coonawarra Cabernet Sauvignon
1990** 17 £E
The colour of crushed blackberries, subtle eucalyptus/leather
aroma, sheer satiny acids and velvet-textured fruit – plus a
lovely tannicky finish. Silk and suede texture.

**Pewsey Vale Adelaide Hills Cabernet Sauvignon
1989** 14 £D

**Pewsey Vale Adelaide Hills Cabernet Sauvignon
1990** 12 £D
Put down for a year.

Ryecroft McLaren Vale Belltrees Merlot 1992 14 £C

Shiraz (Tesco) 13 £C
Excellent value, demurely fruity.

St Halletts Old Block Shiraz 1991 17 £E
Beautifully well-mannered Aussie: balanced, dry, ripe with
fruit, yet not too full of itself. This is an outstandingly smooth
velvety shiraz of seductive construction. Only at a few Tescos.

| **Tarrawarra Pinot Noir Yarra Glen 1990** | 13 | £E |

**Tesco Australian Red, Shiraz/Cabernet
Sauvignon, S. Australia**   14   £B
Brilliant value. The shiraz and cabernet sauvignon grape
varieties combine most attractively and offer a tarry aroma,
excellent fruit with some cherry and plum, and a dryness
which is not too spicy or sweaty.

| **Yalumba Shiraz 1991** | 12 | £C |

| **Yarra Glen Pinot Noir 1992 (Tesco)** | 11 | £D |

AUSTRALIAN WINE – *white*

**Australian Chardonnay, South East Australia
(Tesco)**   14   £C
Has oodles of fruit and finishes with a sly wink of lemonic
acidity.

Australian Colombard/Chardonnay (Tesco)   15   £B
Great combo of grapes offering zest, fruit and acid. Lovely
glass of wine. Very tasty.

**Australian Sauvignon Blanc, SE Australia
(Tesco)**   14   £C
Dry yet with lots of friendly fruit which makes the wine
palatable with salads or on its own.

**Australian White, Rhine Riesling, SE Australia
(Tesco)**   14   £B
Flavour and fruit. Ignore the riesling you may know and hate
– this example has the sun in it.

Australian White (Tesco) 12 £B
Twenty years ago this wine would have labelled itself Australian Hock.

Barramundi Semillon/Chardonnay 15 £C
Rich, fruit-salad nose. Lots of pineapple acidity and great, swinging melon/mango fruit. Smashing wine to let the heart soar.

Brown Brothers Dry Muscat 1992 13 £C

Brown Brothers Dry Muscat 1993 10 £C

Brown Brothers Late-Picked Muscat 1992 13 £D
Aperitif. Wine of some style.

Brown Brothers Late-Picked Muscat 1993 14 £D
Delicious sweet aperitif. Floral and summery.

Cape Mentelle Semillon/Sauvignon Blanc 1993 15 £E
Lush touches of green grass in the melon and citric fruit. Delicious, superb.

Chardonnay (Tesco) 12 £C

Chardonnay Tahbilk Marsanne 14 £D
A rich yet fresh-to-finish concoction for grilled chicken and chilli pepper. Good with Oriental food, especially Indonesian or Thai.

Fumé Blanc, Hunter Valley, Rosemount 1993 12 £D

Hardy's Australian Rhine Riesling, South Australia (Tesco) 14 £B
Elegant, ripe fruit with a touch of acidic butteriness. Good sound stuff. Brilliant with grilled fish.

Hardy's Nottage Hill Chardonnay   14 £C
Not settled yet but give it a few weeks. It's a very stylish wine
with fruit and perfectly evolved acid.

**International Winemaker Oaked Semillon/Sauvignon
Blanc 1992 (Tesco)**   14 £C
Big woody fruit of depth. Great with grilled chicken.

**International Winemaker Semillon/Sauvignon Blanc
1992, McLaren Vale**   14 £C
Delicious woody nose – a white Graves in all but name but
with a lush touch. Excellent food wine.

Jabiru Sauvignon Blanc 1993   13 £C
Not a totally convincing wine. But then nor is the s.b. grape
grown in Australia. Topical fish food label. Very minerally
and fresh. To drink with shellfish and oily fish.

Lindemans Padthaway Chardonnay 1991   14 £E
Lush woody aromas with distant echoes of butterscotch. The
fruit reveals this olfactory blueprint in the flesh, but with
additional weight of sour melon.

Lindemans Padthaway Chardonnay 1992   15 £E
A somewhat quiet chardonnay for an Aussie, but don't mis-
take the purity of the fruit or the keenness of purpose.

**McLaren Vale Chardonnay, Ryecroft 1992
(Tesco)**   16 £D
Elegant, classy, better than all the white burgundies I've
tasted for the money. Has delicious integration of fruit and
acid and has an ineffable touch of haughtiness.

Mitchelton Muscat Late-Picked, Victoria 1992   14 £C
Try it as an aperitif with hard cheese and fruit.

**Mitchelton Semillon/Chardonnay Victoria
1993**   13.5 £C

Nottage Hill Chardonnay 1992   16 £C
Woody and ripe, full yet not aggressive. Good value for a wine
with complex layers of fruit, balanced personality and ver-
satility with food.

Old Triangle Semillon/Chardonnay 1992   15 £C
Terrific style and wonderful citric acid. Vivid, delicious, great
fruit. A pick-me-up of superb style.

Penfolds Koonunga Hill Chardonnay 1992   14 £C
Full lush fruit plus a ticklish dollop of lemon zest. Delicious,
but getting pricey near a fiver.

Penfolds Koonunga Hill Chardonnay 1993   14 £C
Still one of the best-branded white wines around. Has musk,
melon, pineapple and peach.

Penfolds Semillon/Chardonnay 1993   14 £C
Excellent recipe: fruit, acid, wood, but will integrate and
improve mightily over the next 1/2 years.

Pewsey Vale Riesling 1993   13 £C
Delicious aperitif. Not typical.

Preece Chardonnay 1992   15 £D
Delicious classy wine with bags of flavour. Lovely wood and
soft fruit integration plus a touch of lemon.

Rosemount Roxburgh Chardonnay 1991   16 £G
Fabulous. Has the most exquisite marriage of wood and fruit.
Offers flavour, depth, breadth and length. A distinguished
wine.

Roxburgh Chardonnay 1991   17   £G
Magnificent wood/fruit aroma of high quality – better than
many Pulignys. Superb, oily fruit; great balance; delicious,
concentrated.

Sauvignon Blanc (Tesco)   13   £C

Semillon (Tesco)   12   £B

St Halletts Semillon/Sauvignon Blanc   16   £D
Superb style and flavour to the fruit, plus a lovely zest of acid.
Very elegant.

Western Australian Chenin Blanc 1992 (Tesco)   16   £C
'Bags of complexity', said the Tesco buyer and this is true.
But bags of fruit is the immediate impact and you struggle
under a welter of exotic fruits, rich, buttery and finished with
lime and pineapple. Delicious.

Wildflower Ridge Chenin Blanc, Houghton,
Swan Valley 1993   13   £C
Seafood or nothing.

Yalumba Museum Show Reserve Rutherglen
Muscat (half)   14   £D
Considering you get cough mixture, floor polish, oranges,
cherries and herbal honey in your glass, the fact that the stuff
in the glass has cost you £2.30 is probably a fair price. But it is
an acquired taste – and strictly for deep rich desserts and deep
rich pockets. (Adventurous souls, seeking perfumed feet,
could try polishing up the floorboards with it.)

AUSTRIAN WINE – *red*

Winzerhaus Blauer Zweigelt 1992	14	£C

AUSTRIAN WINE – *white*

Austrian Dry White   14   £B
Lovely pear, apple and peach fruit and controlled acidity.
Quite delicious and superb value for money.

Winzerhaus Grüner Veltliner 1993   15   £B

Winzerhaus Pinot Blanc 1992   12   £B

BULGARIAN WINE – *red*

Bulgarian Country Red (Tesco)   13   £A

Bulgarian Cabernet Sauvignon Reserve 1988
(Tesco)   15   £B
More bite than most and less lightweight cherryish fruit. Not
a powerful wine, or an especially tannic or dry one, but a
lovely lushly fruity cabernet at a good price.

Cabernet Sauvignon Reserve (Tesco)   15   £B
Puts those French reds to shame! Aromatic, richly fruity and
soft to finish. Excellent cheese wine.

BULGARIAN WINE – *white*

Bear Ridge Bulgarian White 1993   13   £B
Sound, fruity, drinkable, technically correct. But wears a
bowler hat rather than a baseball cap.

Bulgarian Chardonnay Reserve 1990 (Tesco)   14   £B
Woody as a white Rioja. Rich fruit, slightly sour note on the
finish. Good with food.

Bulgarian Country White (Tesco)   12   £A

Chardonnay Reserve 1990 (Tesco)   12   £B
Under three quid bargain.

CHILEAN WINE – *red*

Chilean Cabernet Sauvignon (Tesco)   14   £B
A lot of deep fruit yet soft and chocolate finished.

Chilean Red (Tesco)   15   £B
Undistinguished aromatically but serious rich fruitiness of the
blackcurrant variety (from the cabernet sauvignon in the
blend) and a touch of dry tannicity (courtesy of the malbec).
Very well-priced.

Cousino Macul Merlot 1989   14   £C

Merlot (Tesco)   13   £C
Attractive rich savoury merlot.

Montes Alpha, Cabernet Sauvignon 1988   14   £E

Santa Rita Merlot, Maipo (Tesco) 14 £C
Delicious – soft and serious at one and the same time. Rich
fruit firmly balanced.

Undurraga Pinot Noir, Maipo 1990 12 £C
How on earth to rate a wine like this? It has some semblance
of style and richness and length but is it really a truly authentic
tasting pinot? Yes and no.

CHILEAN WINE – *white*

Chilean Chardonnay Semillon (Tesco) 14 £C
Not as rich or forward as an Oz specimen but quite stylish
with good fruit and acid balance.

Chilean Sauvignon Blanc (Tesco) 14 £C
Character, style, real class. Fruit and freshness. Flavour.
Great stuff.

Chilean White (Tesco) 16 £B
Was £3.29 – now decidedly cheaper. As good if not better (not
only because of the price but also the concentration of fruit)
than many a fancy Sancerre. Freshness, flavour, bite – great
stuff! Open any time you please wine. Bargain.

Cuvée Ryman-Montes Chardonnay 1993 10 £C
Hugh, the winged Bordeaux-based Englishman, always
makes wines which immediately impact on the nose and this
wine is no exception. However, its hugely inviting aroma of
ripe melon and fresh peach is all foreplay; I failed to reach a
climax worth rating more than 10 points at this price.

Sauvignon Blanc Santa Rita 1991 14 £B

CYPRIOT WINE – *red*

Keo Othello   4   £B
If Shakespeare is to be plundered then 'much ado about nothing' is a neater name for this wine.

CYPRIOT WINE – *white*

Keo Aphrodite Dry White   11   £B
Ye Goddess!

ENGLISH WINE – *white*

English Table Wine NV   13   £B

FRENCH WINE – *red*

Bordeaux Château Michelet (Box) (2 litres)   11   £E

Bourgeuil, La Huralaie, Caslot-Galbrun 1992   15   £C
Black cherries and raspberries richly mixed, very dry, very chunky. Superb food wine. Coal-chewy, dark, and dank to taste, it is hard and tannic, and it needs a little time to soften. Could be brilliant by the time this book is published.

Burgundy, Henri de Bahezre (Tesco)   12   £C

Cabernet Sauvignon Haute Vallée de l'Aude 13 £B
Excellent value for the family get-together with a roast on the table.

Cahors (Tesco) 13 £B
Good.

Chardonnay Serge Dubois, Vin de Pays d'Oc 13 £C
Subtle, woody aroma with a gentle richness to the fruit. Classy in feel but not ultimately in the finish. Remarkable aperitif. Available through Tesco mail order only.

Château Bois Galant Médoc 1989 15.5 £C
Mature, full-flavoured, soft (yet with dry tannins), this is a perfect mid-weight claret, good enough to satisfy any drinker at the price.

Château Cantemerle Haut-Médoc 1987 13 £F

Château d'Arsac Haut-Médoc 1991 11 £G

Château de Goelane 1992 12 £D
Weak finish to the performance lets it down a touch.

Château des Gondats 1992 13 £D
Serious tannins. Must have food, roast or raw.

Château du Bluizard Beaujolais Villages 1992 10 £C

Château Flamand Bellevue Bordeaux 1991 12 £C
(available by the case of 12 bottles)

Château Guillon Graves Rouge 1992 12 £C

**Château Léon Premières Côtes de Bordeaux
1987** 12 £C

Château les Gravières St-Emilion 1990 13 £E

Château les Valentines Bergerac 1984   14 £C
Very dry and still developing flavour in bottle (will improve
2/3 years). Has a meaty edge to a blackberry edge which is
rather serious.

Château Marquis-de-Terme Margaux 1988   13 £E
There is a touch of beefiness about this grand Margaux but I
would prefer to wait a few years before I met it and it and I
had softened.

Château Michelet, Bordeaux (2 litres)   14 £E
A hugely approachable, soft, friendly claret. Very drinkable
and very smooth.

Château Patache d'Aux, Cru Grand Bourgeois
1991   15.5 £D
Splendid little claret with depth of fruit and tannins, and of
surprising class. Great roast lamb wine. Might be even better
if you put it down for three years.

Château Pigoudet, Coteaux d'Aix en Provence
1989   15 £C
Touches of chocolate to the soft berries. A Rhône wine-type
wine without the earthiness.

Château St-Georges St-Emilion 1989   17 £G
A lot of dosh but a lot of posh. Has classic tannin/fruit
balance, with echoes of cedarwood, tobacco and dark
chocolate. Lovely wine.

Château St-Nicholas, Fronsac 1987   10 £D

Château Toutigeac 1992   14 £C
Good, rich, balanced, well-structured.

Château Vieux Castel Robin, St-Emilion   15 £D
Soft and very thick with such accessible fruit you can eat it . . .
I mean drink it . . . with a spoon.

Château Vignolles Peyroulet, Graves 1989   13 £D
(available by the case of 12 bottles)

**Châteauneuf-du-Pape, Les Arnevels, Quiot
1991**   14 £E
Smooth and fruity as ever.

**Châteauneuf-du-Pape, Les Arnevels, Quiot
1992**   12 £E
Touch flabby.

Chinon, Baronnies Madeleine 1990   13 £D
I think this wine is going through a closed stage and in 1/2
years time it will be much tastier.

Claret (Tesco)   14 £B
Lovely soft yet dry example of the genre. Excellent value for a
superbly approachable bottle.

Clos de Chenoves, Bourgogne Rouge, Buxy   13 £D

Côtes de Duras 1993   10 £B

Cotes de Duras (Tesco)   13 £B
Soft with faintly savoury fruit. Very good value.

Côtes de Provence (Tesco)   13 £B
Relatively smooth rustic plonk.

Côtes de Roussillon Rouge (Tesco)   12.5 £B

Côtes du Frontonnais 1990   13 £B

Côtes du Rhône (Tesco)   12 £B
Easy going to the point of absurdity.

Côtes du Rhône Villages 1993   11   £C

Crozes-Hermitage, Domaine Cécile Mussel
1992   11   £D

Domaine Cazelles-Verdier, Minervois 1990   15   £C
Dry, smoky, fruity, rich. A lovely wine. Available through
Tesco mail order only.

Domaine de Conroy, Brouilly, St-Charles 1991   13   £D
Not a bad example, considering how feeble much of the real
thing is nowadays.

Domaine de la Source, Syrah 1992 (Tesco)   14   £B
Tasty, handsome, has hidden riches.

Domaine de Lanestousse Madiran 1989   15   £C
A fascinating red Madiran. This contains cabernet franc and
tannat grapes in which the lead-pencil fruit of the former
combined with the leathery tannins of the latter combine
brilliantly. I have smelt gravies with less of a meaty aroma.
The fruit is so rich and nutty, with a touch of leather to soften
things down, that it's almost edible. I reckon it's better to open
the wine an hour or so before drinking to soften it and bring
out the raspberry edge of the fruit. It's a highly organized
wine, good enough for posh dinner tables with its serious
demeanour. Has great rustic charm. An excellent big wine
with real individuality, flair and flavour. Has a gamey, savoury
fruit, delicious hairy tannins and will accompany roast grouse
magnificently.

Domaine de Prebayon, Côtes du Rhône Villages
1992   13   £C
Grenache and syrah in soft cahoots.

Domaine de Trillol, Corbières 1989   14   £C
Lively and bright with heavy hint of smoker's cough to the
fruit. Available through Tesco mail order only.

**Domaine des Baumelles, Côtes du Luberon
1993**   12   £C

Domaine du Petit Chêne, Corbières 1990   14   £C
Attractive fruit of some depth. Not especially complex. Very
deep fruit with a touch of spice. Dry. Available through Tesco
mail order only – two bottles per case.

Domaine les Hauts des Chambert, Cahors 1988   13   £D

Domaine Maurel Fonsalade, St-Chinian 1990   13   £C

Dorgan, Vin de Pays de l'Aude (Tesco)   13   £B
Has a few rough edges which a good bowl of pasta would soon
smooth out.

**Escoubes Rouge, Vin de Pays de l'Aude, Grassa
(Tesco)**   14   £B
Brilliant value for sheer pizzazz of the fruit.

**French Cabernet Sauvignon, Vin de Pays de la
Haute Vallée de l'Aude (Tesco)**   12   £B
Anyone who says they find cabernet sauvignon too austere will
find a friend in this wine.

French Country Red (Tesco) (1 litre)   13   £C

Fronton, Côtes du Frontonnais 1991   13   £B
Nice baked fruit.

Gévrey Chambertin Marchand 1991   13   £F
Good but pricey.

Grand Carat, Vin de Pays du Comte Tolosan
1993   12   £B

Grenache, Vin de Pays d'Oc 1993 (Tesco)   12   £B

Hautes Côtes de Nuits, Caves des Hautes Côtes
1992   12   £C

Hautes Côtes du Beaune, Caves des Hautes
Côtes 1990   13   £D
A good solid bottle.

International Winemaker Syrah Vin de Pays
d'Oc 1992 (Tesco)   13   £C
Big, dry, earthy fruit of some structure. Excellent food wine.

La Vieille Ferme, Côtes du Rhône 1992   13.5   £C
Highly drinkable, soft and fruity. Exciting? No. But it is all
there.

Les Domaines Buzet, Domaine de la Croix 1989
(Tesco)   13   £C
Tannins in evidence, herby and baked, and maybe it will get
even better over the next 2/3 years.

Les Domaines Château St-Louis La Perdrix
1990 (Tesco)   13   £C
Faint chocolate echoes in dry, gripping fruit.

Les Domaines de Beaufort, Minervois 1992
(Tesco)   13   £B
Some serious wine here. Good with roast vegetables.

Les Domaines des Baumelles, Côtes du
Luberon 1992 (Tesco)   13   £C
Good fruit, softly expressed.

Les Domaines Marmandais, Domaine Beaulieu St-Saveur 1990 (Tesco) 12 £B

Les Forts de Latour, Pauillac 1986 10 £H

Margaux 1990 (Tesco) 16 £E
Gorgeous soft tannins holding up the structure of an immensely (and immediately) drinkable, blackcurrant and serious claret. A terrific roast food wine for elegant dinner parties.

Médoc (Tesco) 12 £C

Merlot, Vin de Pays de la Haute Vallée de l'Aude (Tesco) 13 £C
Don't put pepper on your sausages. Drink this wine with them instead.

Minervois (Tesco) 13 £B
Pleasant cherry fruit.

Morgon, Arthur Barolet 1992 10 £D
Rather dull for a fiver.

Organic Red, Château Vieux Gabiran 1990 (Tesco) 14 £C
Soft, rich fruit, deep and savoury edged. As good an organic red as I've tasted, hic . . . I mean tested.

Pauillac 1989 (Tesco) 10 £D

Pavillon Rouge du Château Margaux 1990 11 £G

Red Graves (Tesco) 13 £C
Some good fruit on offer with a flourish on the finish.

Reserve du Révérend Corbières Rouge 1990   15   £C
Delicious, savoury fruit of depth and style. Burnt fruit, very
dry, herbs and black cherries. Brilliant for roasts. Available
through Tesco mail order only.

Saumur 1991   15   £C
Typical lead pencil, tile and clay, raspberriness. Dry, full of
attractive fruit, and brilliant with barbecued food.

Saumur Rouge 1992   13   £C

St-Emilion (Tesco)   13   £C
Attractive soft fruit finish to a stalwart British favourite.

St-Joseph, Verrier 1989   15   £D
Buy it to pour from a great height into a big jug. Leave it to
aerate for 2 hours. Then . . . bam! Let it coat the tongue with
brambly fruit.

Tesco Beaujolais   13   £C
Light and fruity the label says and this is no lie.

Tesco Corbières   14   £B
Bargain fruity fulfilment.

Tesco Fitou   14   £B
An aromatic, richly-endowed, smooth bottle of fruit.

Tesco Grenache   14   £B
Outstanding value for a fruity wine of real personality. Very
good value for pasta parties.

Vin de Pays de Côtes du Tarn (Tesco)   14   £B
Delicious, modern, soft fruit. Fresh finish. Slightly nutty. Very
good value.

Vin de Pays de l'Aude Rouge (Tesco)   13   £B
Has a pleasing lilt to its voice which recalls sweet cherry.

Vin de Pays de la Cité de Carcassonne (Tesco)   13.5   £B
Lots of flavour here.

Vin de Pays de la Gironde (Tesco)   10   £B

Vin de Pays des Côtes de Gascogne Rouge, Yvon Mau (Tesco)   13   £B
Some bouncey fruit in evidence here.

Vin de Pays des Côtes de Perignan (Tesco)   14   £B
Worth buying just for the Darling Grapes of September label.

Vintage Claret 1990 (Tesco)   13   £C
This is a soft fruity wine with some attractive maturity, but the store's Claret is better value.

FRENCH WINE – *white and rosé*

Alsace Gewürztraminer 1992 (Tesco)   10   £D

Alsace Pinot Blanc (Tesco)   15   £C
The future of Alsatian wine at the lower end of the market (under £4) has to be with non-vintage blends like this. This has muted apricot and greengage fruit admirably well-balanced. A very enjoyable bottle.

Anjou Blanc (Tesco)   13   £B
Good value. Basic fruit.

Beaujolais Blanc 1993   10   £C

Blayais   10   £B

Bordeaux Blanc de Blancs   13   £B

Bordeaux Blanc (Tesco)   15   £B
Brilliant cheapie with lemon, lime and melon fruit softly and
subtly put together.

Bordeaux Rosé (Tesco)   13.5   £C
Excellent little wine for flirting with.

**Cabernet de Saumur, Caves des Vignerons de
Saumur (Tesco)**   14   £B
A good, firm rosé with dryish cherry and raspberry fruit.

**Cépage Terret, Vin de Pays de l'Hérault, Delta
Domaines 1993**   13   £B
If you want the classic earthy fruit of the terret grape, here it is.

Chablis 1992 (Tesco)   12   £D

**Chablis Premier Cru, Montmain, La Chablisienne
1991**   13   £E

**Chardonnay, Domaine des Fontaines, Vin de
Pays d'Oc (Tesco) (2 litre)**   14   £E
Box clever! Brilliant little well-made richly fruited wine of
style and class. Excellent fish wine.

Chardonnay, Vin de Pays d'Oc (Tesco)   11   £B

Chasan 1991, International Winemaker Series   12   £B
Some pleasant melon fruit to this vin de pays d'Oc.

Château de Carles Sauternes 1990   13   £F
A rich dessert wine, or aperitif if you will (and I will with
pleasure, thank you) which I find somewhat expensive. It
would repay cellaring – for a decade.

**Château La Forêt-St-Hilaire,
Entre-Deux-Mers** 14 £C
A touch of greater complexity here, for more money than your average vin de pays and so better with food.

**Château Laquirou, La Clape, Coteaux de
Languedoc Blanc 1991** 11 £C
Dull, doesn't live in the mouth. Will work with grilled fish only. Available through Tesco mail order only.

Château Liot Sauternes (half) 12 £D

Château Magneau, Graves 1990 14 £F
A hugely elegant, richly wooded wine of taste, flair and flavour. Marvellous with grilled fish with a complex sauce.

Château Malagar, Bordeaux Blanc 1993 14 £C

**Château St-Louis la Perdrix, Costières de Nîmes
1990** 12 £C

**Chenin Blanc, Vin de Pays du Jardin de la France
(Tesco)** 15 £B
Has a delicious off-dry honey finish to a crisply conceived wine.

Côtes de Provence (Tesco) 11 £B

Côtes de Roussillon (Tesco) 12 £B
Some pleasant fruit to this.

Côtes du Rhône Blanc 1992 13 £C
Good sound stuff.

Cuvée Reserve Côtes du Rhône Blanc (Tesco) 15 £C
Tesco takes over the 100 per cent bourboulenc (grape variety) crown from Safeway. This is an unusual wine, unusually beautifully balanced, unusually good value for a Rhône white,

and, unusual of all, it's on sale in Britain. Undoubtedly, the winemaker's New World experience has helped, for this is a modern wine, without being horribly tarty and obviously fruity, and very stylish with aroma, finish and class. Great with trout or salmon.

Domaine de la Jalousie, Vin de Pays des Côtes de Gascogne, Late Harvest 1991   11   £D

Domaine de la Done Rosé Syrah 1993   13.5   £B
Full fruited rosé without flabbiness.

Domaine de la Huperie, Muscadet de Sèvres et Maine Sur Lie 1992   12   £C
Basically, I feel muscadet is too expensive for the level of fruit on offer. Nuragus from Italy is so much better value.

Domaine de la Jalousie Chardonnay, Vin de Pays des Côtes de Gascogne 1992   13   £C

Domaine de la Jalousie Sauvignon Blanc 1992   14   £C
Fruit/flower aroma. Good rich fruit – plummy and peary. Excellent.

Domaine St-Alain, Vin de Pays des Côtes du Tarn 1993 (Tesco)   14   £B
Excellent fruit (analogous to nothing yet grown). Mysteriously delicious.

Domaine St-James Viognier, Vin de Pays d'Oc 1992   15   £C
The wine has dried apricot and ripe peach fruit, a subtle citric echo in the finish, and is a thoroughly well-balanced specimen. The structure is sound, and it is fresh and very cleanly made. The only odd thing about the wine is the back label which makes the claim that it comes from the Rhône when they mean the Aude. Still, it's well worth £4.99 and its rating of 15 points.

**Domaine St-Pierre Chardonnay, Vin de Pays
d'Oc 1992**   13 £C

**Domaine Saubagnère, Vin de Pays des Côtes de
Gascogne 1992 (Tesco)**   14 £C
A smooth, non-hysteric Côtes de Gascogne with fruit and
flavour.

Dorgan White, Vin de Pays de l'Aude   13 £B

**Dry Muscat, Vin de Pays des Pyrénées-
Orientales 1993**   11 £B

Entre-Deux-Mers (Tesco)   15 £B
Vividly fruity yet in the end a finely balanced specimen. Good
with fish or a great quaffing wine. Perfect price.

**Escoubes, Vin de Pays des Côtes de Gascogne,
Grassa (Tesco)**   14 £B
A delicious pineapple wine with firm fruit lurking behind a
fresh face.

Floc de Gascogne   14 £D
Made from grape juice with armagnac tossed in to bring it up
to 17%. A simple peasant recipe and I enjoy its rusticity as a
pick-me-up (or should I say as a pull-me-down?) after a hard
day's wine-tasting. The view of my household is that it is
about as toothsome a proposition as old rugby boots pickled in
treacle.

French Chardonnay, Vin de Pays d'Oc (Tesco)   13 £C

**French Country Wine, Vin de Pays des Côtes
de Gascogne (Tesco) (1 litre)**   14 £C
Delicious. Breezy and fruity and very good value.

French Semillon (Tesco)   14 £B
Good value, well-fruited, well-made.

Gaston Dorleans Vouvray Demi-Sec 1992   8 £C
8 points which is remarkable since I actually see little point at
all in the wine. It's not sweet enough for fruit, oily enough for
fish and has insufficient complexity to be good for anything
else.

Graves (Tesco)   15 £C
A richly-edged wine of good fruit, with maturity lurking in the
background. Has some class for the money. Excellent fish
wine.

**Grenache Blanc, Vin de Pays de l'Hérault
(Tesco)**   12 £B

**International Winemakers Blanc de Noirs/Cabernet
Sauvignon Rosé**   14 £B
A vin de pays de l'Aude of unusual frivolity and roseate
deliciousness.

Le Porcii Chardonnay 1992   14 £D
Elegant, quiet, very attractive.

**Les Domaines de la Source Muscat 1992
(Tesco)**   15 £C
Dry yet has rich muscat overtones. Try it with scallops, monk-
fish, sole – with any amount of spicy sauce.

Mâcon Blanc Villages 1993 (Tesco)   12 £C

Monbazillac (Tesco)   12 £C

Montagny Premier Cru Oak-Aged, Buxy 1991   12 £D

Muscadet de Sèvres et Maine 13 £B

Don't think of it as muscadet. Think of it as very pleasant, fruity, uncomplicated wine.

Muscadet Sur Lie, Domaine de la Huperie 1992 (Tesco) 11 £C

Muscat Cuvée José Sala (Tesco) 15 £C

Toffee-nosed and less than £4? Aristocratic sweetness never came so cheap.

Muscat de Rivesalte (half) 14 £B

A light pud wine with soft and subtle marmalade undertones. Excellent with grapes and hard cheese to make a complete meal. Delightful with hard fruit tarts also honey with a raisin undertone.

Muscat de Rivesalte, Les Abeilles 15 £D

Refined, elegant, marmalade fruit. Rather hoity-toity in fact and perhaps too delicate to tackle rich desserts, but fruit tarts would be okay.

Organic White, Entre-Deux-Mers, Château Vieux Gabiran 1992 (Tesco) 13 £C

I'm not entirely convinced this is worth £1 more than the store's excellent VdP des Côtes de Gascogne.

Pouilly-Fumé, Cuvée Jules 1993 9 £D

Premières Côtes de Bordeaux (Tesco) 11 £B

Riesling (Tesco) 14 £B

True varietal vivacity of fruit and acid. Brilliant oyster wine.

Sancerre Alphonse Mellot 1993 (Tesco) 12 £D

Expensive for what the New World, with the same grape (sauvignon blanc), is doing better.

Saumur Blanc, Caves des Vignerons de Saumur
1991 (Tesco)   14   £B
Touch of grassy, buttery fruit and a distant echo of honey in it
– yet this is a very dry wine for all that.

Sauvignon Blanc (Tesco)   13   £B
Has some richness of tone but is it quite as crisp as it might be?

St-Romain, Arthur Barolet 1993   13   £D
This has taste. It has fruit. It also has a price tag.

St-Véran Les Monts, Co-op Prisse 1992   13   £D

Touraine Sauvignon (Tesco)   13   £B
Delicious, fresh, gooseberry aroma but then it fails to punch
home the fruit on the finish. Quiet, understated fruit. Not
shrieking with grassy overtones.

VdP de la Dordogne Co-op Sigoules (Tesco)   15   £B
A modern, melony wine without being brash. Lots of fruit and
flavour and balancing fresh acidity. Superbly drinkable.

Vin de Pays des Côtes du Tarn   11   £B

Vintage Blend Chardonnay Aligoté 1992   15   £B
Excellent, a real bargain. Classy aroma. Excellent structure to
the fruit, rich, not cloying. Fresh fish wine par excellence.

Vouvray (Tesco)   14   £B
Touch of sweet fruit in an off-dry wine of great appeal.
Supremely nice wine for the hock drinker looking for more
finesse and food compatibility.

GERMAN WINE – *red*

Baden Pinot Noir 1990   12   £C
Has a cough-sweet quality you may find useful in darkest
mid-winter.

GERMAN WINE – *white*

Baden Dry (Tesco)   14   £B
There is a faint echo of sticky toffee in this dry fish 'n' chips
wine. Good clean drinking.

Bereich Johannisberg Riesling, Krayer 1991   12   £C

**Bereich Johannisberg Riesling, QbA Krayer
1992**   12   £C

Bernkasteler Kurfurstlay (Tesco)   13   £B

**Binger Scharlachberg Medium Dry Riesling
Kabinett Villa Sachsen 1991**   11   £D

Dry Country German Wine (Tesco) (1 litre)   13   £C

Dry Hock (Tesco)   13   £B
Fresh and straightforward and good with fish dishes.

Grans Fassian, Riesling Trocken 1991   12   £D
Some elegance here but at a price. I would drink this wine in
5 years time.

Hock (Tesco)   11   £A

Kreuznacher Riesling Spätlese, Anheuser 1991   12   £C
Nice fruit. Needs a couple more years to develop. Everything
my wife hates in a German wine. But in 5 years?

Morio Muskat (Tesco)   15   £B
A brilliant thirst-quenching guzzle with a marzipan dry finish
to its fruit. Great solvent for end of the day blues.

Niersteiner Gutes Domtal (Tesco)   12   £B

Piesporter Treppchen Riesling Kabinett 1991   12   £C

**Rauenthaler Rothenberg Riesling Kabinett,
Diefenhardt** 1989   14   £C
Remarkable value for the year with the petal fruit beginning to
emerge. Nice aperitif now but in 3–4 years will be even better.

Rheinpfalz Dry Riesling   12   £B

**Riesling Kabinett Braunerberger Kurfürstlag,
Paulinshof** 1992   13   £D
A fruity Moselle.

Ruppertsberger Hohenberg Riesling Kabinett
1989   13   £D
This is a gentle riesling, well-mannered and dry (although it is
officially a halb-trocken), but it is only beginning to shrug off
its youth and approach impressive middle-age. I'd lay it down
for another 3–4 years.

Scharzhofberger Van Volxem 1990   15   £C
An elegant Moselle and a truly individual piece of work: full of
fruit yet never sweet with gently assertive acidity, it has some
finesse granted it by virtue of the kerosene quality showing
through. You could lay it down for years and it would develop.
A delicious wine to drink by itself or to bring smoked salmon
to life.

Silvaner (Tesco) 12 £B

Slight muted quality to the fruit. Wants some freshness to it and assertiveness.

St Johanner Abtei Kabinett (Tesco) 11 £B

St Johanner Abtei Spätlese (Tesco) 12 £B

Steinweiler Kloster Liebfrauenberg Auslese (Tesco) 12 £C

Steinweiler Kloster Liebfrauenberg Kabinett (Tesco) 10 £B

Steinweiler Kloster Liebfrauenberg Spätlese (Tesco) 11 £C

Stettener Stein, Müller Thurgau 10 £C

Tesco Gewürztraminer 10 £C

It should be a quid less for the simplicity of the style, but I'd raise no objection to it as a quick snifter to tickle the taste buds.

Tesco Müller Thurgau 12 £B

Tesco Riesling Mosel 13 £B

A simple, pretty aperitif in the lightweight Moselle tradition.

Tesco Weissburgunder 13 £C

Delicious earthy fruit bouquet, dry fruit of a vague melon character and a clean finish. Tough competition at £3.99. Good with fish dishes and especially an unspicy fish soup.

Weissburgunder Dry White Wine 11 £B

GREEK WINE – *red*

Nemea 1991   11   £C

GREEK WINE – *white*

Kretikos 1991   12   £C

HUNGARIAN WINE – *red*

Merlot/Cabernet Sauvignon   10   £C

HUNGARIAN WINE – *white*

Hungarian Chardonnay (Tesco)   10   £B

Oreghegyi Chardonnay   10   £C

Tokaji Aszu, 5 Puttonyos (50cl)   16   £D
Brilliant almond and orange marmalade wine with a gorgeous
honey polish to the fruit. Wonderful with soft fruits.

ITALIAN WINE – *red*

Barbaresco Viareggio   11   £D

| **Barolo, Giacosa Fratelli 1988/90** | 12 | £D |

| **Casale Giglio Shiraz** | 15 | £B |

Well, well! The Italians outfruit the Aussies. This is a soft, subtly, spicy, plum and blackcurrant wine with lots of personality. Has smoothness of considerable charm. Has an Italian feel in spite of its Aussie pretensions.

| **Chianti 1992 (Tesco)** | 13 | £B |

| **Chianti Classico 1991 (Tesco)** | 13 | £C |

| **Chianti Classico Riserva 1989 (Tesco)** | 14 | £D |

Excellent.

| **Chianti Colli Senesi 1992 (Tesco)** | 14 | £C |

Soft, delicious, lap-uppable Chianti.

| **Chianti Rufina Grati 1990 (Tesco)** | 13 | £C |

| **Giacosa Fratelli Barolo 1988** | 13 | £D |

| **Merlot del Piave (Tesco)** | 12 | £B |

| **Monica di Sardegna (Tesco)** | 14 | £B |

Dry, cherryish fruit with a lovely rounded feel in the mouth, like gentle rubbery cough syrup. Sounds horrific? Not a bit of it.

| **Montepulciano d'Abruzzo (Tesco)** | 12 | £B |

| **Primitivo de Salento 1993 (Tesco)** | 15 | £C |

A soft, easygoing wine at first and then it leaps on the taste buds like a mad panther. Delicious, curious, maddeningly difficult to describe. Lots of electric hard fruit mingling with bright soft berries. Will undoubtedly develop over the next 2/3 years in bottle.

Rosso del Lazio (Tesco)   12   £B
A merlot/sangiovese blend of some richness and flavour, but
is mildly dull.

Rosso del Piemonte (Tesco)   11   £C
Soft yet faintly tannic. Will it get steadily better in bottle over
the next year?

Rosso di Montalcino 1992 (Tesco)   14   £D
None of your bruised, squashy fruit with this jammy beast.
Delicious and soft as peach fuzz.

Sicilian Red (Tesco)   13   £B
Also comes in a useful 3-litre box for under £11 (equalling
45p a glass).

Viarengo Barbaresco 1986   14   £D
Cherries, figs and blackberries. Lots of fruit, sweet and dry –
delicious wine to drink by itself.

Villa Boscorotondo Chianti Classico 1992   13   £C
Good, very drinkable, but not as ultimately exciting as it might
be with a few more months in bottle.

Villa Cerro Amarone della Valpolicella 1986   16   £D
The most vivid ripe plum, raspberry and blackberry fruit.
Quite lovely. Perfect maturity.

Villa Gaida Lambrusco Rosso DOC   12   £B
Sweet and cherry ripe.

Villa Pigna Cabernesco 1991   15.5 £D
Squashy black cherry, raspberry and plum fruit which is not
top heavy or fat but dry, biscuity (in a subtle way) and very
warming.

Villa Pigna Rosso Piceno 1992   13   £B

Vino da Tavola Rosso, Farli	12 £A

Vino de Tavola 14 £A
Most attractive, soft, cherryade fruited wine for pasta lovers and pizza freaks.

ITALIAN WINE – *white*

Blanco del Lazio 1993 (Tesco) 14 £B
A fruit cake in Lazio! No, not Paul Gascoigne, this wine. Tasty stuff. (And much better value than Gazza.)

Blanco del Piemonte (Tesco) 13 £C
Good wine, lots of attractive fruit, but a touch pricier than it should be.

Chardonnay Alto Adige, E Von Keller 1992 15 £C
Good surge of buttered melon fruit, excellent acid balance. Good value. Relish.

Chardonnay del Veneto (Tesco) 13 £B
Lovely soft citric touch to the fruit.

Colli Lanuvini DOC (Tesco) 13 £B
Excellent value, very fresh and light although not overloaded with fruit. Aperitif.

Coli Toscani 1993 (Tesco) 13 £B

Frascati 1993 (Tesco) 13 £C
A good blend. Good fruit with a nutty touch underlying it. Won't set the world alight but it might kindle an old flame – other circumstances in its consumption being on song, that is.

Italian White Merlot (Tesco)   14   £B
Tastes just like pinot grigio ought to! White merlot – it could
become the rage!!

Nuragus di Cagliari (Tesco)   15   £B
Bargain drinking. Has flint-edged fruit which is soft-centred,
plus good balancing acidity. Lovely fish wine or to enjoy solo.

Orvieto Classico Abboccato (Tesco)   13   £B
Off-dry, but very pleasant fruit. Good aperitif.

Orvieto Classico Vaselli 1993   11   £C

Pinot Grigio del Veneto (Tesco)   13   £B
A pinot grigio with fruit! Alleluja!

Pinot Grigio Tiefenbrunner 1993   12   £C

Sauvignon Blanc del Veneto (Tesco)   14   £B
Delicious fruit and excellent balance. Good value.

Sicilian White (Tesco)   13   £B

Soave Classico 1992 (Tesco)   11   £C

Trulle Chardonnay del Salento 1993   16   £C
A woody, rich, gently buttery chardonnay of surprising complexity for the money. A serious chardonnay for funny money.

Verdicchio Classico 1993 (Tesco)   15.5 £C
Delicious (and surprising) weight of melony fruit with pear
undertones. Has freshness as well, so it's hugely enjoyable
and thirst-quenching. A joyous bottle.

Villa Cerro Soave Recioto 1992   14   £C
An interesting sweet aperitif. Good with hard fruit and a slug
of cheese and Italian sweetmeats and cakes. Also almond
biscuits.

Vino da Tavola Bianco　　　　　　　　13　£A
Fresh with a light finish of lemon. Delicious aperitif.

MEXICAN WINE – *red*

**Mexican Cabernet Sauvignon, L A Cetto 1990
(Tesco)**　　　　　　　　　　　　　16　£C
Bargain bottle. An enriching experience for all serious red wine
nuts: soft fruit of compelling richness. Will age for a while too.
Not as spicy as previous vintages.

NEW ZEALAND WINE – *red*

Cabernet Sauvignon 1990 (Tesco)　　　　14　£C
The fruit's all there, but the bouquet's a bit barking: smells like
a lawnmower grassbox after a downpour. Astonishing con-
tradiction, in fact, for it comes across austere and standoffish and
then comes over all soft, soppy, and instantly fruity with eucalyptus, pine, grass and blackcurrant. Good partner for roast food.

Cabernet/Merlot 1991 (Tesco)　　　　　12　£C

**Coopers Creek Cabernet Sauvignon, Auckland
1990 (Tesco)**　　　　　　　　　　　14　£C
Delicious ripe fruit.

**Riverlea Wines Cabernet Sauvignon/Merlot,
Gisborne 1991 (Tesco)**　　　　　　　　15　£C
Amazingly well-integrated varieties with softness, smoothness
and very effective final delivery. Delicious.

NEW ZEALAND WINE – *white*

Chardonnay (Tesco)   14   £C
Woody, rich and buttery in the mouth, the fruit seems to fight
on the tongue. Great with chicken and rich fruit dishes.

**Coopers Creek Chardonnay, Gisborne 1992
(Tesco)**   15   £C
Distinguished wine where the fruit trips along beautifully with
the wood and the lemony acidity holds both of them. Will age
well, and improve over the next 18 months/2 years.

Dry White (Tesco)   12   £C
Attractive all-round wine with plenty of rounded fruit. Might
be better, in fact, with less fruit and more of that searing New
Zealand grassiness.

Jackson Estate Sauvignon Blanc 1993   15   £D

New Zealand Dry White (Tesco)   13   £C

Nobilo Sauvignon Blanc, Marlborough 1992   10   £C

**Riverlea Wines Sauvignon Blanc, Gisborne 1992
(Tesco)**   16   £C
Zippy, grassy wine, never overdone, of gooseberry/melon/
lime fruit. Great balanced style and length of flavour. Delicious by itself or with seafood.

Sauvignon Blanc 1992 (Tesco)   12   £C

Stoneleigh Chardonnay 1992   12   £D

Timara Dry White   12   £C

Villa Maria Chenin/Chardonnay 1993   12   £D

Villa Maria Sauvignon Blanc 1993 (half)   14   £C

PORTUGUESE WINE – *red*

Bairrada 1989 (Tesco)	13　£B

Borba Alentejo	14.5　£B

Terrific value even at its new just-over-£3 price. Lots of
flavour and style and more concentration of fruit than comparatively priced vins de pays.

Dão 1989 (Tesco)	13　£B

Dom José (Tesco)	14　£A

This rural masterpiece of peasant pulchritude has been
likened to five-day-old lorry driver's socks, but the secret with
this earthy fruit stew is to let it breathe for a bit before tackling
it. Better, pour into a large earthenware vase (removing
flowers first). It has been known to be specially promoted at
£1.99, which is even more endearing.

Douro 1985 (Tesco)	14　£B

This has lost some verve, being 9 years old, but it's very
smooth, rounded (in a figgy sort of way) and remarkably
priced for its age.

Garrafeira Foncesa 1984	13　£D

Raisiny, ripe, very mature. Good with spicy foods.

J.P. Barrel Selection 1991	14　£B

Big, sunny, generous, fat wine of ample fruit and a chocolate
edge. Great sausage and mash wine.

Periquita Portuguese Red 1990	14　£C

Drinkable, fruity, attractive. Simple in some respects, it has
the charm of growing in attractiveness as the bottle empties.

Quinta da Cardiga   13   £B
Brilliant value.

Tinto da Anfora 1990   13   £C
Coffee, catering chocolate and figs up front which fade as they
hit the throat. Doesn't quite deliver the punch its aromatic
and primary palate complexity suggest.

Tinto Velho 1988   13   £C

Velho Reguengos de Monsaraz 1987 (Tesco)   16.5   £C
Rich, chocolatey, chewy, tangy, swirling with fruit and double
cream. Bargain fruitiness.

PORTUGUESE WINE – *white and rosé*

Bairrada 1993 (Tesco)   13   £B
Can't argue with this once fried fish is plonked beside it.

Cova da Ursa Chardonnay 1990   13   £D
Lemon on the pleasant fruity aroma, butter and almonds in
the mouth, some staying power to the finish. An unusual and
attractive chardonnay.

Dão Branco 1993 (Tesco)   13   £B

Douro Branco 1993 (Tesco)   14   £B
Softness of the fruit makes it plump and giving, but there's a
lean, lemony quality to the acidity and this gives the wine a
two-fisted attack. Excellent value.

Dry Portuguese Rosé (Tesco)   12   £B

João Pires Moscato 1992 15 £C
This could replace gewürztraminer at this price. Delicious floral aperitif.

SOUTH AFRICAN WINE – *red*

Cape Pinotage 1992 (Tesco) 14 £B
Sweet, elegantly smokey and rubbery fruit, like a drier style of Beaujolais but tastier.

Kanonkop Pinotage 1992 17 £D
Fabulous crushed blackcurrant fruit which is so rich it's chewy yet it doesn't clog the throat. Expensive but very impressive. Hugely appealing, complex wine. Huge weight of flavour in the finish which turns softly cherryish. Magnificent tannins.

**Oak Village Vintage Reserve Stellenbosch
1992** 14.5 £C
Deliciously serious fruit, yet fun. Dry yet rounded, flexible yet firmly fruited, this is an engaging wine.

**South African Cabernet Sauvignon/Merlot
Winemaker (Tesco)** 14 £C
Mouthy and rich, fresh to finish.

South African Red (Tesco) 14 £B
Excellent value. Bit standoffish at first, but has a firm hand-shake of fruit and a warm, friendly finish.

Stellenbosch Merlot (Tesco) 13 £C
Good fruit. A pleasant, dry plonk.

**Winemaker Cabernet Sauvignon/Merlot
(Tesco)**   15   £C
Lovely brambly fruit – really jammy and delicious. Rich and
full of flavour.

SOUTH AFRICAN WINE – *white*

Boschendal Grand Cuvée 1992   13   £D
Good but not exciting.

Cape Chenin (Tesco)   14   £B
Fruity and fine with it.

Cape Colombar (Tesco)   15   £B
Aromatically a marriage of eau de cologne and apple and pear.
The fruit is a medley of flavours: pawpaw and ripe melon
being the most prominent. Not a serious wine but a joy of
gluggability.

Chardonnay, Robertson 1993   13   £C

Danie de Wet Chardonnay Grey Label 1994 15   £C

Fleur du Cap, Noble Late Harvest 1990 (50cl) 12   £C
Searingly sweet, treacle-tartish wine with not enough solid
botrytis (i.e. noble rot) complexity and concentration of fruit.
This is what that word 'noble' in the name means, referring as
it does to the technique of allowing grapes to rot on the vine
and to become infected with the botrytis fungus before
picking them, so that there is less water in the fruit and the
grape-sugars develop.

Goiya Kgeisje 1994   14   £B
A sauvignon blanc/chardonnay combination with a lovely

fruity backbone and excellent structure. The addition of chardonnay has filled out the wine yet kept masses of freshness
and citric flavour and it is terrific fun drinking. It must be one
of the first '94 vintage wines on sale. It also sports the most
attractively original, and apposite, wine label I've seen in years
commemorating the advent of democracy in South Africa.

International Winemaker South African
Sauvignon Blanc (Tesco) 14 £C
Superb s.b. of freshness and flavour and creamy, nutty, rich-
edged fruit. Terrific shellfish beauty. Delicious style.

Oak Village Sauvignon Blanc 1993 13 £C
Some real fruit in evidence here.

Robertson Chardonnay 1993 (Tesco) 16 £C
Danie de Wet makes this wine, the only own-label he does,
and it is a bargain. A beautifully crafted, appealingly well-
wooded chardonnay of delicacy and flavour. It is staggeringly
elegant wine for the money. With a touch of honeyed hazelnut
on the buttery fruit which is not cloying but has freshness and
vigour, this is a superb wine for the money. A high class act.

South African White (Tesco) 15 £C
Brilliant melony (deep and vivid) and peardrop wine with a
fresh acid cut and an almond finish. Delish aperitif. Quite a
taste bud awakener. Excellent muscat-touched fruit.

Swartland Sauvignon Blanc 1993 (Tesco) 13 £C
Has some elegant restraint but isn't as impactful as it might be.

Van Louveren Blanc de Noirs 14 £B
The slightest blush you've ever seen! Delicious aperitif with
raspberry and strawberry fruitiness. Great fun.

SPANISH WINE – *red*

Campillo Gran Reserva, Rioja 1982	13 £E

Cinco Casas Red (Tesco)   14.5 £B
Lots of fresh young fruit and flavour. Delicious price.

Don Darias   14 £B
It projects like a stage actor. Wonderful company.

Gandia Merlot   14 £B

Gran Don Darias   13 £B

Marqués de Chive (Tesco)   14 £B
Dry, mature, raspberry fruit, rather light but eminently glug-worthy.

Ochoa Tempranillo 1990   14.5 £D
One of the chewiest and most lovable Spanish reds around. Has a gentle coconut dusting to the strawberry and plum fruit.

Rioja Reserva 1987 (Tesco)   17 £C
Baked fruit and herb aroma, assertive soft fruit with no unwelcome intrusion from the wood, and a lush sweet fruit finish. Utterly delicious. A very controlled production from start to finish.

Rioja, Vina Mara (Tesco)   15 £C
Terrific value for money. Controlled, soft, berried fruit, light, not heavy or over-wooded. Lovely fruity style.

Señorio de los Llanos 1989   13 £C

Toro 1990 (Tesco)   15 £C
Soft plums prettily assembled. Dry, not huge, but deliciously satisfying.

SPANISH WINE – *white*

Castillo de San Diego 1993 12 £C
Well, they have to do something with sherry grapes.

Cinco Casas White (Tesco) 14 £B
Highly pleasing little wine of delicious soft fruit with a dash of muted lime.

Don Darias 14 £B
With a spicy fish stew or curry, this is the wine.

Galician Albarino 1992 13 £C
An unknown wine and one of Iberia's great seafood partners. It lacks zip but the fruit has some power and will really shine with a complex spicy fish stew or paella.

Gandia Chardonnay 13 £B
Good varietal character without the sun. Quiet, pale, unfussy.

Marqués de Chive White Wine (Tesco) 12 £B
Vanilla, coconut and fruit which don't quite marry up. But great with Thai food.

Moscatel de Valencia (Tesco) 15 £B
Just under £3 makes this a honey of a bargain. And with it, your Christmas pudding goes down with a broad smile on its face.

Rioja (Tesco) 13 £C

Rueda 1992, International Winemaker Series (Tesco) 11 £B

Rueda 1993 (Tesco) 14 £B
The zinginess to the fruit makes it a perfect aperitif.

Superior Manzanilla (Tesco) (half)   16   £B
Brilliant value. Saline, elegant and very dry. A nutty world-
class aperitif. Or drink with grilled prawns.

Superior Oloroso Secco (Tesco) (half)   16   £B
Just by itself and music. Heaven!

Superior Palo Cortado (Tesco) (half)   17   £C
Rich, very dry camomile fruit, nutty undertone. For drinking
alone with literature – or a superb aperitif. It revives even the
most jaded taste buds – lovely dry fruit.

Viña del Castillo 1992   11   £B

USA WINE – *red*

Californian Cabernet Sauvignon (Tesco)   15   £C
Lovely touches of eucalyptus, soft, unhurried, delicious, to a
firmly fruity and solidly structured specimen. Terrific value
for the money.

Californian Red (Tesco)   13   £B
Interesting what went through the label designer's mind when
(s)he designed this curious blue and somewhat incongruous
townscape on the bottle. Maybe too much of this wine perhaps? Very audacious. The wine only surprises by being soft
and dry and quiet-mannered.

Californian Zinfandel (Tesco)   15   £C
More cabernet in this new blend. Excellent. Sweaty armpit
aroma. Lovely rich, smooth fruit (plums and black cherries,
touch of spice). Good rich finish. Great glug.

USA WINE – *white*

Californian Chardonnay (Tesco) 15 £C
A superb, oily, polished wine. Remarkable value from the earthquake state. Very full, rich yet not cloying.

Californian White (Tesco) 12 £C

SPARKLING WINE/CHAMPAGNE

Australian Sparkling Brut (Tesco) 15 £C
Lovely feathery feel and terrific fruit and acid balance making it impressively elegant in the mouth. Under a fiver it is outstanding value for money.

Blanc de Blancs Champagne (Tesco) 13 £G

Blanquette de Limoux (Tesco) 13 £D
Soft attractive bubbly. Only a weak finish prevents it scoring much higher.

Champagne Premier Cru 1983 (Tesco) 11 £H

Champagne Premier Cru Brut (Tesco) 14 £F
An elegant champagne.

Champagne (Tesco) 13 £F

Chardonnay Frizzante (Tesco) 10 £B

Chardonnay Spumante 15 £D
Great value sparkler with a great touch of Italian bravura on the typical chardonnay fruit.

Chevalier de Moncontour Mousseux Brut   10 £D
Boney, sterile, about as thrilling as a smack in the kisser from
a wet sock.

Crémant de Bourgogne 1989 (Tesco)   18 £D
This is as good ... what am I saying! ... this is better than
many mature, famous marques champagnes. Has biscuity rich
fruit and a rich acidic finish. Brilliant wine for the money.
Perfect age and of great class and style.

**Crémant de Loire Rosé, Cave des Vignerons de
Saumur**   12 £D

Deutz, New Zealand   12 £E
Just like Deutz champagne from the well-known Rheims
company.

Grand Duchess Brut Sparkling Wine, Russia 10 £C
Comradely, but only just.

Henri Mandois Champagne   12 £F

Lindauer Brut   12 £D
New Zealand's champagne copy.

Loridos Espumante 1987   11 £D

Louis Massing Grand Cru Blanc de Blancs   16 £E
Elegant, stylish and a great bargain. Properly mature. A
special purchase this at a special price (and what a price!) and
I cannot guarantee any will be on sale by publication date.
However, there is the chance that Tesco might persuade the
Massing family to release some more at the same price in time
for Christmas and if they do I would like *Superplonk* readers to
be the first to snap the wine up.

Michel Arnould Champagne   12 £G

Moscato d'Asti, Guilio Alfero 1992　　15　£C
Wonderful appley soft fruit bubbles. Brilliant aperitif or with a
bunch of grapes.

Moscato Sparkler (Tesco)　　12　£A
A 5% junior wine for senior tipplers.

Premier Cru Brut Champagne (Tesco)　　14　£F
Classy, delicious and very well made.

Prosecco Spumante (Tesco)　　14　£C
Delicious peachy/strawberry aperitif. Great fun from Italy.

Salinger 1989　　12　£E

Seppelts Salinger Sparkling Wine, Australia　　15　£F
Mature yet fresh finishing. Some elegance. Dry.

Soave Classico Spumante　　13　£D

**South African Sparkling Sauvignon Blanc 1993
(Tesco)**　　15　£C
Excellent value. Up there with Cava and Aussie sparkling
wine, but maybe a touch too elegant.

Tesco Asti Spumante　　10　£C
A sweet muscat wine of little personality. Tesco's Moscato is
much better value.

Tesco Cava　　14　£C
Touch of elegance here. What happened to the tell-tale
earthiness?

Tesco Moscato Spumante　　13　£C
Muscat flavour all the way through. Good fun aperitif.

Tesco Rosé Cava 15 £C
Subtle raspberry here and fruit hints in this brilliant value-
for-money bubbly.

Vintage Cava 1989 (Tesco) 15 £D
Excellent rich-edged fruit of style, purpose and real class.
Good value.

Yalumba Cuvée Sparkling Cabernet Sauvignon 15 £E
Utterly ravishing stuff. Dry fruit, soft to finish. Great fun. Eat?
Nothing. Drinks by itself.

Waitrose

The biggest event in the lives of the Waitrose wine department has come with the acquisition of a mail-order operation, Findlater Mackie Todd. The heady excitement of this revolutionary step aside, the department has carried on as it has always done. In all other respects, Waitrose is still Waitrose. A law unto itself.

It employs Masters of Wine (four men, one woman). It dislikes own-labels. It buys on quality first, price second. It relishes understatement (can you see anyone other than Waitrose calling its basic red bordeaux the devastatingly disarming Good Ordinary Claret?). It woos wine critics with the most delicious luncheon food, served by the most charming waitresses (who, I am sure, would whistle up a full cream tea if asked) and it recognizes the need to offer such journalists a choice of dates on which to attend these food and wine feasts (no other retailer offers this choice, spread over so many weeks). It anguishes when, through customer prejudice, it has to pander to the needs of, say, the burgundy freak, when it is patently obvious no such wine exists any more at a sensible price, and the store will never advertise a £1.99 bottle. Indeed, it will never stoop to the level of shouting about its wares in public *ever*, company rules prevent it, and it will certainly find it impossible to locate a £1.99 wine it could comfortably put on shelf.

It is quite likely that this aversion has something to do with the fact that if the canniest wine buyers on the block, Tesco, cannot make a profit on a £1.99 wine, then what chance does Waitrose stand? The answer is not to compete with anyone else at this level. And so Waitrose doesn't. Waitrose competes with itself.

It offers, on the face of it, a solid range of extremely well-chosen wines. But look at the core of each sub-range. Isn't there always a benchmark of quality in its midst around which the rest revolve? This core may be just one wine, but I have this feeling that the wine department always sets this benchmark wine against the rest, thus stimulating competition to find wines to match it within the same range.

This is tough work. And which are these benchmark wines? In Bordeaux, among the under-a-fiver reds, it has to be Château les Tonnelles de Fronsac 1990, among the whites, Château Carsin Cuvée Prestige 1992. The Aussies have Château Reynella for a benchmark shiraz, and the Rosemount Show Reserve 1992 amongst the chardonnays. The store's own-label champagne serves to keep that lot on its toes, not to mention the Crémant de Bourgogne. The Jackson Estate Sauvignon Blanc is as good a varietal interpretation of this grape as emanates from the New World (and, sad to say nowadays, most of the old) and the store's zinfandel has always been, in the consistent shape of Cartlidge & Brown, a wine it's easy to like.

However, this is not to suggest that Waitrose stands still where wine is concerned and the only revolutions take place around the same old wines, or wines very much like them. It has spread its wings somewhat this year. New wines have piled in from eastern Europe particularly, both red and white, and though the store has no first call on flying winemakers' arts it does offer a few examples of this burgeoning *fin-de-siècle* trend.

But overall nothing much has ruffled the calm surface of the gentlest supermarket wine-buying department of them all, and for that its customers can be truly thankful.

(Even if it does give me very little to write about other than the wines.)

ARGENTINIAN WINE – *red*

Santa Julia Malbec, Mendoza   13   £C
Odd soft fondant cream style of fruit. Very attractive. Open
for three hours to let the raspberry fruit develop.

Trapiche Pinot Noir Reserve 1992   13   £C

AUSTRALIAN WINE – *red*

Brown Brothers Tarrango 1992   14   £C
It takes two to tarrango: the touriga grape of Portugal and a
sultana variety of white table grape called Thompson's seed-
less. There is much to recommend this marriage. The
touriga, rich red in colour, tannin, and flavour, offers a miserly
yield; the Thompson, on the other hand, is fecund to the point
of embarrassment. The marriage was arranged in Australia
and the resultant new grape makes for a deliciously fresh
wine, buzzing with young fruit and offering all the myriad
colours and flavours of summer pudding, and I would certainly rather drink it than a lot of Beaujolais – to which this
Tarrango, chilled and purply in the glass, rubbery and tingly-
supple in the mouth, can be effortlessly compared. I would
urge Tarrango upon anyone interested in the development of
wine, for it is a true talking point. If Brown Bros can get the
price below £3.50, it will become a major drinking point.

Château Reynella Shiraz 1991   14   £D

Coldstream Hills Cabernet/Merlot 1991   14   £E
Sweet thing.

Goundrey Langton Cabernet/Merlot 1992   13   £D
Bit too giving and childlike for the money but hugely quaffable.

Hardy's Southern Creek Shiraz/Cabernet 1993   12   £C

Houghton Wildflower Ridge Chenin Blanc 1993   14   £C
Wildflower Ridge by name, wild flower fruit by nature.

Jacob's Creek Dry Red, Shiraz/Cabernet 1991,
South East Australia   13   £C
Not as vivid as usual but still a mass of dark rich fruit for the money.

Leasingham Domaine Shiraz 1992   13   £D

Ovens and King Shiraz/Cabernet 1991   13   £D

Oxford Landing Cabernet/Shiraz, South East
Australia 1991   14   £C

Penfolds Bin 2 Shiraz/Mourvèdre 1992   15   £C
Plum and black cherries, muted spice. Delicious! Will develop and get even better.

Penfolds Bin 35 Shiraz/Cabernet 1992   15   £C
Ripe, soft fruit with some development ahead of it. Attractive berry flavours, well structured and balanced. Very drinkable now but a 17/18-pointer in 3/4 years.

Peter Lehmann Cabernet Sauvignon 1991   16   £D
So much soft fruit it makes you gag with pleasure. Deep, rich quality of great attractiveness. Lovely wine.

Spring Gully Shiraz/Cabernet Sauvignon 1993   15   £C
Ripe fruit (berries) and rich soft tannins. Lovely wine.

AUSTRALIAN WINE – *white*

**Arrowfield Show Reserve Chardonnay, South
East Australia 1992**   13   £E

**Brown Brothers King Valley, Rhine Riesling
Victoria 1993**   13   £D
Lay down for 3 years? Good stuff, packed with biscuity,
lemon-sherbet fruit but expensive for drinking now. Needs
time.

Currawong Creek Semillon/Chardonnay 1992   13   £C

Hardy's Nottage Hill Chardonnay 1993/4   14   £C

**Hardy's Southern Creek Semillon/Chardonnay
1994**   12   £C

**Mitchelton Reserve Marsanne, Goulbourn
Valley, Victoria 1990**   13   £D

Mitchelton Reserve Marsanne 1992   15.5   £D
Waxy fruit encased in pineapple acidity. Very assertive and
great with rich fish dishes.

Oxford Landing Sauvignon Blanc 1993   14   £C
Rather elegant and classic for the money.

**Penfolds Bin 202 South Australian Riesling
1993**   14   £C
Superb, rich aperitif. Delicious.

Penfolds Bin 21 Semillon/Chardonnay 1993   15   £C
Fresh and lively yet a dollop of pineappley melon keeps
intruding. Delicious refreshing wine. Also available in half -
bottles.

Penfolds Koonunga Hill Chardonnay 1993   13   £C

Stoney Valley Semillon/Chardonnay 1992, **South East Australia**   14   £C
Rich and giving in the fruit department – kind and fresh in the acid department.

Wakefield White Clare Crouchen/Chardonnay, Clare Valley, South Australia 1989   16   £C
Dazzling stuff.

AUSTRIAN WINE – *white*

Grüner Veltliner 1991 **Lenz Moser**   13   £C
Rather less elegant and fresh than in other years.

BULGARIAN WINE – *red*

Bulgarian Country Wine, Merlot/Pinot Noir   13   £B
Newly minted, these Bulgarian country wines seem rather green and even a mite peppery but this character softens in time and this wine is well on the way.

Cabernet Sauvignon Russe 1988   14   £B
Stupendous value: blackcurrant but gooey – gooey and Rioja-like. At this price who's grumbling?

Mavrud Assenovgrad 1988   13   £B

Merlot/Gamza   13   £B

CHILEAN WINE – *red*

Concha y Toro Cabernet Sauvignon 1991   12   £C

Concha y Toro Merlot 1992   15   £C
Excellent value for fairly complex fruit. Delicious rounded
flavours.

CHILEAN WINE – *white*

Caliterra Chardonnay 1994   13   £C

Montenuevo Chardonnay, Maipo 1993   14   £C
Very pleasant, has vivacity and style.

Montenuevo Sauvignon Blanc, Maipo 1993   12   £C
I've tasted worse.

ENGLISH WINE – *red*

Chapel Down Epoch I East Sussex 1992   13   £C
It smells of kidneys cooked with mushrooms and Madeira but
the fruit is less flamboyant and even tasty. Utterly pretentious
wine to serve to visiting French diplomats.

Denbies Surrey Gold 1992   13   £C
Decently made, well structured – you might say as much of a
prefab.

ENGLISH WINE – *white*

Hastings, Carr Taylor 14 £B
Fruit, acidity, perfume, structure, balance, price. It's got the lot in the right proportions.

Priory, Lamberhurst Vineyards 14 £B
Woolly fruit, attractive, subtle. Very pleasant wine at an excellent price.

FRENCH WINE – *red*

**Baron Villeneuve du Château Cantemerle,
Haut-Médoc 1990** 13 £E
California style claret. Delicious stuff now, but liquid velvet in 5 years time.

Beaujolais-Villages 1993 11 £C

Bergerac Rouge AC 1993 13 £B
Seriously good in the middle if not great at the finish.

Cabernet Sauvignon, Vin de Pays d'Oc 1992 12 £C

Cahors Cuvée Reserve 1991 13 £B

Château de la Roche Gamay 1993 14 £C
Tastes like an old Julieñas poured into a jug and let breathe for an hour.

Château de Nages Costières de Nîmes AC 1992 12 £B

Château Lascombes Margaux AC 1990 11 £F

Château Les Tonnelles de Fronsac, Fronsac AC
1990   15   £C
Spicy, bold, mature, dry yet finishing sweetly, this is a terrific
claret for under a fiver.

Château Lyonnat Lussac St-Emilion AC, 1989   13   £D

Château Marseau, Côtes du Marmandais 1991   11   £B

Château Segonzac Premier Côtes de Blaye AC,
1990   15   £C
Seriously good claret at a seriously good price.

Château St-Maurice Côtes du Rhône AC 1991   15   £C
Delicious sweet fruit underpinned by a decisive earthiness.

Châteauneuf-du-Pape, Delas Frères 1990   12   £E

Claret, Patrice Calvet 1990   11   £C

Côtes de Duras 1990   12   £C

Côtes de Ventoux AC 1992   14   £B
As good as ever but not as velvety. Excellent value. Soft fruit.

Côtes du Rhône 1993 (Waitrose)   12   £C

Crozes-Hermitages, Cave des Clairmonts 1991 11   £D

Domaine de Beauséjour, Côtes de la Malepère
1992   12   £B

**Domaine de la Présidente Cairanne Côtes du
Rhône Villages 1990**   14   £C
Delicious.

Domaine de Pigeonnier Corbières AC 1991   15   £B
Superb value for money and will get superber over the next
2 years, as its dry-berried flavour softens voluptuously.

**Domaine de St-Macaire, Vin de Pays de
l'Hérault** 11 £B

**Domaine des Fontaines Merlot, Vin de Pays d'Oc
1992** 14 £B
Handsome, severe, haughty – will improve in bottle for
2 years.

Fleurie AC 1993 (half) 13 £B

**Foncalieu Cabernet Sauvignon, Vin de Pays
de L'Aude 1993** 14 £B
Great value for serious cabernet sauvignon lovers.

Gamay Haut-Poitou 1993 11 £C

Good Ordinary Claret Bordeaux (Waitrose) 13.5 £B
A bargain – also available in a magnum for six quid odd. It's as
good as its name and better than ordinary (thus offering us the
only understatement ever made by a supermarket own-label
bottle).

Hautes Côtes de Beaune 1990 12 £D

Le Secret Vin de Pays de Vaucluse 1993 15 £B
Violet-flavoured fruit to finish, dry overall but never austere.
Great value.

Les Forts de Latour, Pauillac 1985 10 £H
Doesn't take anywhere near so long to reach maturity as its
world-famous relative but it's still got a way to go. But do you
want to wait? Equally, do you want to spend nigh on thirty quid
on a wine which has been on the shelf goodness knows how
long? At a wine merchant, fine wine can be stored properly and
remain unsold and in good nick for years, but how can this be
matched in a supermarket? Even if the bottle isn't completely
upright it's inclined sufficiently for the label to be read, and so

the cork is not completely covered by the wine and it may shrink
and permit oxidation to occur. I would be happier to see fine
wines like this, leaving aside the argument that this soi-disant
example may not be remotely worth the money, being ade-
quately cellared and available for order with one bottle being
displayed on shelf for customers to see but not buy. I do not see
how '85 Pauillacs can be sold off the shelf in the same way as a
£3 Australian bottle which only sits around for a few weeks at
most.

Margaux 1990   13   £E
Lovely classic drinkable Margaux.

Médoc 1993   11   £C

Mercurey AC La Framboisière 1992   13   £E
Lives up to its name fruit-wise.

Minervois AC 1992   14   £B
Lovely dry fruit. A bargain.

**Prieuré de Fonclaire Grande Reserve, Buzet AC
1992 (half)**   14   £A
A £1.99 bottle at Waitrose is something to celebrate even if it is
only a half. Very firmly fruity, dry wine for lone steak eaters.

**Special Reserve Claret 1990 Fronsac AC
(Waitrose)**   14   £C
Excellent. Sweet fruit. Rather forward and soft.

Special Reserve Claret 1989 (Waitrose)   13   £C

St-Chinian   11   £B

St-Emilion   13   £C

St-Joseph, Caves de St-Désirat 1989/90   15   £D
Bouquet developing, and the fruit. Will be 17 points in 3 years.

FRENCH WINE – *white and rosé*

Alsace Gewürztraminer 1993	12	£D

Blanc de Mer   14   £B
Now also in a magnum, for under six quid, this is the wine for large gatherings of the British chapter of the Bouillabaisse Club.

Blaye Blanc 1993	12	£B
Bordeaux Blanc Medium Dry	11	£B

Bordeaux Rosé AC François de Lorgéac 1993   15   £B
One of the best rosés around for the money. Serious, dry, plummy fruit with enough zip and rosé-like fun to make it frivolous. Great stuff. And great with food.

Bordeaux Sauvignon AC 1993	11	£B
Bourgogne Aligoté, Brocard 1993	12	£C
Chablis Gaec des Réugnis 1993	12	£D
Chablis Premier Cru AC Beauroy 1991	13	£E

Chablis Premier Cru, Mont de Milieu 1991   13   £E
Makes a decent stab at depth and class.

Chassagne Montrachet AC 1991	10	£E

**Château Bastor-Lamontagne Sauternes 1990
(half)**   14   £E

Château Carsin Cuvée Prestige 1992   15   £D
Very successful wine at a very attractive price – subtle tropical fruit undertones yet firmly Bordeaux in style.

Château Chaubinet Bordeaux AC 1992   12 £C

Château Darzac 1993   12 £C

Château Haut-Rian Bordeaux AC 1993   11 £C

Château la Cassade Ste-Croix du Mont AC
1991   13 £D

Château La Fonrousse Montbazillac AC 1990   15 £D
Delicious, elegant, honey-toffee exquisiteness.

Château Piada 1989   14 £G
I'd be a very happy bunny with a bottle of this wine, a fruity
novel, a bunch of grapes, and a chunk of hard cheese for
company.

Château Tour Balot Premier Côtes de Bordeaux
AC 1990   13 £D
Curious marzipan undertone to this wine. Good aperitif if
well chilled.

Domaine de Hauret Lalande, Graves 1992   14 £C

Domaine des Fontaines, Rosé de Syrah, Vin
de Pays d'Oc 1992   14 £B
Cherry and pear-drops smell and fruit, good balance, dry,
acidically good. Excellent food rosé (fish, chicken, salads,
vegetables).

Domaine des Fontanelles Sauvignon, Vin de
Pays d'Oc 1993   13 £B
A Ryman wine. Some attractive melony fruit and freshness.

Domaines des Fontanelles, Syrah Rosé, Vin de
Pays d'Oc 1993   15 £B
Brilliant summer wine. Floral overtones. Pinky and perky with
fruit. Delicious to drink on a hot evening.

**Domaine du Temps Perdu, Vin de Pays des
Bouches du Rhône 1992** 11 £B
Nothing Proustian about this wine. Excellent with fish as
you'd anticipate but little complexity and not a lot of fruit.

Domaine Gibault, Sauvignon de Touraine 1993 13 £C
Some rich New World touches to the fruit, but not yet in the
class of the '92. A year of bottle age will sort it out.

**Domaine Petit Château Chardonnay, Vin de
Pays du Jardin de la France 1993** 14 £C

Finesse Blanc (5%) 13 £A

Fortant Chardonnay, Vin de Pays d'Oc 1993 13 £C

Gewürztraminer, Alsace 1990 (Waitrose) 14 £D
Delicious floral gem with subtle lychee fruit. Touch of spice.
Not a hugely concentrated wine but a delicious one.

Le Pujalet, Vin de Pays du Gers 1993 12 £B

Mâcon Lugny, Les Charmes 1992 12 £D

Muscadet 1993 (Waitrose) 10 £B

**Philippe de Baudin Chardonnay, Vin de Pays
d'Oc 1991** 15 £C
Excellent rounded fruit and stylish acid – good balance. A
touch of wood.

Pinot Blanc d'Alsace AC Blanck Frères 1992 12 £C

Pinot Blanc d'Alsace Médaille d'Or 1993 13 £D

Pouilly-Fumé AC 1993 12 £D

Premières Côtes de Bordeaux 13 £C
A pud wine. But the pud needs to be very light.

Prieuré de Fonclaire Buzet Blanc AC 1992   12   £C

Sancerre 1993   11   £D

Sancerre AC Patient Cottat 1992   11   £D

Sauvignon Blanc, Vin de Pays des Coteaux
de l'Ardèche 1992   13   £B
Subtle weight of fruit here, but fails to finish grippingly.

Sauvignon de St-Bris Jean-Marc Brocard 1993   12   £D

Sauvignon Haut-Poitou 1993   12   £C

St-Veran 1993   12   £D

Terret Vin de Pays des Côtes de Thau 1993   12   £B

Tokay Pinot Gris d'Alsace, Cave de Beblenheim 1992
(half)   14   £B
Splendid little half of apricoted fruit.

Tokay Pinot Gris d'Alsace AC, Blanck Frères
1992   16   £D

Vilonds Muscat 1993   11   £C

Vin de Pays d'Oc Chardonnay, Le Gineste 1993   13   £C

Vin de Pays d'Oc Sur Lie 1991   13   £B

Vin de Pays du Jardin de la France Chardonnay
1992   10   £B

Vouvray, Domaine de la Robinière 1993   11   £C

GERMAN WINE – *white*

Avelsbacher Hammerstein Riesling 1988/89	**15**	**£E**

**Avelsbacher Hammerstein Riesling Spätlese,
Ruwer, Staatsweingut 1989**   **13**   **£D**

**Bad Bergzaberner Kloster Liebfrauenberg Auslese
1992**   **14**   **£C**
A superb aperitif, with a glittering touch of honey.

Baden Dry   **14**   **£C**

Erdener Treppchen Riesling Spätlese 1986   **16**   **£D**
Coming along nicely, this wine. Very steely, lemonic Teuton.

Morio Muskat 1992   **15**   **£B**
Brilliant aperitif of great gooey, melony fruit without sweetness. Light (9.5% alcohol), cheap, and with decided personality.

Ockfener Bockstein Riesling QbA 1992/3   **14**   **£C**

Pinot Blanc Trocken 1992   **13**   **£C**

Riesling 1993 (Waitrose) (1 litre)   **13**   **£C**

Westhofener Bergkloster Auslese Pfalz 1992   **13**   **£C**
Very attractive fruity aperitif which will age brilliantly for
7/8 years.

GREEK WINE – *white*

Kouros Patras 1992   **12**   **£C**

HUNGARIAN WINE – *white*

Szeksard Chardonnay 1993	10	£B
Tokaji Aszu 4 Puttonyos 1983 (50cl)	12	£E

ITALIAN WINE – *red*

Campo ai Sassi Rosso di Montalcino DOC 1990 15 £D
Lovely fruity wine, quite squashy and pulpy with warm fruit.

Carafe Red Wine (Waitrose, 1 litre) 13 £C
Adds pizzazz to any pizza.

**Chianti Classico Riserva, Rocca delle Macie
1991** 12 £C

**Dolcetto Vino da Tavola del Piemonte, Gemma
1992** 14 £C
Good brisk fruit, lots of flavour for not a lot of money.

Grifi Avignonesi 1989 15 £E
Very cultured fruit on offer here.

Monica di Sardegna DOC 1992 14 £B
Smelly as an old horse but the fruit's OK.

Montepulciano d'Abruzzo 1992 14 £C

Rosso Conero, Umani Ronchi 1992 11 £C

Teroldego Rotaliano DOC Gaierhof 1991 14 £C
Rounded, figgy, soft-delicious. Great fruit wine.

ITALIAN WINE – *white*

Carafe White Wine (Waitrose, 1 litre)   13   £C
Excellent value for a well-balanced dry white.

Lugana DOC Villa Flora, Zenato 1992   14   £C
Delish, balanced, fruity, lovely.

Nuragus di Cagliari DOC 1993   15   £B
Superb ripe melon fruit enlivened by a freshening breeze of
acidity making the whole effect purposeful, bright and
superbly gluggable.

Orvieto Classico Cardeto 1993   12   £C

Santa Cristina Chardonnay, Zenato 1993   13   £D

Soave Classico, Zenato 1993   12   £C

**Verdicchio dei Casteli di Jesi DOC, Villa Pigna
1992**   10   £C

LEBANESE WINE – *red*

Château Musar 1987   15   £E

NEW ZEALAND WINE – *red*

Montana Cabernet Sauvignon 1991   13   £C

NEW ZEALAND WINE – *white*

Cook's Chardonnay 1993   11 £C

Jackson Estate Sauvignon Blanc, Marlborough
1993   16 £E
Not huge grassiness here, just gentle soothing fruit and
balanced stylishness. One of the most elegantly purposeful of
sauvignon blancs around. Will repay cellaring for 2/3 years.
Very fine.

Villa Maria Sauvignon Blanc, Marlborough
1993   15 £D
Gorgeous cat's pee and cut-grass aroma. Great concentration
of fruit. Brilliant shellfish wine. Cellar for 1–3 years and it'll
get even tastier.

Wairau River Sauvignon Blanc, Marlborough
1993   14 £E
Exotic fruits. Delicious.

PORTUGUESE WINE – *red*

Bairrada Reserva, Dom Ferraz 1989   13 £B
Soft plum fruit of some attractiveness but not as excitingly
boisterous a mouthful as previous vintages.

Perquita, José de Maria de Fonseca 1990   13 £C

Ramada Tinto   15 £B
Brilliant value – lashings of cherries and raspberries, dryly

expressed. Soft creamy touch to this fruit ... stylish, good structure – an excellent mouthful. Delightful quaffing wine.

Tinto de Anfora 1990 15 £C

Hairier, more severely tannic, than previous vintages. Put down for 2/3 years and it will be great.

SLOVENIAN WINE – *white*

Labor Chardonnay 1993 12 £C

SOUTH AFRICAN WINE – *red*

Avontuur Cabernet Sauvignon Stellenbosch 1993 13 £C

Delicious soft fruit.

Avontuur Cabernet Sauvignon/Merlot 1992 15 £C

It is easy to be romantic, exotic, and quite carried away by this wine for it is so soft it is like settling a harem cushion, plump and silken, on the back of the throat; it has less tannin, I declare, than a blackcurrant fool. It is a treat to drink.

Avontuur Cabernet/Merlot Stellenbosch 1993 14 £C

Backsberg Cabernet Sauvignon, Paarl 1990 14 £C

Engagingly fruity wine of great softness and flavour. Good style – a wine to enjoy by itself.

Backsberg Cabernet Sauvignon 1991 15 £C

Superb stuff! Great fruit and structure. A real class act.

Manages that New World style of serious dryness with sweet
blackcurrant fruitiness.

Fairview Estate Merlot 1991   12   £D

Fairview Shiraz Reserve 1991   14   £D

Simonsig Estate Adelberg Stellenbosch 1992   13   £C

Simonsig Estate Shiraz Stellenbosch 1989   13   £E

SOUTH AFRICAN WINE – *white*

Avontuur Chardonnay Stellenbosch 1992   13   £C

Avontuur Chardonnay Stellenbosch 1993   14   £C
A firm delicious wine of style and class.

Backsberg Chardonnay 1992   15   £D
Elegant, rich-edged fruit which is forward without being
gauche, friendly without being overfamiliar.

Cape Selection Chardonnay, Robertson 1993   12   £C
Not bad, not bad at all.

Robertson Sauvignon Blanc 1993   12   £B
Rather melon/pear-drop taste.

Van Riebeeck Cape Dry White 1993   13   £B
Very attractive fruit here, pleasantly shrouded in well-
mannered acidity.

SPANISH WINE – *red*

Agramont Navarra 1990 13 £C

Castillo de Liria Valencia 14 £B
An excellent mix of soft fruits at a bargain price. Also available
in 1.5 litres.

Cosme Palacia Rioja 1989 14 £C
Rich, elegant rather than raffish. A lovely Rioja of considerable style: dry, little ugly vanilla, very smooth.

Don Hugo 14 £B
Turns out regularly for Spain's first eleven, though finicky
aficionados complain at its lack of finesse, but poured into a
common-sense glass and held under a common-sense nose
there is no grumbling at the lush aroma and evident fruitiness.

Ribera del Duero, Callejo 1991 14 £C
Just about scrapes in as a 14-pointer.

Viño Alberdi Rioja 1989 14 £D

SPANISH WINE – *white and rosé*

Cosme Palacio Rioja 1992 11 £C

Don Hugo 15 £B
Full, creamy, banana-y, oaky, coconut-rich fruit yet not boiled
or blowsy but surprisingly fresh and pleasant to roll across the
molars. Perfect for watching flavourless food programmes on
television but equally superb with paellas and fish curries.

Don Hugo Rosé   14   £B
An excellent value-for-money rosé with cherry and melon
fruit.

Solera Jerezana Dry Oloroso (Waitrose)   14   £C
When would you drink it? At funerals. Dull, decaying fruit
which is half in heaven, half in hell.

USA WINE – *red*

California Ruby Cabernet 1992   15   £B
Label like a 4th form instruction booklet for spermatozoa. A
great rousing soup of firm, lovely soft fruit, rounded and very
bright.

Cartlidge & Browne Zinfandel NV   13   £C

Fetzer Valley Oaks Cabernet 1991   14.5 £D
Excellent, lush fruit.

Robert Mondavi Pinot Noir, Nappa Valley 1991 13   £E

USA WINE – *white*

Bel Arbors 1993   14   £B

Bel Arbors Vintage White, California 1992   12   £B

Cartlidge & Browne Chardonnay, California   15   £C
Stylish, forward, very attractive. Delightful oily, fruity chardonnay of interest to grilled chicken.

Villa Mount Eden Chardonnay 1991 16 £D
This is a wine! Beautiful wood/fruit integration, stylish and
purposeful – a gorgeous bottle and great value for the chardonnay lover.

SPARKLING WINE/CHAMPAGNE

Angas Brut Rosé, Australia 15 £C
One of those New World sparklers which deliciously tickle
the nose and only lightly tickle the pocket but send shivers up
the spine of champagne makers.

Anna de Cordoníu Chardonnay 1989, Spain 16 £E
Stunning sparkler of great character: complete, full, elegant,
classy.

Blanquette de Limoux (Waitrose) 13 £D
Very attractive.

Cava Cristal Brut Castellblanch, Spain 12 £D

Champagne Brut Blanc de Noirs (Waitrose) 14 £F
Lovely big wine bubbling over with rich fruit.

Champagne Rosé (Waitrose) 15 £F
The closest the poor teetotaller can come to grasping the
flavour of this scrumptious article is by chewing a digestive
biscuit spread thickly with crushed rose petals and drinking
Perrier water with a microscopically thin slice of lime zest.

Champagne (Waitrose) 14 £F
One of the best supermarket champagnes you can buy.

Clairette de Die Tradition 1992/93 13 £D

Crémant de Bourgogne, Lugny   14   £D
Excellent dry (yet fruitily rounded) sparkling wine to be preferred to many, many champagnes.

Crémant de Bourgogne Rosé   13   £D

Diamantina Brut, Provifin, Brazil   12   £E
Soft and too peachy to be really worth more than 12, at this price not complex enough.

Green Point Vineyards Brut, Australia 1991   12   £E

Krone Borealis Brut Twee Jonge Gezellen South Africa 1988   12   £E
Bit too cloying on the finish for me.

Le Baron de Beaumont Chardonnay   14   £D
Excellent value for a delightful little sparkler.

Liebfraumilch (Waitrose)   13   £C

Santi Chardonnay Brut, Italy   14   £D
Delicious and cheap.

Saumur (Waitrose)   14   £D
Chewy little number of some distinction.

Seaview Brut   15   £D
Where available for under £5, one of the best sparklers on the market: stylish, refined, and quite delicious.

Seppelt Great Western Brut, Australia   16   £C
Superb bargain. A finer fizzer on sale for under a fiver it's difficult to name. Lemony, zingy, zesty. Great style.

Waitrose Champagne Extra Dry 1986   14   £G

Rating guide

10, 11 Nothing nasty but equally nothing worth shouting from the rooftops. Drinkable.

12, 13 Above average, interestingly made. A bargain taste.

14, 15, 16 This is the exceptional stuff, from the very good to the brilliant.

17, 18 Really great wine, worthy of individual acclaim. The sort of wine you can decant and serve to ignorant snobs who'll think it famous even when it is no such thing.

19, 20 Overwhelmingly marvellous. Wine which cannot be faulted, providing an experience never to be forgotten.

PRICE BANDS

A Under £2.50   E £7.00–£10.00

B £2.50–£3.50   F £10.00–£13.00

C £3.50–£5.00   G £13.00–£20.00

D £5.00–£7.00   H Over £20.00